5F $1

Studies in Modern 

The So

## Studies in Modern History

*The Cold War*, Hugh Higgins
*Vietnam*, Hugh Higgins
*Cold War to* Détente, Colin Bown and Peter J. Mooney
*China 1949–75*, Colin Bown
*America Since 1920*, Daniel Snowman

# THE SOVIET SUPERPOWER
## The Soviet Union 1945-80
## Peter J. Mooney

HEINEMANN EDUCATIONAL BOOKS
LONDON AND EXETER

Heinemann Educational Books Ltd
22 Bedford Square, London WC1B 3HH

Heinemann Educational Books Inc
4 Front Street, Exeter, NH 03833, USA

LONDON   EDINBURGH   MELBOURNE   AUCKLAND
HONG KONG   SINGAPORE   KUALA LUMPUR   NEW DELHI
IBADAN   NAIROBI   JOHANNESBURG
EXETER (NH)   KINGSTON   PORT OF SPAIN

**British Library Cataloguing in Publication Data**
Mooney, Peter
   The Soviet Superpower.—(Studies in modern history)
   1. Soviet Union – History – 1953–
   2. Soviet Union – History – 1925–1953
   I. Series
   947.085        DK274

   ISBN 0-435-31600-1 (cased)
        0-435-31601-X (paper)

Printed in Great Britain by
Biddles Ltd, Guildford, Surrey

# CONTENTS

# ABBREVIATIONS

| | |
|---|---|
| ABM | Anti-Ballistic Missile |
| ACC | Allied Control Council |
| ASW | Anti-Submarine Warfare |
| CENTO | Central Treaty Organization |
| CIA | Central Intelligence Agency |
| CMEA (Comecon) | Council for Mutual Economic Assistance |
| CP | Communist Party |
| CPSU | Communist Party of the Soviet Union |
| CSCE | *Conférence de la Sécurité et de la Co-opération Européenne* (European Conference on Security and Co-operation) |
| DDR | *Deutsche Demokratische Republik* (German Democratic Republic, East Germany) |
| EDC | European Defence Community |
| EEC | European Economic Community |
| ERP | European Recovery Programme (Marshall Plan) |
| FTUA | Federation of Free Trade Unions |
| GNP | Gross National Product |
| IAEA | International Atomic Energy Agency |
| ICBM | Inter-continental Ballistic Missile |
| IRBM | Intermediate Range Ballistic Missile |
| KGB | State Security Committee (Secret Police) |
| MBFR | Mutual and Balanced Force Reductions (now called Mutual Force Reductions and Associated Measures) |
| MGB | Ministry of State Security |
| MIRV | Multiple Independently Targetable Re-entry Vehicle |
| MRBM | Medium-Range Ballistic Missile |
| MVD | Ministry of Internal Affairs |
| NATO | North Atlantic Treaty Organization |
| NKVD | People's Commissariat (Ministry) of State Security (Secret Police) |
| NPT | Non-Proliferation Treaty |
| OECD | Organization of Economic Co-operation and Development |
| OPEC | Organization of Petroleum Exporting Countries |
| SALT | Strategic Arms Limitation Talks |
| SAM | Surface-to-Air Missile |
| SEATO | South-East Asia Treaty Organization |
| SLBM | Submarine-Launched Ballistic Missile |
| UNO | United Nations Organization |

# LIST OF MAPS

# PREFACE

In 1978 the government of the People's Republic of China announced a new system of transliterating from the Chinese to the Western alphabet. However, with the exception of specialist publications, the new system is not generally used in its entirety in the West. The old spelling is still widely used for names which were well known in the West before 1978 but it is appropriate that the new spelling is used for names which are relatively new to the West. This is the method that has been adopted here. Therefore, for example, the old name Peking is used in preference to Beijing, but Teng Hsiao-p'ing becomes Deng Xiaoping.

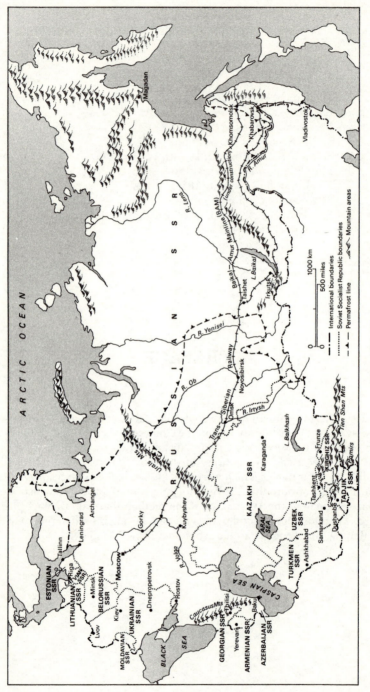

The USSR

Legend:
1000 km
500 miles
International boundaries
Soviet Socialist Republic boundaries
Permafrost line
Mountain areas

ARCTIC OCEAN

Magadan
Khomsomolsk
Khabarovsk
Vladivostok
R. Amur
Baikal–Amur Mainline (BAM) (under construction)
L. Baikal
Taishet
Irkutsk
R. Lena
R. Yenisei
R. Ob
R. Irtysh
Novosibirsk
Omsk
Trans-Siberian Railway
Karaganda
L. Balkhash
Frunze
KIRGHIZ SSR
Tien Shan Mts
TADJIK SSR
Pamirs
Dushanbe
Samarkand
KAZAKH SSR
ARAL SEA
UZBEK SSR
Tashkent
TURKMEN SSR
Ashkhabad
Kuybyshev
Gorky
R. Volga
Urals Mts
R U S S I A N   S.F.S.R.
Archangel
Leningrad
Tallinn
Riga
ESTONIAN SSR
LITHUANIAN SSR
BELORUSSIAN SSR
Minsk
Vilnyus
MOLDAVIAN SSR
Lvov
Kiev
UKRAINIAN SSR
Dneppropetrovsk
Rostov
Dnepropetrovsk
CASPIAN SEA
Baku
AZERBAIJAN SSR
Caucasus Mts
Tbilisi
GEORGIAN SSR
Yerevan
ARMENIAN SSR
BLACK SEA
Moscow

# One

# INTRODUCTION

The purpose of this work is to describe and explain the history of the Soviet Union between 1945 and early 1980 – the period in which she developed from a great power to a superpower. The book is divided into two sections: Part I deals with domestic affairs and Part II with foreign affairs. Within each section there are chapters on the periods of office of the postwar First or General Secretaries of the Communist Party: Stalin, Khrushchev and Brezhnev. There are also separate chapters on some major topics: the economy, minorities, Eastern Europe and the break-up of monolithic communism. The final chapter assesses the extent to which the USSR has become a superpower.

The Soviet Union is one of the dominant forces in the contemporary world. Her power and influence have become enormous not only in the diplomatic, ideological and military fields, but also in the economy, science, performing arts and sport. These aspects alone would make the USSR worthy of study, but she is also the home of an ideology which foretells the inevitable collapse of the Western democracies and their replacement by 'scientific socialism' as practised in the Soviet Union. Therefore, it is essential that the West attempts to understand the policies, preoccupations, and motives of the USSR.

Long before the Russian Revolution perceptive observers noted the potential of Russia and America to dominate the world; to become, in effect, superpowers. In the nineteenth century the Frenchman Alexis de Tocqueville wrote:

> The Anglo-American relies upon personal interest to accomplish his ends and gives free scope to the unguided strength and common sense of the people; the Russian centres all the authority in a single arm. The principal instrument of the former is freedom; of the latter servitude . . . each of them seems marked out by the will of heaven to sway the destinies of half the globe.[1]

Before the Napoleonic Wars Friedrich Grimm wrote to Tsarina Catherine the Great: 'Two empires will divide the world between them, Russia to the east and America to the west.'[2]

Such views reflected the West European view that America and Russia were 'new' countries, little known and with enormous hinterlands into which to expand. It could have been said of imperial Russia, as it has been said of the Soviet Union, that there are no degrees of knowledge, only degrees of ignorance. Russia is different. Her ethnic and cultural make-up is Asiatic as well as European, while her historical experience sets her apart from Western Europe. Unlike the latter, she inherited none of the civilization of Rome. While Western Europe was breaking free of the feudal system and was developing respect for the individual, the paramountcy of law and the beginnings of parliamentary democracy, the Russians were throwing off the yoke of Mongol domination and, in the seventeenth century, formalizing for the first time the institution of serfdom. Even her religion and alphabet separated her from the West, since she was converted by the Greek and not the Roman Church.

Soviet Russia inherited many characteristics from her past, including an admiration for, fear of and mutual lack of comprehension of the West. Both tsarist and communist governments have been autocratic and repressive, and the people have usually been passive. Nadezhda Mandelstam wrote of 'an excruciating capacity for endurance on the part of the ordinary Russian . . . a patience . . . born not of religious faith but of the traditional treatment of the ordinary people as a race apart . . . . the material conditions of the mass of the Soviet people have improved beyond recognition, but a fear of chaos and disorder still persists.'[3]

Despite such common threads in Russian history, the Soviet leadership has portrayed the Revolution of 1917 as a break with the past, claiming that 'classless' communism replaced the inequalities of the old order. According to Marxist–Leninism, the eventual arrival of communism is inevitable. This doctrine claims that all developing societies will eventually pass through the sequence of bourgeois revolution, bourgeois democracy, then the revolution and seizure of power by the working class and the establishment of proletarian democracy or 'the dictatorship of the proletariat'.[4]

Marxist–Leninism claims that under the new system, the old exploiting classes of capitalists and landowners are abolished, turning the USSR into a community of working people: workers, peasants and intelligentsia, where the means of production are held in common. The USSR claimed to be the first 'genuine democracy' because her 'democracy' served the interests of the working people, that is, the majority of the people, unlike the Western 'bourgeois' democracies which served the interests of the middle classes. Marxist–Leninism proclaims the USSR to be the most advanced form of society ever seen and gives the credit to the Communist Party, the vanguard of the working class. Marxist–Leninist ideology explains the laws of history and social development, but the Communist Party interprets the ideology. Therefore, although the USSR has a governmental, administrative and legislative machine of government ministries, departments and soviets, all of which technically enjoy equal status with the party, the decisions of the party prevail. The state administers and enforces policy, but it is the party which mobilizes the people to achieve particular goals.

The Party Programme of 1961 described the party as 'the brain, the honour and the conscience of our epoch of the Soviet people'. The Brezhnev Constitution of 1977 defined the role of the CPSU as: 'The leading and guiding force of Soviet society and the nucleus of its political system, of all state and public organizations.'[5] The party generates an enormous degree of commitment – much of which is sheer patriotism of course – from its 16 million members and 25 million members of the Young Communist League, Komsomol. The CPSU is the seat of power in the USSR, and the key to individual success. To oppose the party is to oppose the state and to risk the charge of treason as a class enemy. Political opposition is minimal, but about 70,000 people are employed by the central censorship organization, Glavlit, to censor the information which is passed on to the masses.

The USSR is a country of contrasts. There is full employment, but this disguises widespread overmanning and underemployment. There is equality of opportunity and equality of the sexes. Women comprise about half the industrial workforce and dominate teaching and medicine where pay levels and status (consequently?) are low. The franchise is held by all over the age of 18 years, even criminals and those in the armed forces. Democracy extends to the fact that in the 1974 elections, 27.8 per cent of those elected to the Supreme Soviet were not party members. But the Supreme Soviet only meets twice a year for four or five days and enjoys little real power.

Marx envisaged the 'withering away of the state' in a communist society because the absence of class divisions would mean that there would be no 'internal contradictions'in society or contending classes among whom the state needed to arbitrate. However, Marxist–Leninism foresaw the continuation of the state mechanism for the forseeable future, both because some system would be needed to regulate consumption, distribution and the development of communism, and because the USSR would need to defend itself against international capitalism.

Soviet ideology proclaimed that communism would inevitably inherit the whole world and called upon Marxist–Leninists to be the conscious agents of revolution. Such a crusading ideology naturally attracted the hostility of those other ideologies and countries which felt threatened by communism. The USSR has continued to proclaim the triumph of communism and support revolution, but the precise nature of the connection between Soviet foreign policy and ideology is a debatable one.

Although nineteenth-century tsars made no major efforts to expand towards Istanbul or the Indian Ocean and although they denied any such ambition, it was thought in the West, and especially in Britain, that Moscow had designs on both. Alternatively, Lord Curzon saw Russian foreign policy differently: 'So far from regarding the foreign policy of Russia as consistent or remorseless or profound, I believe it to be a hand-to-mouth policy of waiting upon events, of profiting by the blunders of others.'[6]

These views, that foreign policy is dictated by grand design or windfall, that it is principled or pragmatic, have continued to the present as the West has wondered if the USSR intends to export her ideology to convert the world. It is even more difficult to perceive a Soviet grand strategy if Lenin's heirs have followed his tactics closely because he argued that the USSR should 'go on zigzags, sometimes retracing our steps, sometimes abandoning the course already selected and trying out various others', and described Soviet foreign policy as the 'ascent of an unexplored and heretofore inaccessible mountain'.[7] Louis Halle described Stalin as: . . . not a crusading ideologist. He was, rather an illegitimate tsar in Russia whose preoccupation had to be that of securing himself in his position.'[8] A later author wrote: 'The men who have ruled the Soviet Union were not and are not merely ideologues with many idle hours to dream about tomorrow's utopia. For the most part they must concern themselves with today'.[9] Yet Soviet policy is couched in ideological terms. Soviet leaders profess a constant unalterable belief in Marxist–Leninism. It may be that the Kremlin has decided not to fight for the millennium, but it would be a mistake to assume that the Kremlin no longer believes in that millennium.

Winston Churchill spoke of Soviet foreign policy as 'a riddle wrapped in a mystery, inside an enigma', and yet the riddle must be unravelled if any understanding is to be achieved of the Soviet superpower. From her actions, motives can be deduced. But, as in the case of the sudden abandonment of support of Somalia in favour of Ethiopia in 1977 (see page 140), motives are difficult to define. Does the USSR support the World Revolution? If so, then her actions in the 1970s in Angola, Ethiopia, South Yemen and Afghanistan are easy to understand, but not so the lack of support for the Greek communists in the late 1940s, Allende in Chile in 1973 and an obvious lack of enthusiasm for the Eurocommunists.

Soviet actions can confuse those trying to discern a pattern in Soviet behaviour, and policy statements by and negotiations with the

*(margin handwritten note: confusing policy)*

leadership are also unhelpful. A British Ambassador to the USSR compared negotiating with the Soviets to playing an old-fashioned slot-machine; you rarely got what you wanted, but you usually got something; you could 'sometimes expedite the process by shaking the machine' but it was 'useless to talk to it'.[10] Even more picturesquely American Secretary of State Dean Acheson once said: 'Negotiating with the Russians was like dealing with a force of nature: you can't argue with a river, it is going to flow. You can damn it up . . . put it to useful purposes . . . deflect it, but you can't argue with it'.[11]

The Soviet system is secretive. American Assistant Secretary of State George Ball wrote of the Politburo as 'a platform covered by a carpet, which is in a constant state of upheaval. It is apparent that a vigorous struggle is in progress under the carpet; grunts and cries of agony and anger are heard, but no one knows who is making the noises or who is doing what to whom.'[12] According to Lenin the crucial question was '*kto-kogo?*', 'who-whom?' or 'who can do what to whom?' This question underlies the relationships of Soviet citizens with each other and also those of the Soviet Union with the outside world, and is a central theme running through the history of the Union of Soviet Socialist Republics since the Second World War.

# PART I

Domestic Affairs

# Two

# STALIN: DIVIDE AND RULE

When Germany attacked the Soviet Union on 22 June 1941, world opinion tended to concur with Hitler's contemptuous dismissal of the prospects of the Soviet state. 'You have only to kick in the door,' Hitler had declared 'and the whole rotten structure will come crashing down.'[1] Certainly the Soviet defences crumbled. Red Army losses in 1941 were enormous, but ultimately, however, far from destroying Stalin's and the Communist Party's hold upon the USSR, the Second World War strengthened it. Courted by the world's governments, her people respected and admired throughout the world, the successful war against Nazi Germany gave the USSR a degree of respectability abroad. It also conferred a wider domestic legitimacy upon the Soviet government that had been lacking hitherto. The successive governments of Lenin and Stalin, imposed upon Russia by revolution, civil war and terror, had received the committed support only of the ideological faithful, but Hitler's attack enabled Stalin to invoke all the old patriotism and mystique of Holy Russia, and to unite the whole country in the desperate endeavour which transcended ideology. However, the united, confident and powerful front that the USSR presented to the world in 1945 masked appalling losses.

The prewar population of approximately 190 million had fallen to 170 million by 1945. One Soviet citizen in *four* had been killed or injured – 20 million killed and 30 million wounded or incapacitated. The population census of 1959 revealed that of the Second World War military age groups, there were 52 million women but only 31 million men.[2] To some extent this population shortfall and sex imbalance was made good by annexations in eastern Europe (see Map 10 on page 150) and by the subjugation of eastern European states, but the lasting impact upon the Soviet mind – individual and collective – of this awesome blood-letting should not be forgotten.

Soviet material losses amounted to about one-quarter of total property. More than 6 million dwellings, 70,000 villages and 1,700 towns and cities were devastated. Thirty-one thousand factories and 84,000 schools were destroyed, while 40,000 miles of railway track were torn up, and 16,000 locomotives and 428,000 railway wagons were destroyed or taken to Germany. In addition 98,000 collective farms, 1,876 state farms and 2,890 machine-tractor stations were wrecked or plundered. Livestock numbers, already low as a result of collectivization, had fallen. In 1945 there were only 87 per cent of the cattle, 76 per cent of the sheep and goats, 38 per cent of the pigs and 51 per cent of the horses (still the motive power in agriculture) that there had been in 1940.[3]

Despite these losses, war production was impressive. In the first half of 1945 industry produced 21,000 aircraft, 9,100 tanks and 82.1 million shells, bombs and mines. The war spurred the USSR's headlong rush to industrialize. Industries and their work forces were moved bodily beyond the Urals, out of reach of German armies and bombers. From this stemmed the postwar development of Siberia and the Far East. Immediate postwar industrial priorities were to rebuild the heavy industry and defences of the Soviet Union. The fourth Five-Year Plan (1946–50) concentrated on reviving agriculture and restoring or building 6,200 large-scale enterprises. It helped that the Red Army was able to send back to the USSR, from Germany and elsewhere, reparations booty in the form of industrial plant and prisoners or 'volunteer' technicians to train Russians in new skills. It also helped that the Soviets were able to impose upon East European states joint stock companies from which Moscow drew the economic benefits, but these were only of marginal significance. In 1945 the Soviet GNP was only 30 per cent of that of America. The USSR's request for a $6 billion[4] loan was refused by Washington, and Lend–Lease ended in August 1945 (see page 81). Unlike the recipients of America's Marshall Aid, the USSR had to finance her economic recovery almost entirely from her own resources.

Economic recovery was swift although relative. By 1948 industrial output exceeded the 1940 level, and was 2½ times greater by 1952 despite a serious drought in 1946 and the consequent failure of the Ukrainian harvest.[5] Indeed, although the postwar average wage was raised by 65 per cent over the prewar rate, when rationing was abolished in 1947 – a year late because of the drought – prices rose to reflect continuing shortages. Bread cost 3½ times the prewar price, but in fact retail prices were reduced every year from 1948–53.[6]

As in the 1920s and 1930s, postwar industrial investment was financed by the agricultural sector. Neither Marx, Lenin nor Stalin viewed the peasants as equal partners in the communist state – at least not until they adopted the same values and urban mentality of the working class, and dropped the social, religious, conservative and acquisitive values traditionally attributed to the peasantry. Stalin always regarded the peasants as potentially hostile to the rule of communism, and therefore any weakness or failure to control them invited potential trouble. In the lands ravaged by war, and even elsewhere, collective and state farms had often virtually ceased to exist. Outside the war zone corruption and the weakening of party control, combined with an inadequate labour force, led to stagnation on thousands of farms as peasants enlarged their own private plots and worked on them to the exclusion of their duties to the state. This wartime laxity threatened the two major benefits which collectivization had conferred on the state: the capacity to plan for a specific nationwide agricultural yield at a preordained price; and the ability to exert party control, through the collective, state farm and machine-tractor station apparatus, right down to grassroots level.

Politburo member Andrei Andreyev was given the task of redisciplining the peasants. On 19 September 1946 decrees were issued on 'breaches of the collective-farm statute'. These cut back private plots and reasserted party control over agriculture. Furthermore, a currency reform, prior to the abolition of rationing, wiped out 90 per cent of the value of savings held in cash (savings accounts and bonds were treated more favourably). Most cash savings were held by peasants and so overnight any limited financial independence that peasants had been able to build up during the war was removed.

Along the USSR's western border, in the newly occupied – or re-occupied – lands the trauma of sovietization and collectivization began again. Polish, Ruthenian and Ukrainian nationalists took up arms against the reimposition of control that was both communist and Russian. In the south-west Ukraine thousands of armed partisans under Stepan Bandera fought pitched battles with Soviet forces in a struggle that continued until the turn of the decade.[7]

The end of the war saw the reimposition of the Stalinist order on the whole of the state, and revenge was taken on those who had been (or had only had the opportunity to have been) traitors. Whole nations were deported to the east because of supposed collective treachery (see Chapter 6). In this period Moldavian Party Secretary Leonid Brezhnev imprisoned, deported to the east, or executed 500,000 or one-sixth of native Moldavians. They were replaced by 250,000 Russian settlers who so effectively russified the republic's towns and cities that of the 300,000 population of the Moldavian republic's capital Kishinev fewer than one-third were ethnic Moldavians by the early 1970s.[8]

Apparently afraid of potential opposition Stalin turned Lavrenti Beria's secret police loose upon the country. Manpower shortages in industry and agriculture were aggravated and popular morale damaged by the deliberate policy of directing demobilized soldiers to work far from their homes, on the principle that they would be less likely to talk to strangers of the material glories of Hungary or Germany.[9] Otherwise loyal citizens and soldiers who criticized the regime were sent to join the millions already in the prison camps of the 'Gulag Archipelago'.[10]

Stalin's revenge was exacted upon up to 3 million Soviet citizens, prisoners of war, slave labourers and Nazi auxiliaries who returned after the war or were returned, often against their wishes, by the British and Americans.[11]

In May 1945 Stalin submerged his own Georgian origins and singled out the Russians: 'The most remarkable of all the nations of the Soviet Union, I drink to the health of the Russian people not only because it is the leading people but also because it has a clear intelligence, a firm character.'[12] Great Russian nationalism became a feature of Stalin's postwar rule. It was the platform from which efforts were made to russify the non-Russian peoples, and it went hand in hand with the growing Cold War climate in which foreigners and their influence were seen as malevolent. In the summer of 1946, Stalin's chief lieutenant and heir apparent, Andrei Zhdanov, set in train the *Zhdanovschina*, the Zhdanov times, a campaign against alien influences on Russian cultural and scientific life.

It was Zhdanov, theoretician of the party, 'dynamo of the Cold War and the scourge of the satellites and foreign communist parties',[13] who launched the Cominform in October 1947 (see page 89), and called upon 'the colonial peoples . . . to expel their aggressors'[14] in parallel with his *Zhdanovschina*, which subjected theatre, film, literature, art and music to party scrutiny. Individuals were threatened, including the poet Akhmatova, and the composer Shostakovitch, who tried to pacify Stalin by publishing an *Ode to Stalin's Afforestation Plan*. The hunt was on for cultural saboteurs, many of whom turned out to be, in line with Stalin's own growing prejudice 'rootless cosmopolitans' or Jews. Ultra-nationalism was required in all Soviet art; 'kotowing before the West' was a crime. Cultural and scientific contacts with the West became minimal, and even international football matches ended after Moscow Dynamo's popular tour of Britain in 1945. In 1947 marriages between Soviet citizens and foreigners were banned. The *Zhdanovschina*,[15] with its vigilance against external influences and their internal tools, continued even after the death of Zhdanov in 1948, although it was but one strand of the web of repression and terror that Stalin wove about his country-men as his years weighed upon him, his health deteriorated and his suspicions and apparent paranoia sharpened.

Stalin had outmanoeuvred his rivals – Trotsky, Kamenev, Zinoviev and others – in coming to power. His intelligence, political acumen, attention to detail, immense capacity for work and utter ruthlessness had fuelled his hunger for power. Supreme by 1928, he continued to use at regular intervals the mechanism of the purge to remove enemies, potential enemies and their families from the party, armed forces and population at large. In 1933–4 over a million members were expelled from the party, and many were imprisoned or worse.[16] Between 1936–8 most of the Central Committee members were arrested on charges of

*Russian nationalism*

*Zhdanov*

sabotage or treason, and by 1938 all Lenin's Politburo still in Russia had been sentenced to death.[17] In the purge of 1937–8, which decimated the officer corps of the Red Army, three out of five field-marshals, fifty-seven out of eighty-five corps commanders and 110 out of 195 divisional commanders were shot. By 1938 as many as 8 million people had been consigned to labour camps.[18] One biographer wrote of Stalin:

> He may have desired to strike out just the leaders of potential treason: those few thousand party officials who in the past had been connected with his rivals. But the mechanics of terror . . . soon acquired its own momentum. The more he killed, the more he was bound to suspect. Since his mind evidently made no distinction between actual and potential treason, slander became a prima facie proof. His passion for revenge was not merely atrocious, it was vulgar. Wives and children of his victims were to suffer, for no one was to curse him, even in silence with impunity.[19]

Stalin's vengefulness was almost total. No one was free from it. His sister-in-law Anna Alliluyeva – whose husband Stanislav Redens had been purged in 1938 – was condemned to ten years' solitary confinement after the war for writing memoirs in which she referred to Stalin with 'impermissible familiarity'. Vyascheslav Molotov, Stalin's most faithful lieutenant, who was slavishly loyal from pre-revolutionary days until he was removed from public life by Khrushchev in 1962, had to suffer the humiliation of his wife Pauline being exiled. She belonged to an official Jewish group, which had proposed to Stalin that the Crimea be made a Jewish Soviet Republic.

By the late 1940s the party hierarchy consisted of sycophants who had achieved prominence by being efficient, obedient, unoriginal and lucky. Even then, the purge and the reshuffle remained essential and regular features of Stalin's ruling style. Without wishing to pursue the analogy too far, they performed some of the functions of a Western election; introducing new blood into the political process – and letting old blood out. One writer argued cogently that purges:

> . . . had integrative effects for the society as a whole . . . . Rapid and violent social and political upheavals require both the destruction of the values of the *ancien régime* and their replacement with a new value system, otherwise society may disintegrate.
>
> The purges and terror isolated and frightened men and broke down old values: at the same time, for those who did not wish to be purged or terrorised, they acted as mechanisms through which they could affirm their loyalty to the new order.[20]

Isaac Deutscher concluded that the permanent terror kept 'the whole bureaucracy in a state of flux, renewing permanently its composition and not allowing it to grow out of a protoplasmic or amoeboid condition, to form a compact and articulate body with a socio–political identity of its own'.[21]

Stalin's subordinates vied with each other to demonstrate their loyalty to him. School children sang songs in his praise; cities, streets and factories were named after him. The press and hierarchy invariably referred to him in superlatives. He was the '*Vozhd*',[22] 'dear father', 'our great leader and patient teacher', 'our guiding light', 'brilliant architect of communism'. In 1944 Khrushchev commissioned thirteen poets to write a paeon: 'To the Great Stalin from the Ukrainian People', which was submitted to the Kremlin with a huge roll of 9,316,973 signatures.[23] This personality cult of Stalin contributed to his air of invincibility after the war when, ostensibly, he gave up some of the trappings of power. He remained General Secretary of the party and Prime Minister, but in September 1945 he abolished the State Committee for Defence – through which he had co-ordinated the war effort – and in January 1947 he handed over the Ministry of Defence to Nikolai Bulganin. Although no party congress was called between 1939–52,[24] the Politburo apparently resumed regular meetings after 1945. Furthermore, 65 years of age by the end of the war, Stalin became ill with heart trouble in 1946–7 following which he spent several months of each year in the warm south,[25] away from Moscow and the seat of power. Despite this, although none of his subordinates can have felt safe from him, there was no apparent attempt to overthrow him. Stalin divided and ruled his subordinates who had as little love for each other as they had for him.

'Stalin's autocratic rule rested on a state of equilibrium between the apparatus of the Party, the machinery of Government, the police and the armed forces . . . [with] liaison provided by his private secretariat.'[26] As the hierarchies of these centres of power were frequently inter-changeable, Stalin's rule also rested upon maintaining an equilibrium between his chief subordinates of the Politburo, and the major city and republican party organizations.[27] Thus, Khrushchev, who was sacked as party boss of the Ukraine in March 1947, was recalled to Moscow at the end of 1949, apparently as a Politburo counterweight to Georgi Malenkov and Lavrenti Beria.[28] In March 1949 the faithful Molotov was replaced as Foreign Minister by his deputy, Vishinsky. Bulganin lost the Ministry of Defence to Marshal Vasilevsky and Mikoyan gave up the Ministry of Foreign Trade to Menshikov. These moves were dressed up as promotions – all three were created, or remained, Deputy Prime Ministers, although such rank had no major departmental power base.

Even earlier, in 1946, Beria's huge security empire had been split into the MGB and the MVD in an apparently unsuccessful attempt to curb the power of the man who, in deploying terror, was one of the keys to

Stalin's rule. A Georgian, like Stalin, and hated by his colleagues and rivals, Beria had the example of his two predecessors as chiefs of the secret police, Yagoda and Yezhov – who were both purged – to teach him to be careful. Nevertheless, it was his empire that ran the prison camps (Map 1), and employed more than half a million border, criminal and secret police. He also commanded a small police air force and fourteen well-equipped divisions of security troops. His slave labour establishments included logging camps in Siberia, canal construction projects in the tundra, the building of the Moscow metro and research laboratories, where Landau and Frank conducted nuclear research, and Korloyev worked on the inter-continental ballistic missile.[29]

As for the armed forces, any spirit of political independence had been quenched in the Great Purge of 1937–8. Any soldier who combined efficiency with style and personality was suspect, and two such were removed from office in 1946. Marshal Zhukov, the hero of Moscow and Stalingrad, was banished to the Crimea, ostensibly for looting jewellery in Berlin, and General Antonov was banished to Transcaucasia for similar reasons. Otherwise, lauded and fêted by state and populace, the army was fully absorbed demobilizing to 2.5 million men by 1948, re-equipping and adapting to its new role of occupier of eastern Europe.

Ultimate power in the USSR rested – and rests – on the party, and power in the party depends upon rank, length of tenure of office and the extent to which patronage is wielded. 'Stalin was a master at using the intricate patronage system to build up support and knock down the other man's props. He knew how to pack the various party and government agencies with enough men dependent upon him to spread the risk and weaken whatever opposition might exist.'[30] Of course, important subordinates were doing similar things at lesser levels; trying to build up bases of support from which they could challenge for higher office when the time came. It may be that the struggle for the succession to Stalin started when his serious illness became manifest in late 1946. The reshuffling of his lieutenants and the subsequent purges appeared to be part of the process by which individuals tried to influence Stalin into doing down rivals. Stalin kept his subordinates politically strong enough to be effective in the roles he cast for them, but not strong enough to act independently of his wishes.

His General Secretaryship allowed him to make appointments to and maintain contacts at the higher levels throughout the party. This he continued to do. Stalin never neglected his own political power base, but may have tried to engineer a situation where Beria had to neglect, or rather damage, his own. While the Leningrad Affair of 1949 (see pages 15–16) and the purge of Titoists in the USSR and Eastern Europe, following Yugoslavia's defection from the Soviet fold in 1948, highlighted the value of the secret police, its chief was having to conduct a witch-hunt for traitors among party officials of the Crimea and Georgia,

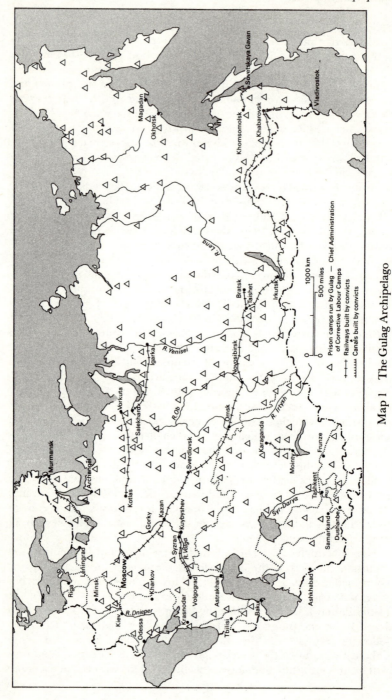

Map 1   The Gulag Archipelago

Legend:
△  Prison camps run by Gulag — Chief Administration of Corrective Labour Camps
+—+  Railways built by convicts
......  Canals built by convicts

Scale: 1000 km / 500 miles

Labels on map: Magadan, Okhotsk, Sovetskaya Gavan, Khabarovsk, Vladivostok, Khomsomolsk, R. Lena, Bratsk, Taishet, Irkutsk, Igarka, R. Yenisei, Novosibirsk, R. Ob, Omsk, R. Irtysh, Karaganda, Mointy, Frunze, Vorkuta, Salekhard, Sverdlovsk, Tashkent, Syr-Darya, Murmansk, Archangel, Kotlas, Dushanbe, Samarkand, Ashkhabad, Gorky, Kazan, Kuybyshev, Syzran, R. Volga, Leningrad, Moscow, Kharkov, Volgograd, Astrakhan, Krasnodar, Riga, Minsk, Kiev, R. Dnieper, Odessa, Tbilisi, Baku his home base. The apparent intention here was to compromise Beria and prevent his aggrandizement which, according to Khrushchev, was beginning to frighten even Stalin.[31]

In the last eight years of Stalin's life, Soviet domestic and foreign politics were conducted against a backcloth of innuendo and intrigue, where important men danced attendance upon the whim of a progressively paranoid autocrat whose word, effectively, was law. After 1946 Stalin shunned publicity as he shunned daylight. He worked at night, and summoned the Politburo to watch American films, have dinner or drinking sessions in the middle of the night. After a full day's work officials would wait in their offices until dawn if there was a chance that the 'Boss' would phone them. Khrushchev said that he regularly managed only a few hours sleep before returning to work after a night with Stalin. Increasingly also no one dared contradict him even when he was patently wrong. In a discussion with Yugoslav comrades in 1948, Stalin refused to accept that the Netherlands was a part of the Benelux countries, and none of his Politburo colleagues dared correct him.[32] In the same year, when the housing situation was almost universally known to be appalling, he announced publicly that Moscow had abolished slums.[33]

As Lenin had been concerned with trivia and detail, such as housing allocations,[34] Stalin, too, dared not delegate where it could be avoided. He read and appended comments to the papers of cases of interrogations by the security forces. He pronounced on ideology, economics, music and literature. In the summer of 1950, when more than enough was happening on the international stage to absorb his energies, Stalin engaged in a polemic in *Pravda* on the linguistic theories of the obscure Professor N. Y. Marr.[35] Then, in 1952, Stalin published a book: *Economic Problems of Socialism in the USSR*. However, Stalin did not see such things as diversions; rather they were an integral part of the one thing that claimed his full attention – the political process. Since he regarded himself as the successor to the ideological and intellectual mantles of Marx and Lenin, he was obliged to wield dialectic and the pen in pursuit of his political goals, as well as the raw power of the Red Army and the secret police. Adam B. Ulam wrote that Stalin 'was easily bored with every game but that of politics'.[36]

In August 1948, Andrei Zhdanov, Stalin's presumed heir, died suddenly and upset the equilibrium of the Soviet hierarchy. His death also removed his protection from his protégés. In a striking parallel with the Kirov Affair, which also centred on Leningrad,[37] between 1948–50 all but one of Zhdanov's closest associates and supporters were arrested and executed, seemingly for involvement in a mysterious conspiracy surrounding his death. Eventually over 2,000 were purged in this way, including Nikolai Vosnesensky, since 1938 head of Gosplan (economic director of the USSR), member of the State Defence Committee in the war and of the Academy of Science and full member of the Politburo; Alexis Kuznetsov, party boss of Leningrad from 1945; and Mikhail Rodionov, Prime Minister of the Russian Federal Republic. The Zhdanov protégé who escaped inexplicably was Finance Minister, First Deputy Prime Minister and member of the eleven-man Politburo, Alexei Kosygin, whose life hung by a thread for the rest of Stalin's years.[38] In 1954 the Minister of State Security from 1946–51, Viktor Abakumov, was executed for having falsified the Zhdanov Affair, and yet he can only have been acting on the instructions of Beria, and ultimately Stalin – both of whom were dead by this time. Interestingly, Abakumov had long been a protégé of Malenkov, the one man who appeared to profit immediately from the affair since he put his own supporters into the recently vacated positions of importance in the Leningrad party and thus strengthened his own power base.

From August 1949 problems accumulated which pressed heavily on Stalin. Although economically the country was recovering, the hardship caused had cost him much of the popular reverence, and even affection, in which he had been widely held in 1945. The Soviet people had faced and overcome enormous suffering and privation in the war, and had experienced the apparent development of a bond between leader and led,[39] between ideology and motherland, but they quickly found out that all was transient. The public exhortations to greater effort and continued self-sacrifice continued, but the camps filled and Stalin's grip tightened on a people to whom no trust or relaxation of control was to be accorded.

Nevertheless, in his final years, his own abilities to keep on top of the myriad details of government declined. The power struggles between his subordinates came out in the open, with the *Vozhd* lending tacit support first to one side and then to the other. Hindsight shows that there were effectively only two sides. Georgi Malenkov and Lavrenti Beria appeared as allies pushing the candidature of the former for Stalin's position. On the other side was Nikita Sergeivitch Khrushchev, not as powerful as the other two, and not taken absolutely seriously as a candidate for the leadership, but strongly supported in the Moscow and Ukraine parties and by individuals like Leonid Brezhnev. The other major figures in the Politburo – Molotov, Bulganin, Kaganovitch and Voroshilov – had no major power bases from which they could attempt to gain the leadership. However, they aimed at preventing anybody else from having it, by holding the balance of power between the two factions with a view to 'returning' to a collective leadership after Stalin's death. Certainly they had good reason to fear the possible consequences of a continuation of one-man rule. After the Leningrad Affair Stalin would stalk the corridors of the Kremlin at dead of night nursing his paranoia, and muttering that Molotov – the slavishly faithful Molotov – and Mikoyan were British spies. The state of mind of these two, given Stalin's penchant for summary justice, can only be guessed at, but it must have affected all who were within reach of Stalin's suspicions.

Between 1950–53 agriculture became a centre of controversy between the factions in the party leadership. On 24 March 1951 *Pravda* published an article by Khrushchev which advocated building *agrogorods* and effectively revolutionizing peasant life by creating a 'town' and therefore 'worker' ambience in the countryside. The following day *Pravda* announced that the article had been published in error: it was not an editorial, and was for discussion only. Official approval, that is, Stalin's, had been withdrawn from Khrushchev's scheme, and Beria and Malenkov weighed into the attack on the agrotown concept and, by extension, its author.

Khrushchev's set-back was temporary however. Eighteen months later he was to be the tool by which Stalin would effect far-reaching changes in the party at the Nineteenth Congress of the Party. By and large Stalin ignored the Supreme Soviet, the Politburo and the Central Committee. He ruled through his General Secretary's office and through a caucus of senior figures. In 1952, however, he called a congress of the party, the first since 1939.

In October 1952 1,192 voting delegates, from all over the USSR, met in Moscow at the Nineteenth Congress of the CPSU. Stalin played little direct part in the Congress and although he had, effectively, scripted the proceedings, the major speeches were made by Malenkov and Khrushchev. As its final act the Congress elected a new 125 man Central Committee as the repository of authority until the next congress. This is the reason for which the Congress had been summoned, and following this, Stalin showed his hand. The new Central Committee was packed with younger, more reliable men, and when it first met on 16 October under Stalin's chairmanship it approved his proposals to enlarge the Politburo (renamed Praesidium) from eleven to twenty-five full members plus eleven non-voting or candidate members, and to enlarge the General Secretariat from five to ten members.[40] Stalin then stepped down as General Secretary, a post he had held since 1922. Further, the Central Committee unanimously approved his nominations to the Praesidium and Secretariat. He had achieved his aim. The two crucial organs of the party were so enlarged with his undoubted supporters as to dilute the importance and power of the old guard, against whom he could now move when the time was right. In his Secret Speech of 1956 (see Chapter 3) Khrushchev said that Stalin's proposal at the Nineteenth Congress '. . . was a design for the future annihilation of the old Politburo'. It undoubtedly was. After all, this was the same Stalin who had presaged the 1937–8 Great Purge at the Central Committee meeting of 1937 where he was applauded with frantic enthusiasm when he told members that treason was rife in the party and elsewhere, and that *all* party officials must promptly select two understudies and have them fully trained within six months. In other words, two out of three party *apparatchiki* were to be liquidated.

On 13 January 1953 came the starting pistol for Stalin's new purge. It was announced that nine doctors (of whom seven were Jews), who had all attended the Soviet élite, had been arrested on charges of murdering Zhdanov in 1948, the Moscow party boss, Scherbakov, in 1945 and others. Confessions were published from some of the doctors, who were arrested in November 1952, soon after the Nineteenth Congress. Two had died under interrogation, 'proving' that they were acting under orders from a Zionist organization at the behest of the British and Americans. Diplomatic relations with Israel were severed and a witch-hunt began for traitors. Many Jews in public life were arrested, including Palgunov, the head of the news agency *Tass*, and Molotov's wife, Pauline. At least 8,000 people were arrested in the two months the purge lasted, many of whom died. It seems that Khrushchev was privy to the plot details and that if Stalin had lived, the purge may have claimed Molotov, Mikoyan, Beria and Voroshilov, and might even have touched Malenkov.

Within two days of Stalin's death, the old guard reversed the decisions of the Nineteenth Congress. Politburo membership was cut from thirty-six to fourteen (ten full and four alternate members) and the Secretariat from ten to seven members. All the younger beneficiaries of the Congress, such as Brezhnev, were demoted, and on 3 April, Beria, who was in a position to know, announced publicly that the Doctors' Plot had been a fabrication and those responsible would be punished.

The 73-year-old dictator died of a stroke on 5 March 1953 after a brief illness. On 6 March *Pravda* announced that 'the heart of Lenin's comrade-in-arms, the standard bearer of his genius and his cause, the wise leader and teacher of the CPSU has ceased to exist'. Distrustful of each other, and with no accepted succession procedures, the collective leadership feared the unknown that lay ahead of them. The Moscow garrison commanders were arrested, Beria's MVD troops sealed off the city, and on 7 March *Pravda* appealed that there should be 'no panic and disarray'.

Although many people breathed easier (and longer) once Stalin was gone, and although his successors quickly dismantled the terror machinery, many felt as Khrushchev did: 'Far from looking forward to Stalin's death, I actually feared it. I was afraid of the consequences.'[41] They agreed with his comment to the American Ambassador: 'Like Peter the Great, Stalin fought barbarism with barbarism, but he was a great man.'[42]

It is true that Khrushchev's great man industrialized, urbanized and politicized Soviet society. He educated the USSR, waged war upon the peasantry, committed awesome atrocities against the Soviet people and made the Soviet state strong, respected and feared. A product of the Bolshevik Party, he institutionalized party rule, and manipulated the party as he saw fit. Scholars have debated whether Stalin corrupted Lenin's Revolution or whether he was Lenin's direct heir. Was Stalin's Russia inevitable once the Revolution had happened? Was he the master of the system or the victim of it? These questions are frequently answered with conviction but they remain hypothetical.[43]

Although Stalin's successors demoted him in the Soviet pantheon, he retained support among those who approved of his brand of communism and who had benefited from his rule. Moscow cinema audiences still sometimes applaud his image on the screen.[44] In 1976 Defence Minister Dmitri Ustinov was twice prevented by applause from continuing a speech to an audience of 6,000 in the Kremlin's Great Hall of Congress when he referred to 'Comrade Stalin'. Stalin's regime was brutal and its passing was marked by a grisly incident which occurred when his body was placed on public view in the Kremlin a few days after his death. Crowds queueing in the half-light and subzero cold of the Moscow winter rioted, and scores were trampled to death in the snow.

# Three

# KHRUSHCHEV: THE UNEASY SUCCESION

*Маленков*

Stalin died politically intestate, as had Lenin before him, and the succession crises which followed both deaths pointed to the central fact of Soviet politics: that the *fons et origo* of political power was the Communist Party and he who controlled the party machine had the potential to attain supreme power. Supreme power did not follow automatically upon accession to the First Secretaryship; this power derived from the influential positions held at all levels by party members, their numbers, commitment and privilege. The First Secretary deals directly with the republican parties, transmits central policy to them and reports to the Central Committee on behalf of the CPSU. He appoints candidates – technically with the approval of the Politburo[1] – to the important posts in republican party organizations and naturally appoints his supporters. He is in a position to gauge the mood of the party and to mobilize it. He can claim that as guardian of the party, bequeathed as the repository of political truth by Lenin, he is also the guardian of the tablets of Marxist–Leninism.

Possibly the potential of the First Secretaryship was not grasped by the Praesidium in March 1953. Possibly it was felt that Stalin's victories over Trotsky, Kamenev, Zinoviev and Bukharin owed as much to his predilection for political intrigue as to his control of the party. Perhaps Malenkov and his supporters felt that times were changing and the party could now become the servant of the state rather than its master. Whatever the reasoning, on 14 March 1953, Malenkov chose the Premiership rather than the First Secretaryship when he was forced to decide between the two offices by his Praesidium colleagues, who feared that he might become another Stalin. Khrushchev, his chief opponent, received the First Secretaryship, even though he was not publicly referred to as First Secretary until September 1953. Before this date he was known just as the first in the Secretariat, by virtue of seniority. The power struggle between Khrushchev and Malenkov was to continue until 1957, but essentially Malenkov lost the race on 14 March 1953.

Within twenty-four hours of the announcement of Stalin's death, all those who had benefited from Stalin's expansion of the Praesidium and the Secretariat at the Nineteenth Congress – like Brezhnev and Kosygin – were summarily demoted. The Praesidium was reduced from thirty-six to fourteen members and the Secretariat from ten to seven members. Government ministries were reduced from fifty-two to twenty-five.

The death of Stalin occasioned a power struggle but it was just that, a struggle for power since disagreement over policy was more apparent than real. All Stalin's heirs had risen to pre-eminence as his creatures who had grown in his shadow, but they recognized that they could safely relax some of the harsher controls over a cowed populace and win public support in so doing. On 28 March 1953 an amnesty was announced for most prisoners serving terms of less than five years and the prison and labour camps began to release untold thousands of a prison population which at its height may have numbered up to 15 *million*.[2] On 3 April it was announced that the Doctors' Plot had been a fabrication and those responsible were to be punished for their part in 'this criminal provocation' and for using 'impermissible methods of investigation'.[3] In the words of one who was there: 'This was a bombshell of unprecedented dimension. Never before had the secret police been officially accused of doing what everybody knew they did but nobody dared mention even in a whisper.'[4] Furthermore, 8,000 people were cleared (many posthumously) of complicity in the plot,[5] and the Praesidium limited the power of the secret police.

Apparently this threat to his power base made Lavrenti Beria make his move in June 1953. Hitherto he had supported Malenkov, but Beria had always been one of the major contenders for supreme power. He had regained control of his old empire of the MGB and MVD which had been split by Stalin. The only counterweight to Beria's strength was the army, which had no cause to support him. The generals distrusted Malenkov for the role he had played in the Great Purge, the way he had reported on them to Stalin during the war and for his 'new course' policies (see page 22). It was Khrushchev, the man who engineered the *coup* against Beria, who drummed up army support. During the war Khrushchev, unlike Beria, Malenkov, Molotov and others, was not based in Moscow. He had been a political commissar and had served as a lieutenant-general in the field, where he had earned a degree of popularity in the army and had got on well with some of the senior generals, including Marshal Zhukov.

On 27 June 1953 Red Army units surrounded the Kremlin and prevented the security forces from supporting their chief, who was arrested, tried and shot, as were many of his subordinates in the next few months.[6] The unlamented Beria became the scapegoat for the Doctors' Plot, the Leningrad Affair, the split with Yugoslavia and the Berlin uprising (see Chapter 8). But with Beria gone, Malenkov had lost his chief supporter.

Georgi Malenkov was intelligent, able and ambitious and had succeeded Zhdanov, in 1948, as Stalin's favourite. An educated man of some sophistication, he represented the rising breed of 'technocrats' who possessed skills and not just ideological purity, for whom the party was a means not an end, who wanted to better living standards and to move away from the hard-line doctrines of continuing stark confrontation with the capitalists. Much of the 'thaw' in the Cold War (see Chapter 8) which followed Stalin's death was of his doing. Malenkov presented his 'new course' to the Supreme Soviet in August 1953, advocating more production of food stuffs and consumer goods at the expense of heavy industry. This alienated still further the military who saw the prospect of a diminution of spending on arms if funds were diverted to light industry and agriculture. Moreover, the 'new course' offended the Stalinists, such as Molotov, for whom any variation from the Stalinist path was heresy. They also did not accept Malenkov's theses that more could be spent on raising living standards and relatively less on heavy industry and defence *because* war with the West was no longer inevitable. More importantly, Malenkov alienated part of his power base in the party.

Malenkov had the backing of the technocrats and government ministries, as well as parts of the Leningrad and Moscow parties. Since purging the former in 1948 he had made his supporter Adrianov boss of Leningrad, while the Moscow party had been run by Malenkov until Khrushchev took it over in 1949. Khrushchev, too, had the support of part of the Moscow party. He had not been in charge long enough to winkle out all Malenkov's men. He could also call upon the Ukraine party and the benevolent neutrality of the armed forces. However, when Malenkov presented his 'new course' to the Supreme Soviet without having first referred it to the Central Committee of the CPSU, then career party members, the *apparatchiki*, began to turn to Khrushchev to defend their interests. It was said of Malenkov that 'his weakness was his unconscious Menshevik liking for parliamentary institutions and the rumour, gaining ground, that he would subordinate the Party to the Supreme Soviet if given the chance.'[7]

Khrushchev condemned Malenkov's foreign policy ideas as revisionist and became the spokesman of the military–industrial complex 'metal-eaters' in his attacks on the 'new course', but only until the power struggle was over. Afterwards Khrushchev adopted Malenkov's programme wholesale and became the champion of 'coexistence' with the West and 'goulash communism'. Allied with Foreign Minister Molotov and others in the Praesidium, Khrushchev forced the resignation of Malenkov from the Premiership on 8 February 1955; but Khrushchev had already won. In December 1954 he went to

Peking and negotiated the supply to China of capital equipment, the manufacture of which in the USSR necessitated the diversion of any extra funds previously earmarked for light industry. This effectively killed off what was left of the 'new course'. In the same month, Victor Abakumov, Malenkov's man, was executed for his role in the Leningrad Affair.

Khrushchev's defeat of Malenkov did not make him all-powerful. The rest of the Praesidium were careful to prevent that. In fact Malenkov, the technocrat and manager, was appointed Minister of Electric Power Stations and stayed in the Praesidium where his influence remained strong, if diminished.

The Premiership went to Nikolai Bulganin, and Bulganin's old Ministry of Defence to Khrushchev's ally, Marshal Zhukov. But Khrushchev had become the man to stop, and his tacit alliance with Molotov broke down as the Foreign Minister opposed any departure from Stalinism – in particular Khrushchev's attempted *rapprochement* with Yugoslavia (see Chapter 8).

Born to Russian peasant parents in 1894, Nikita Sergeivitch Khrushchev had no formal education and owed everything to the party, luck and his native wit and ability. He joined the party in 1918 and moved up the ladder in the Ukraine and Moscow on the coat-tails of Lazar Kaganovitch by showing prodigious abilities to work, organize, learn and survive until, in 1938, he was appointed First Secretary of the Ukrainian CP, one of the most powerful posts in the USSR.

Although Khrushchev lacked social polish he was unique among his Kremlin confrères in that he had charm, humour and spontaneity. A short, fat, avuncular figure, his image was deceptive. He was not the cuddly Russian bear portrayed by Western cartoonists, but a steely-willed *apparatchik* who had been a party to and had profited from the Great Purge. He had himself purged the Ukraine before and after the war when he must have connived at, if not directed, the deportation to Siberia of surviving Ukrainian Jews. Khrushchev came up through a hard school of privation, war, purge and intrigue. He saw his first wife die of exhaustion in the famine of 1920. Although he was utterly ruthless in his pursuit of power, he was prepared to abandon terror in the mid 1950s, feeling that it had served its purpose.

Khrushchev differed from his Praesidium colleagues in his willingness to do the unexpected and to take risks. At the Twentieth Congress of the CPSU in February 1956, he delivered his 'Secret Speech'[8] in which he denounced Stalin's abuse of power, shifted the thrust of Soviet foreign policy from 'confrontation' to 'coexistence' and lifted an edge of the carpet which covered the horrors that had been committed in the name of communism. In fact, destalinization and the 'thaw' with the West had been taking place quietly and undramatically since Stalin died.

Khrushchev also introduced some liberalism into the arts, economy and life of the individual, although this could probably have been effected without shaking the foundations of the Soviet state; for that is what Khrushchev did. He denounced Stalin's personality cult and his instigation of the Great Purge and later purges. He blamed Stalin for the USSR's military unpreparedness and defeats in 1941. He criticized the deportation of whole nationalities to Siberia (see Chapter 6). But this was all blamed on Stalin personally and no criticism was levelled at the system which Stalin had created. Also, no criticism was made of Stalin's actions before 1934, nor of his destruction of Trotsky, Bukharin and others, nor of the millions of deaths which resulted from his enforced collectivization of agriculture.

Truly Khrushchev had opened a Pandora's box. Until 1956 all communist parties, even China's, took their lead from Moscow. All had owed fealty to Moscow and to Stalin. Yet many of the congress delegates, both Soviet and foreign, had benefited from Stalinism, believed in it and practised it. Communists had lived through the frightening circumstances of collectivization, industrialization, purge, war and Cold War, but throughout there had been the immutable Stalin to whom the faithful could turn. Doctrine could change, for Stalin had changed it, but in his last decade, his personality cult had transcended doctrine. He was the constant, the *icon* to which the communist world bowed the knee, but if Stalin could be challenged, what then was sacred?

The speech, intended only for the congress delegates, was leaked to the USA, which published it to the world in June 1956. The speech and the congress itself had more immediate effects in other communist states (see Chapter 10) since the Soviet people remained uninformed. Nevertheless the domestic impact of the speech was considerable. Many local party officials destalinized enthusiastically. Equally, many simply went through the motions, for if one First Secretary had been shown to be a falsifier of history and a mass-murderer, how trustworthy was another? Many *apparatchiki* must have echoed the Italian CP leader, Palmiro Togliatti, who suggested that 'the Russian comrades should surely, in the light of Khrushchev's revelations, be asking themselves some heart-searching questions about the very nature of the Soviet system and, in all humility, seeking ways and means of changing it'.[9]

There was change, of course: not only had the Twentieth Congress instigated it, but in cutting the powers of the secret police, Khrushchev denied himself some of the means of preventing change. As Alec Nove wrote: 'Fear greatly diminished. Personal feelings of security increased'.[10] Prisoners returned to their families and there were few political arrests. Debate increased, and party organs met more frequently and were required to operate more constitutionally. New men moved towards the higher reaches of the party. The Twentieth Congress elected fifty-three new members (mostly Khrushchev supporters) to the 133 seat Central Committee, and the press began to carry edited reports of its proceedings and some criticisms of ministries. However, there was no criticism of the party leadership, nor of general policy.

In the party leadership itself, the hostile reaction to the speech – by Molotov, Malenkov, Kaganovitch and Voroshilov – was strong enough to hobble Khrushchev for the next twelve months. The Central Committee resumed some of its early authority *vis-à-vis* the Praesidium, and the shocks of Poland, Hungary and Suez (see Chapters 8 and 10) convinced many hardliners that Khrushchev had gone too far. Isaac Deutscher wrote in 1967: 'Since the Twentieth Congress, people have been aware how much of what they once believed was made up of forgeries and myths. They want to learn the truth but are denied access to it . . . . The ideological edifice of Stalinism has been exploded: but, the structure still stands; and people are required to live in it.'[11] It was not just the Stalinist bubble that had been burst of course; destalinization went much deeper. A French journalist wrote that:

> No other society . . . has ever claimed to be the result of objective social laws, which the proletariat interprets and applies, under the guidance of the party, in order to arrive at the Revolution. For communists, history is merely the analysis of this process and they cannot twist it round without the risk of reaching a point where the justification for the Revolution, and its title to continue in being are lost. As a result, a communist society is more shaken than any other when it finds that its official history had been deformed and falsified. It then feels that both its past and present . . . have been thrown into doubt.[12]

Furthermore, although the Twentieth Congress highlighted some falsifications of the past, it did not replace them with truths, but instead introduced other falsifications. History was rewritten to downgrade Stalin's role, as he had downgraded the role of others. Beria was 'unpersoned', as Stalin had 'unpersoned' Trotsky before him.[13] Indeed after Khrushchev returned to the attack on Stalin at the Twenty-second Congress of the CPSU in 1961, Stalin's remains were removed from the Lenin mausoleum in Red Square and interred without ceremony at the wall of the Kremlin. Since then, except in his birthplace of Georgia, Stalin's statue has largely disappeared from public view.[14] His name was virtually expunged from literature, history and the Soviet map (Stalingrad became Volgograd). References to him became guarded, but he could not be written out of history altogether. Anyway, the CPSU went no further in condemning Stalin after 1964 than had Khrushchev before.

The doubts and hostility engendered in the party and abroad – especially in China – towards destalinization must have been anticipated by Khrushchev even if the hardliner backlash generated by Poland and Hungary was unexpected; so why did he take such a risk? A contemporary observer put it simply:

Khrushchev and his associates were trying to modernise the Soviet state and free it from the ossified rigidity into which Stalin had fixed it. But obviously this process could not succeed if those hostile to it could at any time appeal to Stalin's actions and writings as holy writ. It was necessary to demolish Stalin's moral authority if his policies were to be repudiated.[15]

Nevertheless, although Khrushchev's motives may have been of the highest, many felt that his actions were irresponsible, designed to further his political cause in the Praesidium even if, by so doing, he undermined the whole Soviet system. Furthermore, he built up enmities which contributed to his fall eight years later for he had 'cast doubts on the deeds and personal sacrifices that millions had made in Stalin's cause with Stalin's name on their lips. He had made so many look so foolish or so guilty for their silent adulation of Stalin.'[16]

In terms of power balance in the party leadership, the immediate outcome of the Twentieth Congress was favourable to Khrushchev. The new men on the Central Committee were mostly his nominees, as were the five newly created candidate members of the Praesidium who included Leonid Brezhnev and Marshal Zhukov. Also, Molotov, one of his most ardent Praesidium opponents, was replaced as Foreign Minister by Shepilev in June 1956. But Poland and Hungary changed this situation, and in November 1956 the Stalinist Molotov was again promoted to be Minister of State Control with the power to examine all aspects of government. The hardliners had opposed the reconciliation with Tito, and when Belgrade condemned the Soviet invasion of Hungary, Khrushchev's foreign policy was seriously damaged.

Although he had dominated the Twentieth Congress, Khrushchev did not speak at the Central Committee meeting of December 1956 and was so much on the defensive that he began to defend Stalin publicly. On 31 December he declared: 'Stalin was a great Marxist. He made mistakes but we are all responsible for the mistakes which were made at that time.' On 17 January 1957, at a reception at the Chinese Embassy, he went further: 'I wish that God [sic] would help every communist to fight like Stalin.'[17]

Khrushchev's Praesidium opponents did not attack his destalinization policies openly, after all, Stalin had been officially declared a mass murderer. However, one of the major objections to Khrushchev was the pace of change he sought to introduce. Also, he was the one man who could still step into Stalin's shoes. In fact, Malenkov, Molotov, Kaganovitch and the others of the Anti-Party Group were able to attack Khrushchev's record not just because of destalinization and his power hunger, but also on the more tangible issues of foreign affairs, the economy and administration.

The Secret Speech was seen to give rise to the crises of Poland and

Hungary, in which Soviet authority was only restored by the display of military strength so naked that it shocked many foreign communists and Third World countries into a reappraisal of their attitudes towards Moscow. In addition, the mutual distaste of Khrushchev and Mao Tse-Tung, fuelled by the ideological differences between Moscow and Peking which had been revealed by the speech, exacerbated and accelerated the great schism of the communist world (see Chapter 11). Furthermore, the 'neo-imperialist' spasm of the Suez crisis made many in the Kremlin wonder if they could peacefully coexist with the Western powers.

By December 1956 the sixth Five-Year Plan adopted by the Twentieth Congress had already proved unworkable, and was soon to be abandoned. It was replaced two years later by a Seven-Year Plan which granted sweeping powers to the industrial ministries but not enough power to the co-ordinating agencies. This resulted in lopsided economic development as the strongest ministries cornered most resources. The December 1956 Central Committee meeting made Mikhail Pervukhin, one of Malenkov's allies, government minister in charge of the whole economy, thus reducing the power of Khrushchev and the party *apparat*. This then was the Anti-Party Group, the allies of Georgi Malenkov who intended to run the state and economy through the government ministries – on technological and managerial, rather than ideological or party lines.

Once again the party *apparatchiki* gathered to Khrushchev, and in February 1957 he fought back and decentralized economic management by creating *sovnarkhozy* or regional economic councils. The effect of this was to undermine the ministerial power bases of the Anti-Party Group by returning economic control to the party *apparat*.

At a Praesidium meeting on 19 June 1957, Khrushchev was accused of pursuing opportunist and Trotskyist policies and was voted out of the leadership by seven votes to four. Malenkov, Molotov, Kaganovitch, Bulganin, Voroshilov, Saburov and Pervukhin voted against him. The four votes in Khrushchev's favour were his own and those of Mikoyan, Suslov and Kirichenko. However, it is a measure of how civilized, or naïve, or confident, Soviet government had become that not only was Khrushchev not tried or throttled (*vide* Beria), but that his colleagues accepted his argument that he had been elected First Secretary by the Central Committee and only the Central Committee could depose him.

The Central Committee was convened and the power of the First Secretary to appoint to senior party posts came into its own. Khrushchev's supporters then staged a filibuster: 215 of the 309 members present by 22 June had spoken for him, of whom Madame Furtseva spoke for six hours. This gave Marshal Zhukov time to deploy military aircraft to fly Khrushchev supporters in from the provinces. Khrushchev won the vote, but his need for wide support limited the extent of his victory. The Central Committee refused to accede to his request that the Anti-Party Group be disgraced and dismissed. Malenkov, the technocrat, was sent to Kazakhstan to manage a power station. Molotov went as Ambassador to Mongolia. Kaganovitch, the longest serving member of the Praesidium (1930–57), was sent to Sverdlovsk to manage a cement works. Pervukhin became a divisional chief of Gosplan, Saburov sank into obscurity. Bulganin was only removed in March 1958, but after he had denounced his co-conspirators he received a pension and a dacha near Moscow where he lived until his death in 1975. Of all the Anti-Party Group, Marshal Kliment Voroshilov was so popular that he was only denounced in 1962 and immediately rehabilitated.

After the defeat of the Anti-Party Group, the Praesidium was increased to fifteen full members – including Zhukov, Furtseva and Frol Kozlov, soon to be Khrushchev's heir apparent – and nine candidate members. Most of them were Khrushchev supporters and after March 1958, as First Secretary and Premier, he ruled relatively supreme; although never as unchallenged as Stalin. Thereafter, successful challenge could only come from those whom he had promoted. But although the Anti-Party Group was defeated, its views remained influential. Kozlov was warning against 'goulash communism' when he said that Malenkov 'made crude political mistakes distorting the Leninist line on the preferential development of heavy industry'. On 5 July 1957, at the height of Khrushchev's victory, the army newspaper, *Red Star*, warned: 'Enormous harm to our state would occur if . . . the tempos of further development of industry . . . were weakened.'[18] Many factors aided Khrushchev's victory, but the help of Zhukov and the military was invaluable. Zhukov was the first serving soldier to sit on the Praesidium and he quickly made his mark. He called for an investigation into Stalin's repressions and wanted to give military training priority over political instruction in the armed forces. The former threatened to take the destalinization issue out of Khrushchev's hands and thus upset the delicate Praesidium consensus on how far destalinization could safely go. The latter threatened the primacy of the party. Besides, Zhukov was a conventional, if brilliant, general of the old school of mass armies, armour and the Russian 'steamroller' concept. But a radical change in Soviet strategic thinking came about when the launching of sputnik inaugurated the era of the inter-continental ballistic missile and rendered obsolescent ideas of defence based simply upon weight of numbers.

At the beginning of October 1957 Zhukov was sacked from the Praesidium and the Ministry of Defence. He was accused of creating a personality cult, 'adventurism' in foreign policy, 'Bonapartism' and complicity in Stalin's negligence at the beginning of the Second World War. The USSR has always been wary of influential soldiers in politics, but it is difficult to imagine the bluff Zhukov as a Boulanger[19] or even an Eisenhower, much less a Bonaparte. Zhukov went quietly and was replaced as Defence Minister by the almost equally distinguished Marshal Malinovsky.

From the time that he became Premier until he was deposed in 1964, Soviet domestic and foreign policies were largely, although not entirely, shaped by Khrushchev. He radiated confidence and optimism, some of which rubbed off on others. He cracked down on dissenting intellectuals after Hungary, and he persecuted Boris Pasternak, refusing to let him accept the Nobel Prize for Literature in 1958. But in May 1959, Khrushchev declared at the third USSR Writers' Congress that the 'revisionists' had been defeated and that the party would now let writers settle their own internal problems. This did not lift censorship but made it less restrictive. Khrushchev personally sanctioned the publication of Solzhenitsyn's *One Day in the Life of Ivan Denisovitch*, about a day – a good day – in the Arctic cold of one of Stalin's labour camps. After Stalin's death, Ilya Ehrenburg had published *The Thaw*, in which he showed up the barren cultural values of his countrymen. After the Twentieth Congress Vladimir Dudintsev's, *Not by Bread Alone* attacked the 'new class' of the non-ideological bureaucracy which had become a haven for narrow-minded, unprincipled self-seekers.[20] Konstantin Simonov's *Victims and Heroes* dealt openly with the tragic days at the beginning of the war, and the literary journal *Novy Mir*, under the editorship of the poet Alexander Tvardovsky, continued to push at the bounds of the permissible. Intellectual freedom was limited but also erratic because it depended upon the whim of Khrushchev, who liked literature but detested experiments in art. On 1 December 1962 he visited the Manezh exhibition in Moscow and thundered against the abstract art he saw there: 'This is art for donkeys . . . . You're a nice-looking lad, but how could you paint something like this . . . . Why aren't you ashamed of this mess?'[21] A crack down followed which spread to music and literature but by the summer of 1963 *Novy Mir* was still publishing pieces by Pasternak and Yevtushenko despite the fact that both writers were in disgrace.

The freedoms extended to intellectuals in the early 1960s incensed the orthodox in the Soviet hierarchy. The regime had difficulty deciding how much freedom the artist should have. Since he used media that were susceptible to wide publication and circulation, the artist was dangerous if his message could not be controlled by the state. Khrushchev's biographer, Edward Crankshaw, wrote: 'The cultural battlefront offers the deepest insights into the minds and the expedients of the Soviet leadership . . . . the only [opposition] politicians as we understand the term in the Soviet Union are the artists of all kinds.'[22] The censorship curtain came down after Khrushchev's departure leaving the intellectuals as one of the few groups in the USSR to mourn his passing. Nevertheless, relative intellectual freedom was not matched by a similar attitude to religion for Khrushchev was impatient that this continued to attract adherents (see Chapter 6).

But then, Khrushchev and many of his compatriots viewed freedom differently from the Western perspective. On one occasion he declared: 'Under the dictatorship of the proletariat there can be no such thing as absolute "freedom",' and on another: 'Most people still measure their own freedom in terms of how much meat, how many potatoes or what kind of boots they can get for one rouble.'[23] This was the kind of freedom, of destalinization, at which Khrushchev aimed for the USSR; the material well-being of 'goulash communism' where the staple meal would be goulash (which has meat and a variety of vegetables in it) rather than the traditional bortsch (which frequently only had cabbage in it). The agricultural abundance and distributive efficiency needed to give goulash to everybody were to be achieved partly through the harvest increases which followed his Virgin Lands scheme (see Chapter 5), and partly through administrative reorganization, such as the introduction of the *sovnarkhozy* in February 1957, but also through exhortation.

Khrushchev stumped the country, blustering, encouraging and cajoling the people to raise production so that more consumer goods would be available which would create a favourable popular climate for the reforms of industry and agriculture, which would in turn create higher productivity, and so on. Once the wheel was turning, Khrushchev believed that the cycle of increased production, better living standards and greater personal freedoms would be self-sustaining, but he apparently also thought that public statements of success (even if not yet true) could so enthuse the listeners that they would go away and make the statements true.

In November 1957 he claimed that heavy industry had reached such levels that more resources could be diverted to light industry (the very thing for which he had earlier criticized Malenkov).[24] At the Twenty-first Congress of the CPSU in January 1959 he declared that the USSR was moving from socialism towards full communism and that the process would be complete when 'we shall have provided a complete abundance of everything needed to satisfy the requirements of all the people. Communism is impossible without this.'[25] At the Twenty-second Congress in 1961 he announced that there was no longer a dictatorship of the proletariat, that the triumph of socialism in the USSR was complete and that communism would be achieved by 1980. The state had now become a 'state of the entire people, expressing the interests of the will of the people as a whole', which meant that there was no longer any danger of its overthrow by internal enemies. However, although the Twenty-second

Congress declared that 'capitalist encirclement' (an idea basic to Stalinism) was at an end, the military forces of the state were to remain intact.

These were revolutionary pronouncements which appealed to the *stakhanovite*[26] work ethic and ideological enthusiasm of the 'new socialist man'.[27] However, they did not describe the state of the USSR as it was then. Meanwhile, Khrushchev failed to carry the other Soviet leaders with him. Besides, the agricultural miracle of the virgin lands, which was to pay for the transition to communism, had already run into difficulties.

In fact, the only significant way to switch the Soviet effort away from heavy industry was to cut the cost of the military. In parallel with the contemporary American Radford Plan he accepted Eisenhower's idea that a nuclear weapons-based defence allowed savings in military man-power.[28] In 1960 troop cuts of 1.2 million were announced, but, after the split with China and the Berlin and Cuba crises Khrushchev's opponents refused to accept that the international situation was peaceful enough to allow the USSR to demobilize part of her armed forces. In fact, the very next year Khrushchev had to climb down. Defence spending was increased by one-third and the release of troops stopped.

In other fields Khrushchev achieved greater success. Maternity leave was increased from 70 to 112 days, a minimum wage law benefited the lower-paid, pensions and disability allowances were increased and the law forbidding workers from changing jobs without permission was repealed. The sixth Plan provided for more housing and some increases in consumer goods. In September 1958 he tried to root out privilege from the education system. In secondary and higher education he abandoned the tuition fees that had been introduced by Stalin in 1940, and tried to promote more vocational courses and ensure that the bulk of those entering higher education had at least two years' work experience. This latter was so unpopular in the world of education and among the privileged that it failed to work and was abandoned.

The destalinization drive led to the appearance in 1958 of the Fundamental Principles of Criminal Legislation which reduced the number of crimes punishable by death. Such measures showed that although Khrushchev was a man of vision, it was frequently not a coherent vision. After Beria's removal, the leadership abolished the dual system of public order under which, alongside the regular courts, police tribunals could ignore the criminal code and deal with suspects. Instead, the principle was established that no one should be punished except by a duly constituted court of law. Khrushchev flouted this principle when he argued for the creation of 'comrades' courts', a volunteer 'people's guard' and the 'anti-parasite' laws. This raised the spectre of vigilantes meting out summary justice to those guilty of street crimes and vandalism which started to increase in the 1960s.

Certainly Khrushchev contributed much to the Soviet Union, but at a price that his colleagues became reluctant to pay until, on 14 October 1964, the Central Committee accepted his resignation from all his offices 'in view of his advanced age and the deterioration of his health' as *Tass* announced the next day. This was a palace revolt but, in effect, Khrushchev was voted out of office by the body to which he had so successfully appealed in 1957, the body constitutionally equipped to elect or remove a First Secretary. He retired on a pension to a dacha outside Moscow where he died in obscurity in September 1971. The West was sorry to see him go, but not so the communist world. On 17 October *Pravda*, without naming Khrushchev, summed up his faults when it attacked the cult of personality as one of 'subjectivism and drifting in communist construction . . . hare-brained scheming, hasty decisions, actions divorced from reality, phrase-mongering and commandism'.[29] An American journalist wrote: 'It came to me as a discovery that Stalin had great latent prestige among ordinary people and that Khrushchev was widely regarded as a boor and a bungler practically without redeeming attributes except among the liberal intelligentsia and the rehabilitated victims of the purges who had been direct beneficiaries of his policies.'[30]

He had much to answer for. The communist world was no longer the monolith of Stalin's day. Yugoslavia had come no closer. China and Albania were heading towards open schism. Relations with Romania and Cuba were problematic. Added to which, in August 1964, *Pravda* published the 'testament' of the veteran and much respected leader of the Italian Communist Party, Palmiro Togliatti. This document was highly critical of Khrushchev's style and his split with China. He had blustered, gambled and lost over Berlin and Cuba – publicly. The Congo episode reflected no credit on the USSR. His accent on consumer production and attempted cuts in the armed forces had antagonized the 'metal-eaters' and some of the military, as had his boasting about the USSR's new 'most powerful weapon in existence with a limitless destructive power' in September 1964.[31]

There was no Zhukov to support him in 1964, and Khrushchev had alienated the nuclear and conventional wings of the army by accepting a strategy of minimum deterrence, or nuclear inferiority to the USA, and by planning to cut the defence budget again. Further, he resurrected plans to reorganize the army by reducing conventional forces which would have deprived half the junior officers of career and promotion prospects. In anticipation, the Ground Forces Command ceased to exist as a separate command shortly before his fall. These measures were all reversed after October 1964.

His occasional lack of dignity had annoyed those colleagues who felt that the USSR should present a more sophisticated face to the world. The incident at the UN in 1960 when Khrushchev interrupted British Premier Macmillan's speech by banging his shoe on the desk may have been 'partly high spirits, partly the desire of one ham to upstage another ham', but 'the faces of the rest of the Soviet delegation, their expressions of shame and outraged dignity'[32] put his actions into their domestic perspective.

The Chinese were on the verge of exploding their own bomb, and there was the fear that West Germany might also acquire a finger on the nuclear trigger. As the strategic situation became more complicated, many must have wanted the Soviet forces to be commanded by a less erratic character. In October 1964, shortly after the June 1964 signing of a new USSR–DDR treaty of friendship, Khrushchev was preparing a new European initiative with West German Chancellor Erhard. It may be that the rehabilitation of the Volga Germans in August 1964 (see page 66) was connected. Interestingly, Brezhnev and Suslov made speeches reassuring the DDR in early October 1964.[33] The prospect of a *rapprochement* with Bonn must have disturbed some of the Praesidium to whom Bonn still ranked with (or above) Washington as the arch-enemy. Failures in foreign affairs (see Chapter 8) created an atmosphere in which Khrushchev's colleagues were prepared to oust him. However, these had little impact on the ordinary citizen from whom detailed, objective knowledge about affairs in general was hidden; but Khrushchev's domestic policies and actions had directly affected the lives of the citizen and party members.

In 1964 the economy (which he had said would overtake that of the USA by 1980) was in difficulties. Between 1958–64 growth had fallen to 5.3 per cent per annum, whereas between 1950–58 national income had increased by 7.2 per cent per annum. The big harvests from the virgin lands had fallen off as soil became exhausted and Khrushchev's efforts to switch investment into the chemical industry, which produced fertilizers, had been thwarted by his opponents. Indeed, the economy was under such strain that, in June 1962, butter and meat prices were raised by up to 30 per cent. This took place in the middle of and not as a part of the current plan. Shortages and bread queues followed, as well as serious riots in Novocherkassk near Rostov. To increase food supplies Khrushchev even tried to cut back on the private plots which must have damaged his name with the peasants. So serious was the situation that the death penalty was reintroduced for economic crimes. At the time of his departure, he may have been preparing another major reorganization of agriculture.

Facing major problems, Khrushchev had sought major solutions, but he never solved or began to solve the central dilemma of the Soviet economy: how to release productive energies in a command economy dominated by the Plan; and how to do this while maintaining party control. In 1957 he abolished some 140 all-union, union republic and republic ministries and replaced them with 150 regional economic councils, *sovnarkhozy*, the task of which was to run the economy on the basis of geographical regions, rather than economic sectors as had previously been the case. Even though overall economic control was vested in Gosplan, there was always a danger that the reform might actually foster regional identities and economies. From May 1960 Khrushchev's power began to wane, and Frol Kozlov and Kosygin began to recentralize. Furthermore, thousands of lower and middle ranking *apparatchiki*, traditionally Khrushchev's supporters, had to leave their jobs in Moscow and move themselves, their families and their careers away from the attractions of the capital to run the *sovnarkhozy* in the provinces.

Then, in 1962 when the previous reform had ground to a halt, Khrushchev introduced changes even more sweeping. He divided the party into industrial and agricultural wings. The aim was greater party control over the economy and an attempt to halt the damage that his earlier decentralization had caused. In effect his moves were widely seen as downgrading the party from its rightful position as one single body distinct from the state. Chaos resulted, and the scheme created thousands of disgruntled *apparatchiki* whose careers were again being tampered with and who felt insulted by this disregard of their interests. In dividing the party, Khrushchev reduced the power of many party secretaries. Interestingly, this policy was paralleled by a drive to recruit more party members. Khrushchev may have realized that he was losing his grip on the party. This party reform was short-sighted: all the secretaries threatened by reorganization at the higher levels of the two largest republics, Russia and the Ukraine, were Central Committee members or candidates, whereas none of the new secretaries (who may have felt grateful to Khrushchev for their promotion) were on the Central Committee.[34] The party reverted to a unitary organization as soon as Khrushchev was gone.

In 1956 Khrushchev had created a special Central Committee Bureau for the Russian Republic, the object of which was to increase his hold upon the heartland of the USSR and create important jobs for supporters. Yet by 1964 he had become complacent or careless or had ignored the central issue of his power: the ability to pack the Central Committee with his men. The Central Committee elected in October 1961 had 107 new members out of 175, but the significant point was that almost all of them survived Khrushchev's fall and were re-elected in 1966. They weren't his men at all.

The distinguished French correspondent Michel Tatu[35] argued that there must have been a last straw that led to Khrushchev's dismissal. Incensed at his policy failures, reorganizations, foreign adventures, personal style and growing personality cult, the Praesidium also objected to Khrushchev's use of his son-in-law Adzubei as a personal emissary in trips abroad, but that was a minor matter. The power struggle among Khrushchev's lieutenants which had been taking place since the defeat of the Anti-Party Group had resolved itself by the summer of 1964. The supposed heir Kozlov had retired owing to illness and on 15 July 1964 Leonid Brezhnev was appointed First Deputy Secretary (and heir apparent) and allowed to surrender his duties as President to Anastas Mikoyan. There was now in the Praesidium a balance of different factions led by Brezhnev and Kosygin with influential, independent corners held by senior party ideologist Suslov, President Mikoyan and Deputy Premier Nikolai Podgorny.

Relatively secure in the knowledge that Khrushchev would be succeeded by at best an oligarchy and at worst a troika of Brezhnev, Kosygin and Podgorny, Khrushchev's colleagues were prepared to oust him when the opportunity offered in October 1964. It seemed that the Central Committee meeting summoned for November 1964 was to witness a reshuffle of the party leadership and a purge of those who posed a threat to Khrushchev. The Central Committee was mobilized against him while he was out of Moscow. He was brought back from Sochi under escort and hustled out of office – but constitutionally. His biographer wrote: 'He went not because he was reactionary and not because he was liberal, but because he was erratic, unpredictable, unmanageable, now increasingly dictatorial.'[36] A delegation of the British CP visiting Moscow was told: 'There had been many discussions and disagreements with Khrushchev in the Praesidium which finally felt that his methods had exceeded all possible limits and had become an obstacle.'[37]

# Four

# BREZHNEV: FIRST AMONG EQUALS

Meeting between the 14–16 November 1964, the Central Committee ratified the removal of Khrushchev. His 'division' of the party was abolished, the *sovnarkhoz* system of regionalizing the economy was disbanded and his son-in-law Adzubei was voted off the Central Committee. Leonid Brezhnev, who succeeded Khrushchev as First Secretary, promised the Central Committee that there would be no more agricultural 'campaigns'. Frol Kozlov retired on health grounds. Otherwise none of Khrushchev's senior colleagues was dismissed with him and most of his basic policies remained unchanged; only method altered. Defence expenditure was cut and consumer production was stressed. The new government established a State Committee for Science and Technology to arrange intergovernmental deals to exchange scientific and technological knowledge with the West (deals were concluded with France in 1965, Italy in 1966 and the UK in 1970).[1]

In March 1965, the Central Committee approved the changes that had taken place. The Twenty-third Congress of the CPSU in March and April 1966 formally ended the interregnum. The Praesidium was renamed the Politburo and Brezhnev was confirmed as General Secretary of the CPSU. Alexei Kosygin was Prime Minister and Head of Government and Nikolai Podgorny was Head of State. To the West it appeared that the triumvirate ruled the USSR on behalf of a Politburo of almost equally powerful men, but in the ensuing power struggle, Nikolai Podgorny was never a serious contender. Born in 1903, of the ideological centre, in favour of more consumer production and with a background in the Ukrainian party, Podgorny was bundled upstairs when, in December 1965, he replaced Anastas Mikoyan as President of the USSR – a largely symbolic role – and had to surrender his membership of the Secretariat of the Central Committee – a more substantial post. Podgorny was an occasional ally of Kosygin until ousted and succeeded as President by Brezhnev in 1977.

Kosygin, born in Leningrad in 1904, had been at the centre of affairs in the USSR for over twenty years by 1964. Self-effacing and very able, his career was in government rather than party and he never had the opportunity, unlike Malenkov, Khrushchev or Brezhnev, to build up a circle of loyal party supporters. He had co-ordinated the food industries during the Second World War, was a Deputy Premier of the USSR at the age of 36, Prime Minister of the Russian Republic at 39 and a full member of Stalin's Politburo at 42. That he survived the Stalin and Khrushchev years was a tribute to his political skills. He inherited from Malenkov the advocacy of a free hand for the managers and technocrats to run the economy.

Like Kosygin, Brezhnev occupied the ideological middle ground in the CPSU.[2] Apart from war service as a colonel and political commissar in the Red Army, his career was in the party. Born in 1906, he became an engineer and joined the party in 1931. A member of the generation of Soviet *apparatchiki* who saw the rungs of the party ladder above them cleared by purge and war, Brezhnev was given great responsibility at a young age. He rebuilt the industries of Zaporozhe and Dnepropetrovsk after the war and as party boss of Moldavia in 1950 reintroduced orthodoxy before becoming party boss of Kazakhstan.[3] A protégé of Khrushchev, he promoted his own 'Dnieper mafia' so that of the 195 full members of the Central Committee elected by the Twenty-third Congress in April 1966, 25 were Brezhnev's men.[4] By assuming Khrushchev's role as party chief in November 1964, Brezhnev had an edge on his rivals, but his most serious challenge took a decade to defeat fully.

In December 1964 Alexei Shelepin, ex-head of the Komsomol and the KGB, was promoted to full membership of the Praesidium without first having to serve as a candidate member. This was apparently his reward because the security service had allowed the *coup* to go ahead. For a time Shelepin's power was very great and more broadly based than Brezhnev's. He was a member of the Praesidium, a First Deputy Premier in the government, a member of the Party Secretariat, and head of the independent powerful watchdog Committee of Party State Control.[5] He retained much support in the Komsomol and the new KGB chief Vladimir Semichastny was Shelepin's supporter.

Brezhnev and Kosygin appeared content to allow much – but not all – of Khrushchev's liberal attitude towards the arts to continue but Alexander Solzhenitsyn wrote that in the summer of 1965 'an abrupt return to Stalinism was being prepared under the leadership of "Iron Shurik" Shelepin'.[6] Alexei Rumyantsev, the 'liberal' editor of *Pravda* was dismissed. *Pravda* denounced 'excessive criticism' of the Stalin era and Sinyavsky and Daniel were arrested (see Chapter 6). Stalin was partially rehabilitated although not glorified.

Shelepin was dangerous, very powerful and harked back to a Stalinism that his major colleagues did not want. The Praesidium therefore united to clip his wings in December 1965 when the Party State Control Committee was abolished and he lost his Deputy Premiership. Shelepin was too powerful to be defeated outright even had that been the intention. Although the reasoning remains obscure, he was partly blamed for the Arab defeats in the June 1967 war. He lost his position in the Party Secretariat and was made head of the trade unions organization where he could no longer protect his major clients. Semichastny was replaced at the KGB in 1967 by Brezhnev's friend, Yuri Andropov, who, in turn, was provided with Brezhnev supporters as his deputies and senior assistants. Only in 1975, at the peak of his power, was Brezhnev able to remove Shelepin from the Politburo.

The Twenty-third Congress of the CPSU blessed the new order. 'The Congress of silences'[7] discussed nothing controversial. China, Khrushchev and destalinization were not mentioned. Instead delegates heard an eight-hour key-note speech from Brezhnev and learned that the 1966–70 Plan intended to increase consumer goods and produce colour televisions and more cars. The Congress warned writers and film and theatre directors that they should exercise less liberty than Khrushchev had allowed and, symbolic of the end of Khrushchev's liberalism towards the arts, the editor of *Novy Mir* Alexander Tvardovsky, who had published Solzhenitsyn and Pasternak, was removed from the Central Committee. The Congress approved Brezhnev's plan to increase the minimum wage, pay higher old-age pensions, reduce income taxes and introduce a five-day working week.

Initially, Kosygin held responsibility for foreign affairs, Brezhnev for the party and domestic matters, and they shared a role in the economy. Kosygin appeared to conduct Soviet diplomacy. He mediated between India and Pakistan in 1966 and met President Johnson in 1967. In fact Brezhnev played a role in foreign affairs from the start. He led a delegation to Poland in April 1965 and although Kosygin and Podgorny appeared at public functions with French President de Gaulle when he visited the USSR in June 1966, it was Brezhnev who did nearly all the negotiating.

In turn, both Stalin and Khrushchev had been criticized for creating their own personality cults, but on his 60th birthday, in December 1966 Brezhnev's own personality cult began. But there was opposition to the growth of Brezhnev's power. In February 1969 the influential magazine *Partinaya Zhizn* (*Party Life*) argued that 'glorification of any one person . . . undermines the very basis of party democracy'.[8] But by this time, his *détente* was bearing fruit with the new American President Nixon and as General Secretary of the CPSU he had had five years in which to introduce his supporters into positions of importance within the party. By increasing the defence budget in 1967 and by making his own appointee, Marshal Grechko, Defence Minister in April of that year Brezhnev earned support from the armed forces. The value of military support had increased with the invasion of Czechoslovakia in 1968 and the armed clashes with China in 1969.

It was Brezhnev who dominated the Moscow International Conference of Communist Parties in June 1969, and Brezhnev, whose discussions with West German Chancellor Brandt, in September 1971, led to the European Security Conference (see pages 131–2) and further *détente* in Europe. It was Brezhnev who tamed the Soviet military by cancelling the traditional military display in the May Day parade in 1969 and giving the speech, instead of the Defence Minister, from the Lenin Mausoleum. It was also Brezhnev who personally and unprecedentedly broadcast New Year's greetings to the USSR at midnight on 31 December 1970. This was the signal to the Soviet people that he was in sole charge even if he had failed during the preceding year to win the premiership from Kosygin. At the beginning of April 1970 Kosygin, Shelepin, Suslov, Polyansky and Podgorny all had appointments cancelled, disappeared from public view and were proclaimed ill. When he returned to Moscow from Budapest on 6 April 1970, Brezhnev was met by only three Politburo colleagues: Kirilenko, Mazurov and Voronov (of whom only Kirilenko was a noted Brezhnev loyalist). It appeared that Brezhnev faced and overcame a major challenge, but his opponents kept their positions in the Politburo for he was not yet strong enough to move against all of them.

From this time, Brezhnev was increasingly able to get his own way on important policy initiatives. This was not just because he was leader of the party and a skilled operator who had more personal support in the higher reaches of the party than anyone else, but because, as a man of the Kremlin's centre, he reflected the political instincts of most of his colleagues. He was able to build up a consensus in favour of *détente* and its domestic parallel of increased consumer production. Although frequently strained by Politburo hardliners this consensus nevertheless held together throughout the 1970s. It was Brezhnev's good fortune, or perhaps his genius, that his policies were approved by different members of the Politburo as opportune or necessary or inevitable. None of his policies involved sharp breaks with the past; so none of them disturbed too many of his colleagues at once. They were evolutionary, not revolutionary. *Détente* simply put into practice the peaceful coexistence that Moscow had preached since the death of Stalin. The 33 per cent increase in real income per head, promised in the Five-Year Plan of 1971–5 and announced by Brezhnev on 30 March 1971 at the Twenty-fourth Congress of the CPSU, involved giving for the first time priority to consumer goods over heavy industry. Malenkov and Khrushchev had faced severe problems when trying to shift investment in this way. By 1971, however, the metal-eaters had learned the lesson of Poland in December 1970 when large-scale riots reversed the government's economic policies, brought down Wladyslaw Gomulka and convinced the Kremlin that living standards must be raised if similar unrest was to be avoided at home.

The Twenty-fourth Congress gave Brezhnev a mandate for his policies. The elections to the Central Committee provided him with broad-based support, but Central Committee support did not extend to the elections to the Politburo: where all were re-elected, including Shelepin and Shelest, Brezhnev's severest critics. Brezhnev solved this problem by enlarging the Politburo by four new members, thus diluting the strength of the opposition. The policy of *détente* (see Chapter 9) had built up much domestic support not just among Brezhnev loyalists but also in the government machinery, the service and consumer industries, and the cultural and scientific worlds. Attempts were made to gain the support of the military and the security services. The immediate significance of the former diminished if international tension lessened, while the latter was essential to the control of a population made less easy to control by virtue of its contact with the ideas and goods of the West.

If anything was likely to unite opposition to Brezhnev, then the May visit of Nixon to sign SALT I was it. Before the visit the party hierarchy stumped the country to drum up support for *détente* with America which included the emotive issue of limiting arms at a time when American aircraft had mined North Vietnam's harbours and caused Soviet casualties. Defence Minister Marshal Grechko spoke of the 'growing aggressiveness of imperialism and primarily of American imperialism' and KGB chief Andropov declared: 'We certainly have no illusions and are not exaggerating the possibilities of co-operation.'[9] However, the Nixon visit was a huge domestic as well as foreign affairs success for Brezhnev (see page 127).

On 27 April 1973 the Central Committee approved the policy of *détente* in word and in deed, for in the first Politburo reshuffle since 1964, it dropped two of *détente*'s major critics, Pyotr Shelest and Gennady Voronov, and elected in their place three new members, Foreign Minister Andrei Gromyko, Minister for Internal Security Yuri Andropov and Defence Minister Marshal Grechko. In one respect Brezhnev was offering hostages to fortune for although Andropov and Grechko were not opponents, neither were they proponents of *détente*, and none of the three had a rank that entitled them to a Politburo seat.

The Soviet leadership invariably presents a picture of unity to the outside world, and the Kremlinologist, with no Hansard or investigative Kremlin lobby correspondents to help him, is reduced to deducing significance from the otherwise insignificant. But in Soviet official life, the formality of relationships, the importance of precedence and the sheer conservatism of the political system mean that departures from accepted or past practice can, in fact, signify underlying changes. For example, from 1964 the Soviet press always printed the names of Politburo members in alphabetical order, but by a happy accident

Brezhnev's name came first, even in the Cyrillic alphabet. When Brezhnev's name still came first after the elevation to the Politburo of Yuri Andropov, commentators rightly inferred that Brezhnev was dominant. Although supreme, Brezhnev was not impregnable. When his visit to the USA in June 1973 failed to produce the trade concessions and 'most favoured nation' status with the West, seen as a major domestic justification of *détente*, some of his colleagues may have tried to sabotage his *Westpolitik* by treating Soviet dissidents in such a way as to alienate Western liberals who might then have halted the progress of *détente*. Coinciding with Brezhnev's summer holiday and ending on his return, the press launched a campaign to vilify Alexander Solzhenitsyn and Andrei Sakharov. A Stalinist-type show trial of two other prominent dissidents, Piotr Yakir and Victor Krasin, was also staged. It could be, of course, that the short anti-dissident drive was mounted with Brezhnev's approval as a hint to the West of what Soviet reactions would be if *détente* did not continue to develop. Whether this is true or not, opposition to Brezhnev certainly coalesced around *détente* when it failed to deliver the military security and flow of foreign capital and advanced technology it had promised. Furthermore, the departure from politics of his two major *détente* partners, Brandt in 1973 and Nixon in 1974, weakened the chance of pursuing *détente* much further.

The strength of the opposition took different forms. The publication of the draft Brezhnev Constitution which he had promised for 1975 was held up until June 1977 by continuing internal debate, and Brezhnev's grandiose 'Fifteen-Year Plan', which was due to be presented to the Twenty-fifth Congress of the CPSU in February 1976, was also blocked. The loss of status in the Politburo of Brezhnev's protégé Fyodor Kulakov in December 1974 was matched by a resurgence in the fortunes of Alexander Shelepin[10] which, however, lasted only until he left the Politburo 'at his own request' in 1975.[11] Brezhnev had finally succeeded against the man who had probably been his major Politburo opponent. Presumably the opposition was able to capitalize upon the fact that although Brezhnev's phrase 'proletarian internationalism' underlined his claim that the USSR led the international communist movement, *détente* had apparently given rise to the Eurocommunists who spurned Moscow's leadership (see Chapter 11).

But Leonid Brezhnev had built his inner circle consensus well and, unlike Khrushchev, did not rock the boat unduly or become complacent in his control of the party. When Dmitri Polyansky, the Minister of Agriculture, was dismissed from the Politburo in March 1976, as a scapegoat for the bad harvest of 1975, the criticism missed Brezhnev who held overall responsibility for agriculture. The Congress elected two new men to the Politburo; a Brezhnev protégé, Grigori Romanov, who had been boss of the powerful Leningrad party, and Dmitri Ustinov who, although a civilian, succeeded to the Ministry of Defence following the death of Marshal Grechko in April 1976. The break with the tradition of having a military man as Defence Minister was thinly camouflaged by making Ustinov a Marshal of the Red Army, but it may have indicated that Brezhnev no longer needed military support as much as he had done when Marshal Grechko was brought into the Politburo. Shelepin had gone, and taken potentially serious opposition with him. An inner caucus of Brezhnev aided by Alexei Kosygin, Mikhail Suslov and Andrei Kirilenko dominated the party.

When Podgorny disapproved of some aspects of the Brezhnev Constitution, he was dismissed from the Politburo with little fuss on 24 May 1977 and lost the Presidency to Brezhnev on 16 June 1977.[12] While never acquiring or possibly even seeking as much personal power as Khrushchev had, Brezhnev gradually came to possess far more trappings of power than his predecessor. Apart from his General Secretaryship, the Presidency and the chairmanship of the shadowy State Defence Council, Brezhnev amassed more awards and honours than any other Soviet leader. He won the Lenin Peace Prize in April 1973, was awarded two Gold Stars of the Hero of the Soviet Union and five Orders of Lenin. On 10 May 1976 he was promoted to Marshal of the Soviet Union (a rank that Stalin, but neither Lenin nor Khrushchev, had enjoyed) and on 31 March 1980 earned the Lenin Prize for Literature.

On his 70th birthday on 19 December 1976, there was an enormous outpouring of adulation. For seven days *Pravda* devoted a page to him and the two issues of 19 and 20 December consisted largely of birthday greetings, many of them on the lines of a speech given by Andrei Kirilenko two months previously:

The Party and people love you, Leonid Il'ich. They love you for your humanity and warmth, for your wisdom and limitless devotion to Leninism. All your life your wisdom and talent have given you the possibility to acquire and absorb the precious qualities of a Party leader and statesman which are distinctive to the great man of our time, the *Vozhd* of our Party and of all the peoples of our native land.[13]

The celebrations ended with an award to the *Vozhd* of a ceremonial sword.

The personality cult made it that much harder for Brezhnev to be criticized, but it was also a tactic which, by elevating him, made it easier for his supporters to bring about the retirement of independents like Shelepin and Podgorny and their supporters.[14] It also meant that the new constitution, which was ratified by the Supreme Soviet in time for the October 1977 celebrations of the sixtieth anniversary of the Russian Revolution, became known as the Brezhnev Constitution.[15]

The new Constitution did not differ markedly from the old. Its 173 articles proclaimed that the USSR had a socialist society, that the state was a state of the whole people and that therefore, the aims of the dictatorship of the proletariat had been accomplished. It declared that: 'The CPSU is the leading and guiding force in Soviet society and the nucleus of the political system, of all state and public organizations. The CPSU exists for the people and serves the people.' The Stalin Constitution had merely said that the party 'is the vanguard of the working people . . . and the leading core of all organizations . . . both public and state . . .'. The Soviet people were guaranteed freedoms of speech, press, assembly, conscience, privacy of correspondence, artistic, scientific and technical creation. However, 'exercise by citizens of rights and freedoms must not injure the interests of society and the state and the rights of other citizens . . . [and] shall be inseparable from the performance by citizens of their duties.' Citizens had rights to a dwelling, work, leisure, health care, etc. Peasants had rights to private plots.

Despite the freedoms offered, the Brezhnev Constitution altered little the lives of Soviet citizens, but at least it was not immediately violated as Stalin's purges had violated his constitution. The approval of the Constitution served to carry destalinization a stage further. It enshrined Brezhnev as President and undisputed leader of the USSR, was good propaganda at home and abroad,[16] and provided a focus for widespread expressions of patriotism and loyalty.

As a society in which order was highly prized, the Soviet Union had come a long way in the Brezhnev years. Societal stability, relative to Western societies, was matched by stability at the top. The advancing age of Leonid Brezhnev, together with his frequent illnesses and the age of most of his senior colleagues, led to speculation in the West of a possible succession crisis in the USSR. But the overall impression was one of smoothness and constitutionality. Veteran diplomat Vasily Kuznetsov was elected to the new post of Vice-President in October 1977. First Deputy Premier Mazurov was dropped from the Politburo in November 1978 and replaced in December 1979 by 74-year-old First Deputy Premier Nikolai Tikhonov. Unlike the rapid turnover of the Stalin and Khrushchev years, the pattern emerged under Brezhnev of deputies succeeding to their superiors' jobs when the latter were promoted, retired or died.

The turnover of local party leaders in the fifteen years between 1964–79 was half of that of the previous eleven years, 1953–64.[17] By the spring of 1978 only twelve of the fifty-eight ministers and deputy premiers in 1966 had retired or been replaced, despite an average age of 70 in 1979. Similarly, only six of the twenty-three Central Committee Secretaries and department heads appointed in 1966 had moved by 1979. Although there were some changes in the Politburo between 1972–9 the average age increased from 62 in 1972 to 69 in 1979.[18]

Reflecting its age and conservatism, the leadership allowed a limited official and popular recognition of the centenary of Stalin's birth on 21 December 1979. This was, to an extent, symptomatic of the return to domestic control, order and orthodoxy that marked the Brezhnev years. Apart from major dissidents whose names were news in the West (see Chapter 6), the dissidents issue had been brought under control by 1980. Preparations to receive foreign visitors to the Moscow Olympic Games in July 1980 were accompanied by the evacuation of school children and students from Olympic venues for the duration of the Games, so as to keep them out of reach of contaminating contact with foreign visitors. Also, employers had to submit lists of drunkards, psychotics, disorderly people, and Jews waiting to emigrate, so that the party could decide who to move when it also made its decision on dissidents and religious groups, such as Baptists, who were similarly threatened with temporary resettlement.

The Soviet Union remained a police state, where the rights of the individual were subordinated to the rights of the state, but where, as one writer put it: 'At least three-quarters of the country's population . . . given the hypothetical opportunity of doing otherwise would vote for the existing system.'[19] The civil police were augmented by the KGB which was responsible for preventing all major crimes against the state. On the KGB's 60th anniversary in December 1977, Brezhnev described its work as 'hard but honourable', and with the 'broadest support of the working people'.[20] The day of the bloody purges had been replaced by selective arrests and blacklisting. The personnel section of every organization possessed full dossiers on its people. The individual needed a *kharakteristika*, or reference including a KGB security clearance, every time he wanted to change job, be promoted, travel abroad or do something out of the ordinary. All this meant that state control was pervasive and inescapable even if it was no longer bloodthirsty. Nevertheless, where Khrushchev emptied the camps Brezhnev filled them again with 2 million,[21] or even 5 million (out of a population of 262 million) according to dissident Dr Yuri Orlov,[22] including 10,000 to 20,000 prisoners of conscience.[23]

In Marxist theory crime is a product of class inequality and will disappear, since there will be no need for it in the classless communist society. However, the USSR has a long way to go for it shares not just the crimes committed the world over but admits to crimes previously ascribed only to the decadent West. On 26 July 1966 a Central Committee decree on hooliganism gave the police summary powers to fine hooligans on the spot. In a state where alcohol tax yielded $25 billion in 1972, equivalent to half the defence budget, addiction to vodka creates major problems. With fewer vehicles than Western countries, 600,000 drunken drivers were sentenced in 1974.[24] But probably more symbolic of Brezhnev's Russia was the continued growth of corruption and illegal private enterprise.

Where the official economy creaked and was inefficient, a counter-economy partly balanced this by handling goods and providing services of all descriptions. This blackmarket accounted for up to 10 per cent of Soviet GNP and meant that the individual could frequently have jobs done *na levo* ('on the left'), that is, illegally, by someone using state-owned tools and materials for his own profit-making purposes. Such jobs were done for cash, or more often as part of a complex web of interlocking reciprocal services. An American correspondent in Moscow wrote in 1976:

> Russian friends tipped me off that it was not money that really mattered, but access or *blat* (the influence or connections to gain the access you need) . . . The more rank and power one has, the more *blat* one normally has. But actually almost everyone can bestow the benefits of *blat* on someone else – a doorman, a railroad porter, a cleaning lady in a food store, a sales clerk, an auto mechanic or a professor – because each has access to things or services that are hard to get.[25]

To some extent *blat* and *na levo* dealings only extended to ordinary people the opportunity to bypass the official clumsy system, that was enjoyed by the upper ranks of society, in any sphere, but especially in the party, armed forces and government. These were the people who enjoyed the far-reaching privileges of special shops, imported and high quality goods at special prices and better access to education, culture, housing, holidays, etc.

The Soviet system extolled honesty, but the prevalence, usually unchecked, of unMarxist corruption, blackmarketing and moonlighting, must have weakened the moral underpinning of the state, as ordinary citizens adopted and practised values that seriously departed from the ideology of the state. Nevertheless, as the USSR entered the 1980s the Brezhnev administration had reduced wage differentials, increased living standards and educational opportunities, strengthened the constitutional system and involved more people in decision-making. According to Brezhnev some 400,000 'mass' meetings were held to discuss the new Constitution and suggest amendments before its ratification – approximately 150 changes were then made.[26]The 1980–85 Five-Year Plan aimed to increase wages below the national average figure of 150 roubles per week and freeze those above it.[27] In anticipation of this, prices of consumer goods were raised by up to 50 per cent in July 1979. In the unbalanced Soviet economy where housing and food costs were held down by subsidies, luxury goods cost a market price that would have been unacceptable in the West. In July 1979 the Zhiguli saloon, with its two to three years' waiting list for the unprivileged, retailed at over $9,850, but its superior export version, the Lada, was sold in Britain at between $4000–$5000.

The 1961 programme of the CPSU proclaimed that the basis of communism would be laid in the 1970s and that full communism would be achieved in the 1980s. This prophecy has not been mentioned by Khrushchev's successors for the schedule went wrong. Apart from the failure to produce changes in character and behaviour, in effect the new socialist man, the economy, which was supposed to generate the impetus needed to create full communism, faced serious problems in 1980. Since 1965, $500 billion has been invested in agriculture, but in the same period grain imports cost about $15 billion; nearly the amount of Moscow's hard-currency debt of $17.2 billion at the end of 1978. Economic growth slowed to less than 2 per cent per annum in 1979 as planning became more complex and less effective. A bureaucratic and compartmentalized society and economy, the USSR has a workforce that is 20 per cent larger than America's and which produces three times as many engineering graduates – many more than it effectively uses. New legislation, however, aimed to correct this mismatch by making higher education produce graduates in needed disciplines.[28]

In the late 1970s 4 per cent of GNP was spent on research and development by 3.5 million scientists and technicians. This was a much larger effort than in the West, but whereas the US and West Germany put more than 50 per cent of inventions into practice within about a year, it took three years in the USSR. Capital equipment was allowed to become obsolete before it was replaced. Replacement investment accounted for 30 per cent of the total investment, but this was only half the rate of American replacement investment. An importer, as well as an exporter of oil and gas, the USSR faces an energy crisis by the late 1980s because, although Siberia and the Soviet Far East have the largest reserves in the world, the USSR does not have the drilling capacity to develop existing fields and drill for new ones at the same time.

The 1970s saw a growing labour shortage. Also, a low birthrate in Europe and burgeoning growth among the Muslim Asiatics meant that educated skilled workers who retired in Europe were frequently not replaced at the other end of the age range, or were being replaced by unskilled Muslims whose peasant background, culture and language difficulties often made them more difficult to train than Europeans.[29] Moscow's economic and social problems were potentially very serious but they were no worse than those of some Western countries and they were offset partly by the cohesion of Soviet society.

In July 1977 membership of the CPSU stood at 16,203,446, including 658,349 candidate members; an increase from the 11,022,369 members of 1964 and representing over 10 per cent of the adult population.[30] Party and Komsomol Young Communist League members were required to maintain high levels of *partynost*, or commitment to the party, and *aktivnost*, that is, political activity. Membership purges weeded out the weaker brethren but, when members' families and other committed groups are taken into account, it probably meant that a conservative minimum of at least 30 million citizens were actively engaged in promoting the existing system at all levels of society. This included the inculcation and reinforcement of loyalty and conformity through the formal curriculum of schools, colleges, and universities. In the West disparaging remarks were made about the rigidity and the *conformity* of the USSR which were extraordinary by West European standards. But in his excellent book David Lane argued: 'Soviet politics is effective politics: major interest groups are able to articulate their needs. It is a *united* government: decisions are not questioned in public. It is an accepted government: its processes and structure are legitimate in the sense of being taken for granted by the masses.'[31] Leonid Brezhnev's achievement was to have consolidated stability and acceptance by society in a state which was founded on revolution.

# Five

# INDUSTRY AND AGRICULTURE IN A PLANNED ECONOMY

The Soviet Union has a command economy. The state controls the means of production and allocates all investment. The Five-Year Plans, inaugurated by Stalin in 1928 and drawn up by Gosplan, the State Planning Commission, set growth targets, prices and minimum wages. However, it seems that the Five-Year Plan, *pyatiletka*, has become only a moral goal, setting general objectives, but regularly modifying its targets. Of more immediate importance are the annual plans produced by individual ministries in conjunction with Gosplan. They allocate to specific enterprises, specific quantities of raw materials, and require, in turn, specific quantities of finished goods.

Gosplan's operations are enormously complicated. More than 9 million prices are fixed for each Plan and each enterprise has its monthly plans. The Plan dominates the working lives of Soviet citizens and, despite changes of emphasis from the mid-1960s onwards, it is still geared to producing quantity rather than quality. Consumer demand is not yet very significant. What matters is plan-fulfilment, or over-fulfilment, for which a manager can increase his salary by 30 per cent and a worker can get a thirteenth month's pay. However, although the Plan allocates a factory the resources to meet its targets, allocation is no guarantee of receipt. Tiny planning errors can reverberate throughout the economy, and have led to enterprises protecting their own plan-fulfilment potential through another unofficial economy. Enterprises indent for quantities of materials in excess of their requirements. These are then hoarded as insurance against future demands. Some enterprises engage a *tolkach*, or fixer, who travels the country locating raw materials and arranging deals *na levo*, on the side. Bonuses are paid for over-fulfilment of the Plan, but frequently, over-fulfilment ought not to be possible. So absolute is the Plan that it has helped create an economic system which is resistant to change. Innovation comes from above, as few managers are willing to risk their chances of plan-fulfilment and its bonuses by interrupting production or accepting the short-term production losses that accompany the introduction of new techniques and processes. However, only minimum wages are fixed and in the 1970s labour turnover became high as workers sought jobs with better pay. Increasingly in the 1970s, managers became sandwiched between the dictates of the Plan and the market forces of consumer choice and labour mobility because these affected the level of sales which affected bonuses.

Where full employment is virtually a reality, skilled labour is scarce and quality is not the first determinant of production, there has emerged the phenomenon of *shturmovshchina*, 'storming the target' – if a factory has to produce *x* tables to meet its monthly plan, then it does not matter when in the month the tables are produced. In 1971 the First Secretary of the Azerbaijan party said that the average factory in his republic produced only 10–15 per cent of its production in the first 10 days of the month, but 50 per cent in the last 10 days.[1] Workers sometimes have to put in unpaid days or shifts at the end of the month when quality control is inadequate because there is too much for the controllers to check. As consumer goods bear a production date tag, Soviet citizens avoid goods produced after the 15th of the month, especially in December when annual plans are completed. The 1975 Nobel Economics Prize winner Leonid Kantorovich estimated that national income could go up by 50 per cent if 'storming' were replaced by the efficient use of resources.[2]

The authorities have recognized that central control has its drawbacks, but it also conveys important benefits upon the leadership. Because the Plan is ordered and impersonal and 'serves the working people', it is the *sine qua non* of a state that preaches the scientific nature of Marxist–Leninism. Planning gives the Kremlin control over the whole of the official economy. Despite its defects the Soviet planned economy protects its citizens from the unemployment and cyclical recession that are apparently endemic in the West.

Workers are organized in trade unions. Membership is voluntary, but in 1977 113.5 million or 97 per cent of the workforce belonged to a union. Union dues amount to 1 per cent of earnings, much higher than in Britain. Soviet unions share some functions with Western unions: 9 million unionists on 160,000 standing production committees negotiate with management on increasing production, labour problems and wages.[3] Yet their basic function is different. Unions are partners with management and the state in fulfilling the Plan. Together they promote efficiency, maintain discipline and reject confrontational politics.

Strikes are not banned by law and they occur, if only infrequently. But all strikes are wild-cat strikes of workers who, in the workers' state, are technically striking against themselves. Strikes range from the minor local dispute, which is usually amicably settled, to the Novocherkassk strike in the DonBas coalfield on 1 June 1962 when tens of thousands of workers rioted against food price increases. They were severely put down by the Red Army and several hundred were reported killed.[4]

The importance of Soviet trade unions lies elsewhere. They control the social security system, handle pension funds, allocate extra allowances and provide crèches, kindergartens, holiday centres and sports facilities. They have a national daily newspaper, *Trud* ('labour'), and are an important element in the Kremlin's control over the populace. Whereas party membership is exclusive, the unions allow everybody to enjoy the benefits of 'club membership'. They are safety valves that allow the workforce to participate in enterprise-level decision-making. The parallel with the soviets is obvious, but the top union leadership is appointed by the party leadership rather than being elected by the rank and file.[5]

Soviet unions buttress the system and change, even of wages, comes from outside the union machine. Yet change in the economic system has been publicly recognized as essential since the Khrushchev era.

Immediately after the Second World War the head of Gosplan, Nikolai Vosnesensky, argued for more free play for market forces in the economy. Both he and his views were purged by Stalin, but in *Pravda* on 9 September 1962 Professor Yevsei Liberman echoed Vosnesensky's essential ideas. Liberman argued against concentration on quantity rather than quality. He proposed that bonuses should relate directly to the quantity of production sold. In effect he wanted to give enterprises more control over their own affairs and introduce profitability as the measure of economic success. A similar debate over the 'link system' was occurring in the world of agriculture (see page 59).

In March 1964 an eminent economist, Academician Vassily Nemchinov, attacked the red tape which crippled the efficiency of enterprises and suggested that the price of an article should accurately reflect the value of labour, materials and capital that had gone into its manufacture.

Apparently the merits of the Liberman–Nemchinov ideas were widely recognized, but in proposing free play for some market forces they challenged the basis of scientific socialism and party control. Nevertheless, on 19 October 1964, only four days after the fall of Khrushchev, the new Premier Kosygin declared: 'It is impossible to overtake the high level of productivity of the more developed capitalist countries without increasing the initiative and autonomy of the workers.'[6] Khrushchev had applied the new ideas to pilot plants and Kosygin extended the scheme to 400 more in January 1965.[7] The Kosygin reforms were endorsed by the Central Committee on 29 September 1965. Management was given greater latitude to make local decisions. Instead of receiving central instructions on up to fifty of a factory's 'indicators', such as price levels, delivery dates, production schedules, etc., managers would receive only five or six. Economic performance was to be measured by sales and profits, not by gross output. Enterprises were to retain 40 per cent of profits for capital investment, social services or incentives.

Out of more than 200,000 Soviet enterprises, 25,000, accounting for 70 per cent of industrial output, had been reformed by the end of 1968.[8] The reforms, which boosted consumer production, were combined with the 1966–70 Plan to raise industrial output in its first two years by 20 per cent and labour productivity by 13 per cent. Thereafter, however, the reforms slackened off.

Against opponents of the reforms, Liberman insisted that there was no question of a return to capitalism since the means of production, distribution and exchange remained in the hands of the state. But Brezhnev and the party ideologists opposed the reforms because of the damage they threatened to the role of the party.[9] Kosygin was alive to all the arguments and indeed, he appeared to embody them. In 1957 Khrushchev had partly decentralized the economy by scrapping the controlling national ministries and replacing them with republic-level economic councils, *sovnarkhozy*, which were to be responsible for planning, but within the general framework of the Plan. The Kosygin reforms reversed this and so gave autonomy to managers on the one hand and more authority to the centre on the other.

These contradictory elements of the Kosygin reforms struggled against each other during the 1966–70 Plan. The profits and incentive fund elements prospered so that in 1976 44 per cent of profits remained for distribution within enterprises, 11 per cent went on capital investment, 16 per cent on incentives and 11 per cent on social services.[10] Otherwise, the reforms were bogged down and even reversed by the inertia of bureaucracy and by the vested interests of the planning machine and the party.

The economy fared badly in 1969. Agricultural production dropped by 3 per cent and industrial production increased by only 7 per cent – the worst figure since 1928. Wages and savings had grown faster than expected and caused inflationary pressures. Although the Kosygin reforms were blamed, there were many reasons why the Soviet economy slowed down in the late 1960s. Planning, which was largely uncomputerized, was increasingly complex and difficult. The catch-up period after the Second World War was largely over. Economic performance was being distorted by artificial prices. Agricultural growth between 1953–8 had boosted the whole economy, but this could not be repeated, and by 1969 the USSR had the highest agricultural price support bill in the world. This was estimated to be 13.3 billion roubles in 1975. The economy was no longer able to milk the peasants as Stalin had done, and there was no longer a reserve pool of labour waiting to be drafted into industry. The industrial week had been shortened from 47.8 hours in 1955 to 40.7 hours in 1971 with longer paid holidays.[11] By 1970 almost everybody who could work, did work: this amounted to 92.4 per cent of the able-bodied population of working age (excluding students) compared with 76 per cent in the USA. Labour turnover had increased and consumer demands were being heard. The service sector was being developed. New sources of raw materials in Siberia were expensive to exploit.[12] All these factors contributed to Brezhnev's wider strategy of seeking *détente* with the West and the economic advantages that would flow from it.

A *Pravda* editorial of 13 January 1970 virtually abandoned all the reforms. Brezhnev appealed not to incentives but to patriotism and 'moral stimulants' to re-invigorate the economy. He called for discipline of workers, management and administration; for penalties for slackers, absenteeism and drunkenness. Hours and outlets of sale of vodka were restricted and the price increased. The *subbotnik*, annual day of unpaid work, was reintroduced.

This return to orthodoxy was ended in December 1970 by the Polish riots which ousted party leader Gomulka and showed what could happen if a population was no longer cowed by Stalinist repression and was dissatisfied with its economic lot.

When the ninth Five-Year Plan appeared in 1971, for the first time a *pyatiletka* promised faster growth in the consumer sector than in heavy industry. The Plan's 'main task' of the future was 'to ensure a significant increase in the material and cultural standard of living'. At the Twenty-fourth Congress of the CPSU in April 1971, Brezhnev said: 'The long years of heroic history when millions of Communists and non-Party people deliberately made sacrifices and underwent privation . . . lie behind us . . . What was explicable and only natural in the past . . . is unacceptable under present conditions.'[13] The reforms had gone, and Brezhnev effectively wrested economic grand strategy from Kosygin's hands, but although Brezhnev called for quality in production, higher minimum wages and bigger pensions, there was no question of a return to Libermanism, although local party organizations were given more authority to supervise and control economic activity in their areas.

The measures of 1970 were a hurried reaction to circumstances and were quietly reversed by 1972. Brezhnev's grip on the leadership had tightened and he survived the poor economic performance of 1972. The harvest was poor, productivity fell and butter and potatoes were rationed in some areas, but Brezhnev, apparently preoccupied with foreign affairs, continued with *détente*, bought grain from the USA and prepared his own scheme to raise efficiency while maintaining party control.

In April 1973 he announced plans to create industrial associations to combine related factories and include research and development and design organizations. Most of the decision-making powers granted to management in 1965 were conferred on these industrial associations as were most of the detailed planning and control functions of the national ministries. Once again the Soviet leadership was tinkering with the issue of command and control; once again some powers were being decentralized, and once again these reforms did not take adequate account of the unvoiced wishes of the great constant of Soviet society: the deeply conservative party and governmental machines, or *apparat*. As the *apparat* thwarted Kosygin's reforms so too it was partly responsible for thwarting Brezhnev's. By 1975 the new associations accounted for only 12 per cent of industrial capacity.

Factors that had led to the economic slowdown in the late 1960s persisted into the 1970s and were compounded by a shortage of skilled labour, unsophisticated management, a poor productivity record, the beginnings of an energy problem, imported inflation from the recession-hit West and erratic performance by the agricultural sector. Also, despite outproducing the USA in steel by 155 million ton(ne)s to 117 million ton(ne)s in 1977, high quality cold-rolled steel, tinplate and large-diameter pipe still had to be imported at a cost of $2 billion in 1977. A precision instruments industry was only in its infancy. There was little spin-off from space and military research into the civilian economy. Compared with 170,000 computers and 138 million telephones in the USA, there were only 15,000 computers and 17 million telephones. There was an information bottleneck compounded by a communications bottleneck caused by inadequate production of freight cars and locomotives; only 91,263 miles (146,842 km) of railway track against America's 202,775 miles (326,265 km); 901,763 miles (1,450,937 km) of road against America's 3.8 million miles (6.1 million km); 63 billion domestic air passenger miles (101.4 billion km) against America's 162.8 billion miles (262 billion km).[14] Moscow had to spend enormous sums simply on opening up its huge hinterland through projects like the northern spur of the Trans-Siberian Railway, the Baikal-Amur Main Line Railway, to be completed in 1982, and ice-breakers for the northern ocean.

GNP growth fell to only 3.3 per cent per annum between 1976–80, with gloomier forecasts for the future. But personal consumption accounted for a steady 57–8 per cent of GNP during the 1970s.[15] Nevertheless, although Soviet consumer products were seen as inferior to East European or Western goods, at least they were becoming available. In 1977 the USSR produced 5.6 million refrigerators and 1.2 million cars against American production of 6 million refrigerators and 6.7 million cars. More significantly, the average American spent only 4.3 months income on the average car whereas the average Russian spent 51 months income.[16]

*Détente* brought Western credits, trade deals and a $17.2 billion hard-currency debt, but Western trade remained a small part of the economy. East Germany took 11 per cent of Soviet exports in 1977 whereas the biggest Western share was West Germany's 3.7 per cent. Imports from the West consisted mainly of technology, often involving whole industrial plants. In 1977 Japan won $380 million contracts for three chemical fertilizer and ten ammonia plants, and Britain gained $475 million contracts for two methanol plants, a polyethylene plant and a materials reprocessing plant.[17] In return the USSR exported mainly raw materials in the form of oil and oil products, wood and wood products and gold, apart from some machinery and a huge volume of arms.

Whereas industry employed 38 per cent of the active population and produced 53 per cent of national income, agriculture employed 22 per cent of the working population and produced only 17 per cent of national income.[18] This is despite agriculture's share of investment, increasing from 22 per cent in 1970 to 27 per cent in 1977.[19] In 1975 it was estimated that 37 million agricultural workers produced 5.3 ton(ne)s of grain per head and 0.63 ton(ne)s per acre (0.405 hectare), whereas 4.3 million American farmers produced 50.8 ton(ne)s per head and 1.41 ton(ne)s per acre (0.405 hectare).[20] In Stalin's time agriculture financed industrialization, but agricultural performance has been so erratic since that, despite a long-term growth trend of 3.5 per cent per year,[21] five-year and even annual plans have been badly thrown out by the vagaries of the weather and the failures of the system as Table 5.1 indicates.

Table 5.1 Soviet Grain Harvest, 1972–9                              *millions of ton(ne)s*

| | 1972 | 1973 | 1974 | 1975 | 1976 | 1977 | 1978 | 1979 |
|---|---|---|---|---|---|---|---|---|
| Grain harvest | 168 | 222.5 | 196 | 140 | 224 | 195.5 | 237 | 179 |

The 179 million ton(ne)s of grain gathered in 1979 meant that the Plan target, which at best would only have provided the Soviet citizen with an average 1.5 oz (42.5 g) of meat per day, had fallen short by 48 million ton(ne)s or 21 per cent.

Harvest shortfalls led the USSR to import grain from the USA after the disastrous harvest of 1963 and again in 1972 when a Soviet *coup* bought 19 million ton(ne)s of American grain at subsidized prices before Washington realized what was happening.[22] In September 1975 Moscow entered a five-year agreement with the USA to buy a minimum of 6–8 million ton(ne)s of grain per year. This guaranteed grain supplies upon which the promise of increased production of meat and dairy products could be based: but at huge cost. Food subsidies cost 25 billion roubles per year by 1979 out of agricultural production valued at 130 billion roubles.[23]

Agriculture's failings were partly due to the climate and latitude of the

USSR. Sixty per cent of the grain fields lie north of the 49th parallel (the US–Canadian border) where the season is short, the frosts harder, the sun weaker and the rain more sparse. Nowhere in the USSR are there growing areas as richly favoured as Ohio, Iowa or Kansas. Favourable weather conditions prevail only every four years. Frost reaches much of Siberia early in September and there is a constant susceptibility to drought. The most productive area, the Ukraine, has only 20 in. (50 cm) of rain per year.

When harvests have been unexpectedly good, inadequate transport and storage have lost huge quantities of grain. Furthermore, the theories of Stalin's favourite geneticist, Trofim Lysenko, who argued that the genetic constitution of wheat strains could be altered by controlling their environment, delayed the introduction of proper hybrid strains by about twenty years so that Soviet grains still yielded 50 per cent less than American grains in the mid-1970s.[24] Nevertheless, the basic failures of Soviet agriculture must lie in the system of collectivized agriculture itself, a system which Poland and Yugoslavia rejected and which only the satellites of Mongolia and Bulgaria have adopted uncritically.

The Revolution broke up the large estates leaving about 25 million, usually very small, farms. In 1928 Stalin made war upon the Soviet peasants by dispossessing and destroying the 2 million *Kulaks*, or 'rich' or efficient peasants, and collectivizing all land, livestock and equipment. Peasants destroyed livestock and equipment, fields were left unploughed, famine followed and millions died in opposition to the enforced collectivization. By 1940 all agricultural land was grouped in 235,500 collective farms, *kolkhozy*, and 4,159 state farms, *sovkhozy*, apart from the tiny private plots owned by individuals.

It must be remembered that Marxist–Leninism was an urban ideology with little sympathy for the rural masses. Lenin frequently warned against enforced collectivization, and the peasants were not collectivized until 1928 because the Kremlin feared their actual or potential hostility to communist rule. Collectivization allowed Moscow to exert over the countryside the same detailed political control that existed in the towns.

Believing in economies of scale, Stalin allowed Khrushchev to reduce the number of agricultural units. There were 121,400 *kolkhozy* and 4,988 *sovkhozy* in 1950. In 1960 there were 44,000 *kolkhozy* and 7,375 *sovkhozy* and in 1976 Brezhnev continued the process so that there were 27,700 *kolkhozy* and 19,600 *sovkhozy*.[25] The declining number of farms reflected the trend towards the more ideologically correct *sovkhoz*. Technically, a collective is a co-operative, leasing nationalized land, electing management, conforming to the norms and quotas decided for it by the district soviet, selling to the state at fixed prices the produce of collective effort, the proceeds from which are then distributed by a farm meeting. Peasants were paid a share of the proceeds according to the number of 'work days' they had done, but after 1966 and the movement to merge collective and state farms *kolkhozniki* were paid fixed rates with end-of-year bonuses.

The *sovkhozniki* was a worker whose factory happened to be the land. His management was appointed from above. He was unionized. He received a wage just like a factory worker, and his wage did not suffer if the harvest failed. Both the *kolkhoz* and the *sovkhoz* were required to meet quota targets of produce which were then delivered to the state at fixed prices. The state paid higher prices for deliveries above quota. Khrushchev hoped to raise peasant living standards and when he advocated the merger of collectives in 1950 he claimed that the resulting enormous farms would be able to build fine villages. On 4 March 1951 he wrote in *Pravda* that the new collectives would be able to build 4-roomed houses in new *agrogorods* which would have amenities similar to industrial towns. *Pravda* printed a retraction the next day and nothing came of the idea until the Central Committee called for the formation of farm conglomerates linking agriculture with industry in June 1976. The decree announced that 'conglomerates will provide a good basis for further development of agro-industrial integration, joining agricultural production with industry and creating a wide network of agro-industrial enterprises to which the future belongs'.[26] The net result by 1980 was that rural squalor had gone. Even so the relative absence of paved roads (only 200,000 miles (321,800 km)) and adequate transport meant that the spring thaw and autumn rains cut off large numbers of villages in seas of mud or *bezdorozhie* ('roadlessness'). However, the ever-increasing size of the agricultural unit, apart from being more difficult to manage, was an engine of social change as it removed the peasant from his traditional village and cultural environment.

It is party policy for membership to reflect the occupational divisions within society, but in 1977, although *kolkhozniki* represented 16.4 per cent of the population, they only represented 13.6 per cent of party membership. Nevertheless, the party has always sought control over all sectors of agriculture. In 1930 Stalin established machine tractor stations which possessed, serviced and loaned out agricultural machinery to collectives, as well as ensuring produce deliveries for the state. These stations controlled the collectives and issued their instructions, but even then, Khrushchev felt the need in the mid-1950s to appoint 30,000 selected party members as collective chairmen on the grounds of their ideological correctness even if they knew nothing about agriculture.

From the state's point of view, the peasants needed watching. After the war Andreyev's new Council for *Kolkhoz* Affairs seized 14 million acres (5.7 million hectares) which had been annexed to private plots from the parent collectives. Approximately 500,000 non-productive personnel were returned to work in the fields and 213,000 names were removed from collective payrolls. The machine tractor stations served to prolong suspicion between village and party, and Stalin began to internalize party control to the collective. From 1953 party organizations developed in the collectives and in the local areas, so that in 1958 Khrushchev scrapped the machine tractor stations. He handed their political control to the local party. Their machinery was bought by the collectives and 1.7 million machine tractor station personnel joined the collectives. The garage function of the stations was retained by repair tractor stations, but these failed, and the repair service collapsed as many collectives suffered grave financial problems in acquiring machinery. By 1966 thousands of collectives still had not bought their own machines.

Khrushchev's reforms of the system, his reshuffling of personnel, the creation of the *sovnarkhozy* and the division of the party into agricultural and industrial wings, all played their part in disorganizing and disenchanting the agricultural sector. Brezhnev recognized the importance of stability and at the March 1965 meeting of the Central Committee he announced the restoration of the Ministry of Agriculture and an end to Khrushchev's reorganizations. There were to be no more campaigns: Khrushchev's maize campaign had increased land under maize even though much of this land was unsuited for the crop. There was to be no more pressure upon private livestock.[27] Sizeable food price increases were given and compulsory delivery quotas were reduced. Brezhnev's programme included more mechanization of agriculture and increased fertilizer output, but by 1970 tractor production was 19 per cent, farm trucks 35 per cent and fertilizer 15 per cent below the planned level.[28] It was only in the ninth and tenth Plans in the 1970s that Brezhnev got his way in the Politburo and agricultural investment increased to 27 per cent of total investment in order to accommodate his ambitions to improve diet, consumer choice and peasant living standards, as well as to eliminate the ideologically unattractive and inefficient collectives by submerging them in the new conglomerates.

Structural reorganization of agriculture was designed to increase party control and efficiency, but other ways had also been tried. Khrushchev announced to the Central Committee in February 1954 plans to increase grain production by one-third by putting to the plough the virgin grasslands of western Siberia, the lower Volga and Kazakhstan. By 1956 500,000 volunteers had moved to Kazakhstan. Khrushchev boasted that 90 million acres (36.45 million hectares) were ploughed up in 1954 alone, equal to the cultivated areas of France, England and Spain.[29] The new farms were created on the *sovkhoz* principle, and the state's propaganda machine offered high pay and appealed to the party loyalty and patriotism of the young and the skilled to bring in the new harvests.

The first year of the Virgin Lands scheme called for 5,000 combine harvesters – 10,000 trucks and 50,000 tractors – as well as the housing and tentage needed by the *sovkhozniki*. The scheme was a gamble, for the Kazakh party leadership opposed the pace of development which was to destroy the Kazakh herds and nomad traditions and eventually reduce the Kazakhs to a minority in their own republic. However, in February 1954 the Kazakh party Secretary Shayakmetov and the Second Secretary Afonov were replaced by Brezhnev and Ponomarenko. More intractable was the climate, the marginal soil and the sheer size and inaccessibility of the region. There were virtually no roads, railways, electricity or airstrips. Almost all the modern infrastructure had to be provided from scratch.

Initially the scheme paid off. It confounded Malenkov who had opposed it, and the 16.1 million ton(ne)s of Kazakh grain in 1956 offset the drought in the Ukraine. However, by 1960 the thin soil and inadequate fertilizer failed to sustain yields. Dustbowls were created, topsoil was lost and harvests fell, culminating in the double disaster in 1963 of harvest failures in the virgin lands and the Ukraine. Nevertheless the scheme had yielded about 155 million ton(ne)s of grain by 1964, equivalent to a whole annual harvest; and it had opened up, colonized and russified some of the grasslands on China's borders. Brezhnev remained committed to the virgin lands, but more fertilizer, better grain strains and more scientific husbandry made better use of the new lands. When the Ukraine harvest failed in 1972, Kazakhstan produced its biggest crop of 27 million ton(ne)s, 16 per cent of the Soviet total. Brezhnev argued that the 2.1 billion roubles invested in Kazakhstan between 1954 and 1977 were value for money in producing more than 250 million ton(ne)s of grain.[30]

The Virgin Lands scheme was a stopgap gamble to raise production without tackling the ideologically difficult questions of raising product-ivity and motivating the peasants to work harder for the common good on land and with machinery that was not their own. The relationship between the prices of agricultural produce and consumer manufactures were traditionally unfavourable for the peasant. Between 1932 and 1952 agricultural prices remained basically unchanged, but the price of consumer goods increased nearly tenfold.[31] Only by the late 1970s had rural and urban incomes converged, if profits from private plots are included. By then, too, the state had stopped 'exploiting' agriculture for the benefit of industry.[32]

Only after the July 1964 Supreme Soviet did peasants enjoy old-age pensions and other social security benefits that workers had long had. Even then, at $20 per month rural pensions in the mid-1970s were only, half the national average. From November 1974 child allowances of $15 per month were paid to families where annual *per capita* income was less than $800. Education facilities were poorer and standards lower in the countryside. Even more revealing of the peasants' standing in the USSR was the fact that in 1945 Stalin allowed freedom of movement of workers from job to job and place to place, but only in 1975 did the government agree to issue to peasants, by 1981, the internal passport without which travel is illegal.

Between 1939–49, Andrei Andreyev's Council for *Kolkhoz* Affairs encouraged the *sveno* or 'link' experiment, but Andreyev was dismissed in 1949, and when Khrushchev took over responsibility for agriculture he propounded the 'brigade' system. The 'link' was a unit of up to twelve peasants who were responsible for certain areas of a farm. The 'brigade' was a unit of peasants so large and impersonal as to take advantage of economies of scale and of the limited machinery available without allowing individuals to cultivate the psychology of private ownership of the land they worked – which was the major criticism levelled at the *sveno*.

The idea was revived in summer 1965 in the Communist Youth League newspaper, *Komsomolskaya Pravda*, which argued that the fundamental weakness of Soviet agriculture was the absence of an 'organic link' between the peasant and the land. It proposed that 'links' of five or six be given long-term control of parcels of land for which they would have responsibility and from which they would reap the benefits.[33]

Many farms developed their 'links', but the bureaucracy opposed the idea because it might expose overmanning in agriculture. Also the government's attitude was ambivalent, for the scheme offered to raise production, ensure the agricultural health of the state and dispense with the need for private plots, but at a cost of enshrining the profit motive and recreating something akin to private land and risking the break-up of the collective and state farms with the resultant loss of party control over the countryside. The most noted practitioner of the *sveno* was Ivan Khudenko who, in 1972, on a tract of marginal land in Kazakhstan, demonstrated that labour productivity was twenty times higher than on neighbouring farms. Khudenko was an embarrassment. His experimental farm was closed down and he was imprisoned for the alleged theft of 1000 roubles from the state.

The *sveno* remained an experiment disliked by conservatives, but the only part of the state system which could compete with the private plots. Both the Stalin and Brezhnev Constitutions allowed peasants to possess private allotments. Although Stalin and Khrushchev squeezed the plots, to dispense with them could have invited disaster. Brezhnev even encouraged them. In October 1977 the Ministry of Agriculture ordered local authorities to consider higher quotas for private livestock. The Ministry also promised regular supplies of feed from state sources. The private plots were owned by the 34 million farmers in individual plots of 1.24 acres (0.5 hectare) or less and usually had one or two cows plus pigs and small flocks of fowl. Covering less than 1 per cent of the USSR's cultivated area, the plots supplied more than 25 per cent of total farm output and 30 per cent of all livestock products.

These surpluses were either consumed at home or sold in the 8,000 free farmers' markets. The plots were simply more efficient. Public-sector growers needed 11 lbs (5 kg) of feed to produce 2.2 lbs (1 kg) of goose, but the private plots produced the same weight of meat from 6.6 lbs (3 kg) or even 4.4 lbs (2 kg) of feed.[34]

Agriculture remained a weakness of the Soviet economy but after Stalin the peasant's lot improved immeasurably: diet became better and food production soared. As one writer commented: 'Agriculture is often described as the Achilles' heel of the Soviet economy. But while this is true, it is less often remembered that Achilles could after all, walk upon his heel.'[35]

# Six

# RELIGIOUS, ETHNIC AND POLITICAL MINORITIES

The USSR aims at the ideal of a classless society in which the internal contradictions and antagonisms of the bourgeois state are replaced by communism and 'proletarian homogeneity'.

To a large extent, the USSR is a meritocratic society and its federal structure counters some of the effects of the economic, legal and cultural hegemony exerted by Moscow. Nevertheless, it continues to have problems with religious believers and the churches, ethnic groups and dissidents whose traditions, cultures and aspirations remain distinct from the rest of the country. However, these problems are not great; although they could become great. Their interest lies in the persistence of minorities whose treatment and standing provide a perspective through which the theory and practice of Soviet ideology can be viewed.

Marx and Engels wrote: 'Religion is the sigh of the oppressed creature, the heart of a heartless world, just as it is the spirit of a spiritless situation. It is the opium of the people'.[1] Lenin continued: 'Religion is a kind of spiritual gin in which the slaves of capital drown their human shape and their claims to any decent life. All modern religions and churches . . . Marxism always regards as organs of bourgeois reaction serving to defend exploitation and to stupefy the working class.'[2] Lenin's atheism was profound: 'Every religious idea, every idea of God, every flirting with the idea of God is unutterable vileness.'[3]

Yet Lenin compromised with his ideals, as did his successors. The Constitutions of 1936 and 1977 both guaranteed freedom of belief. But by preaching 'freedom' and expecting religions to fade away, the authorities have been trapped by their own rhetoric, and although the Kremlin actively encouraged the disappearance of religion, it stopped short of attempting to extirpate it altogether.

Where Soviet law guarantees freedom of religion it also guarantees freedom of anti-religion, and the authority and resources of the state and the party have been mobilized against religious observance. 'Anti-religious propaganda' is co-ordinated, official and pervasive. Members of the Society for the Dissemination of Political and Scientific Knowledge, known as 'Knowledge', delivered 738,188 lectures on anti-religious and natural science topics in 1965 alone.[4] About 200–300 anti-religious books and brochures are published annually and there are 'rooms of atheism' (350 in the Ukraine in 1967) and anti-religious museums.

Against this constant onslaught, the churches could offer nothing comparable. There is no freedom to propagate religion publicly and Sunday schools and religious instruction outside seminaries are banned.

In January 1960 Khrushchev invoked the full force of law against any religious practice that could be regarded as illegal. In effect this meant that un-registered congregations could be closed down and the licensing of churches made very difficult. The anti-religious campaign was emphasized by Khrushchev at the Twenty-second Party Congress in November 1961, and again in 1964: 'Now that the building of communism has been broadly undertaken . . . the Party has put into its programme the task of fully and completely overcoming religious prejudices [*sic*].'[5]

Khrushchev was apparently disturbed by an increase in church weddings among Komsomol members and his campaign, led by Leonid Illichev, was directed at churches. Before the Revolution there had been 22,000 Orthodox churches. By June 1964 there were about 17,500, but within a matter of months nearly 10,000 were closed. Five out of eight seminaries and fifty-four out of sixty-seven monasteries and convents were also closed. The number of Baptist congregations was cut by a half to 2,700. Out of 400 synagogues, 338 were closed and 7,600 out of 8,000 mosques. A law was also passed in 1962 banning religious meetings in private, and in 1961 the Patriarch of Moscow 'voluntarily' surrendered to the state, administrative and economic control over the parishes of the Orthodox Church.

Some of Khrushchev's excesses were counterproductive and increased numbers of believers. Furthermore, thrown out of their official churches, some congregations – especially Baptist – took to meeting privately and, therefore, to conspiring regularly to break the law, in which defiant guise they were more trouble and danger to the state than before. The Brezhnev leadership changed tack; the campaign eased off; emphasis shifted from attacks on churches, clergy and believers to attacks on religious beliefs. Church closures stopped, and since then, numbers of new churches have opened, so that there were about 11,000 Orthodox churches in 1979.

Brezhnev established a church–state equilibrium of sorts. An amnesty was given to some imprisoned Baptists in 1965, but this was paralleled by the imposition of stiffer penalties from March 1966 for 'the preparation for the purposes of mass dissemination or the mass dissemination of handbills, letters and leaflets and other documents making appeals for the non-observance of the legislation on religious cults'.[6]

Religions survived not only because of the strength of faith of their adherents and the policies adopted towards them by the state but because of their own approach to the state. Lacking formal voices in public life, the churches do not attract attention to themselves. Opposition to the state tended to be by individual Orthodox and Catholic clergy and lay people: their Churches have traditional roles in Russia proper and the south-western fringe respectively, and have continued, in modified form, their subservient relationships to the state which existed before 1917.

The Russian Orthodox Church inherited from its parent Greek Church the old caesaro-papism relationship in which church was subordinate to and effectively an arm of the state. Throughout its existence, Orthodoxy reinforced secular power by preaching submission to the state. The Orthodox hierarchy regularly speaks out in support of Soviet policy,[7] and the Church even had something of a revival in the 1970s when there were occasions on which up to half the marriages in some areas were in church and more than half the new babies were baptized.[8]

Out of 262 million Soviet citizens, between 30 and 40 million are members of the Orthodox Church, although few are young. Orthodoxy is complementary to the state and serves as a vehicle for expression of Russian national consciousness. Catholicism can also act as a vehicle for national feeling, so it is handled carefully where it exists in Lithuania and parts of Belorussia and the Ukraine, for the example of strongly Catholic Poland has been constant and was reinforced in 1978 by the election of a Polish pope.

Opposition to the state by religious groups rather than by individuals tended to come from the small Protestant denominations, of which the 500,000 strong (and growing) Baptists are the largest. In 1961, with the closure of some of their churches, Baptist dissent took shape and the authorities received so many requests for a relaxation of the measures aimed at them that President Mikoyan received a Baptist delegation in September 1965. On 16–17 May 1966 Baptist delegates from 130 towns staged an unprecedented sit-in outside the Central Committee in Moscow for a day and a half demanding to see Brezhnev. Their immediate demands were refused. Some delegates received short prison sentences and legislation was quickly passed penalizing those who organized or participated in 'group actions which grossly violate order'.[9] Since then, Baptists have shared in the easier official attitude towards the churches.

The issue of the Jewish religion is submerged in the wider issue of Jews in the USSR and is discussed below. The other major religion, Islam, has resisted russification by tsar and communist alike. Frequently nomadic by tradition and Muslim by religion the Kazakh, Uzbek, Kirghiz, Tadzhik and Turkmen peoples share ethnic, linguistic and cultural bonds across the Iranian, Afghan and Chinese frontiers.

The cities of central Asia have been settled by Russians and Ukrainians, but the countryside remained Muslim by religion or at least by background. Even with only 300 mosques and four officially approved *muftis*, Islam remained strong. Few Muslims were allowed to make the hajd, the pilgrimage to Mecca, so they made pilgrimages to local shrines. This has consequently reinforced national and religious identities. They are also relatively cut off from Russian culture and politics by a language barrier: 40 per cent of Kazakhs, 20 per cent of Kirghiz and even fewer Uzbeks, Tadzhiks and Turkmen speak Russian as a second language.[10] Coupled with an unwillingness to move away from their homelands, even preferring higher education in their own languages, despite the fact that fluent Russian is essential to a good career, Muslim national exclusiveness has meant that, by and large, Muslims have not married outside their faith. One result has been the rapid growth in numbers of the Muslims. In 1970 the five central Asian republics made up less than 14 per cent of the Soviet population, but by 1978 this had increased to 15.5 per cent and was expected to reach nearly 25 per cent by the year 2000. In the 1970s the central Asians showed population growth rates of up to 30 per cent, and the Tadzhiks had a crude birth rate of 48 per 1,000; compared with 13.1 per 1,000 in England and Wales, and 34.6 per 1,000 in India.[11]

The unassimilated Muslims do not have the technological skills or ideological values of the Europeans. They present a worry for the Kremlin, but they also illustrate the success of Moscow's religious policies. The USSR has been transformed in two generations into a secular state where, although between 50 and 80 million (19–30 per cent) Soviet citizens are practising believers, religion has no public voice and no official say in formulating public policy and attitudes unless expressly invited to do so. With one of the largest Muslim populations in the world the USSR can claim a voice in the counsels of Islam. In 1961 the World Council of Churches accepted the Russian Orthodox Church, which, with its claimed 40 million followers, became the biggest voice on the Council. Thereafter its policies came in part to reflect Soviet wishes.[12] So the World Council of Churches began to support national liberation movements. But it blocked discussion of such matters as human rights, and although it condemned Soviet action in Hungary in 1956, it did not condemn Soviet action in Czechoslovakia in 1968.

The census of January 1979 revealed that of the 262 million Soviet citizens, 137 million or 52.4 per cent were Russians, compared with 129 million or 53.3 per cent in 1970. The USSR is a multicultural and polyglot country matching its enormous size. Slavs make up over 70 per cent of the total, but there are 131 nations and nationalities ranging from the Russians, the 40 million Ukrainians and 12.5 million Uzbeks, to tribal fragments of only a few thousand.[13]

Whole families of languages are found, ranging from the Indo–European Polish, Romanian and Tadzhik, to the Ural–Altaic Uzbek and Estonian, and to the Caucasian and Palao–Asiatic languages. There are Germans in the USSR from the settlements of Catherine the Great, as well as Crimean Greeks, Bulgarians, Koreans, aboriginal Ainu from the once Japanese Kurile islands and Chukchi, who are also found in Alaska.

Such variety created difficulties for the Soviet as it did for the tsarist state. The tsars tried to 'russify' their non-Russian subjects and it was inevitable that after 1917 an unannounced 'creeping russification' should have continued. Russians or educated russified communists, such as Georgians like Stalin and Beria, and Armenians like Mikoyan, have dominated the party and government in all the republics of the USSR. Russian is also the language of administration, science, advanced education and commerce.

The USSR is a federal state where each of fifteen major ethnic groups, from the Russians to the Estonians, have their own union republics. Twenty smaller groups have their own autonomous republics, and there are, in addition, eight autonomous regions and ten national areas. These groups have a voice in the second chamber of the Supreme Soviet, the Council of the Nationalities. Soviet ideology originally proclaimed the eventual, inevitable voluntary amalgamation of the peoples of the USSR. Khrushchev alarmed many by talking of a 'merging' of the nations of the USSR, and the Twenty-second Congress of the CPSU in 1961 predicted the rapid diminution in significance of the boundaries between the republics.

In support of this policy republic party Secretaries were disciplined for 'nationalist tendencies' in their cadres' policies, that is, promoting to high office local rather than Russian officials. In 1959 the First Secretaries of the Uzbek, Turkmen and Azerbaijan parties, and in 1961 those of the Tadzhik and Armenian parties were sacked for this reason. But Brezhnev replaced talk of a merger. In 1969 he declared: 'The *rapprochement* of Soviet nations and their internationalist unity should not be regarded as the merger. The removal of all national differences is a long process, which cannot be achieved except after full victory of communism *in the world* [author's italics].'[14] Such a long term view offered stability to the ethnic minorities. Moscow has done much to encourage the survival and revival of minor languages and cultures and to reverse some of the injustices that Stalin meted out to over 1.5 million people of nine ethnic minorities.

In his Secret Speech, Khrushchev revealed some of the atrocities committed in Stalin's name. In 1943 and 1944 the Crimean Tatars, Kalmyk Tatars and four Caucasian tribes – the Chechen, Ingush, Karachai and Balkars – were deprived of autonomous status and deported to the east for alleged wholesale collaboration with the German forces. About 500,000 Volga Germans were deported in 1941 as a precautionary measure so that they could not collaborate with the *Wehrmacht*. Soon after, German groups in the Crimea and Caucasus were also exiled. Also deported as a precaution, but accused of nothing, were the Turkic Meskhetians from the Turkish–Georgian border. The Crimean Greeks were uprooted to Kazakhstan, presumably for alleged collaboration.

Huge numbers of Soviet citizens – and other Europeans – collaborated willingly or unwillingly with Hitler's forces. Up to 1 million Soviets served in the Vlassov 'Free Russia Army' or in auxiliary units attached to the *Wehrmacht* or SS. Of these there were units of Crimean Tatars, just as the same nationality provided Red Army heroes and anti-German partisans, just as there were Ukrainian, Latvian, Cossack and other units attached to the German forces.[15]

All the deportees suffered in the process of deportation. The Crimean Tatars claimed that 46 per cent of their 250,000 died in the deportation or the next 18 months.[16] All were subject to conditions of 'special settlement' in their new homes. They were restricted to the immediate area to which they had been deported on penalty of a 25-year sentence for unauthorized departure, and had to report every month to the local police chief. It seems that there was an Ingush rising in Kazakhstan in spring 1945 and a Chechen break-out from a penal camp in October 1954.[17]

The four Caucasian tribes, the Kalmyk Tatars and the Volga Germans were released from security police control in 1955. In his Secret Speech, Khrushchev condemned Stalin's actions towards the five former groups and on 9 January 1967, their autonomous territories were re-established and they were repatriated. The Meskhetians were quietly rehabilitated in 1956, but the Volga Germans had to wait until 1964, and the Crimean Tatars until 1967. However, these three groups did not regain their national autonomy and were not allowed to return to their homelands despite their rights as Soviet citizens to settle anywhere in the USSR 'in accordance with the existing legislation on employment and the passport regulations'.[18]

The desire of the Crimean Tatars to return to the Crimea was espoused by some leading Soviet dissidents. On 22 May 1969 fifty-five noted Moscow intellectuals, led by Piotr Yakir, appealed on their behalf to the UN Commission on Human Rights. A retired General, Piotr Grigorenko, pursued their case so vigorously that he was committed to a mental home in 1969. By 1977 only between 2,000 (according to the Moscow-based Helsinki Human Rights Group) and 8,000 families (the official figure) had returned to the Crimea. The January 1979 census no longer listed the Crimean Tatars separately.

The Meskhetians only came to Western notice in 1971 when some of them approached the Turkish embassy in Moscow and the UN

Secretary-General to ask for permission for Meskhetians to emigrate to Turkey.[19] They were refused, but they had identified a course of action that Germans and Jews, with influential foreign friends, were to pursue with more success. Part of West Germany's price for *détente* with the USSR was that those ethnic Germans who so wished should be allowed to leave Eastern Europe and settle in West Germany. Only small numbers are involved, for of more than 1.5 million Soviet Germans, only 8,200 were allowed to emigrate in 1977 and 8,500 in 1978, together with another 50,000 from the satellites.[20] But this was apparently enough to keep Bonn more or less satisfied without unsettling the Soviet–German communities unduly, although it has probably allowed the USSR to rid herself of those ethnic Germans who might have stirred up national consciousness and caused trouble.

As the self-proclaimed promised land of socialism, it was difficult for the USSR to acknowledge that some might want to emigrate, much less actually to let them go. Nevertheless thousands of Germans, some individual dissidents like Alexander Solzhenitsyn and over 125,000 Jews were allowed to emigrate in the 1970s. Only 1000 Jews left in 1970, but 43,000 in the first ten months of 1979. Even more might have been allowed to leave if the failure in January 1974 of the US–Soviet trade bill had not cut Jewish emigration from 35,000 in 1973 to less than half that in 1974. The next two years saw a further decrease. Soviet willingness to allow 10 per cent of the 2.1 million Soviet Jews to leave consistently undermined the credibility of Soviet support for the Arabs against Israel and invited criticism of Russia from China and the Arab world that the 40–50 per cent of Jewish *émigrés* who went to Israel bolstered that country's manpower skills and technical resources against the Arabs: which, indeed they did.

Nevertheless, emigration allowed the USSR to get rid of the embarrassment of widespread disaffection amongst its Jews. By Soviet standards, Jews did well in the USSR out of proportion to their numbers. In 1970, 134 Jews per 1000 but only 22 per 1000 Russians received higher education. They did well in the arts, science and administration, and discrimination was milder than in the past. They were the most 'party-saturated' group with more than twice the Soviet average of party membership – 13 per cent of the Jewish population.[21] But they were effectively excluded from the higher ranks of the party, armed forces and diplomacy. Unlike any other major ethnic group they have no geographic region as a base for their cultural identity.

The Jewish Autonomous Republic of Birobidjan in the Far East, had only 15,000 Jews out of a population of 191,000[22] and Stalin's 1947–8 bans on Yiddish language theatres and publications remained in force in 1980. The monthly government-controlled *Sovetish Heimland* is the only Yiddish publication and there is only one small Yiddish theatre group. Latent discontent with their cultural and national vacuum was fanned by Israel's victory in 1967. This raised the national consciousness of Soviet Jews just as the 1968 suppression of Czechoslovakia convinced many Jewish intellectuals that there was no hope for liberalism in the USSR. Jews mounted demonstrations in Moscow and elsewhere, and attracted and kept foreign attention. Only brute force could have silenced them, but that would have jeopardized *détente* and would have meant a return to Stalinism, so the Kremlin solved its dilemma by letting Jews go. Many difficulties of cost, delay, harassment and humiliation were imposed upon those who applied to leave, but the figures speak for themselves. It must also be said that Jewish flight served the propaganda purpose of 'proving' that Jews really were 'rootless cosmopolitans' with no loyalty to the motherland as they had been accused in the *Zhdanovschina* (see page 10).

Otherwise, the vast majority of Soviet citizens appeared reconciled, indeed content with their national identities. Stirrings of discontent occurred in the 1970s in the Ukraine and the Baltic states – especially Lithuania – but these were small groups protesting not so much against the political system but against the growing cultural and economic dominance of Moscow. Educational reforms in 1959 attempted to weaken republican languages in favour of the teaching of Russian, but these reforms were made optional following protests in the Supreme Soviet from the Baltic and Caucasian republics. When it was proposed in 1978 to replace Georgian as the sole official language and give equality to Russian, mass demonstrations in Tbilisi persuaded the authorities to abandon this reform.

Although expressions of minority nationalism have been frowned upon, it has frequently been difficult to distinguish between official promotion of Soviet and Great Russian nationalism. Stalin encouraged the revival of old tsarist heroes like Peter the Great and Alexander Nevsky, and successive regimes promoted Russia's past and identity at the inevitable expense of other nationalities. This policy may become even more pronounced as the non-Russians increase faster in numbers than the Russians, the ethnic balance of the state tilts and when 35 per cent of military recruits come from central Asia and the Transcaucasus by the year 2000.[23]

Modern political dissidence was born in the USSR in February 1966 with the arrest, trial and sentencing of Yuli Daniel and Andrei Sinyavsky to five and seven years respectively in labour camps for having published abroad 'anti-Soviet propaganda' and 'lampoons and slanders on Soviet society'. This partial return to Stalinism was enshrined in law in September 1966, when three-year sentences were decreed for those guilty of 'the systematic spreading of intentional fabrications orally or in written form if harmful to the Soviet state'.[24] Thereafter, not just the traitor or opponent of the regime but the dissatisfied grumbler could be caught in the net of repression.

But repression sparked off more dissent. On 5 December 1965, 100 people demonstrated in Pushkin Square, Moscow, against the Sinyavsky–Daniel trial, and sixty-two members of the Moscow Writers' Union appealed to the Twenty-third Party Congress for a review of the case. More significant was the arrest in January 1967 of Alexander Ginzburg, Yuri Galanskov and others, after Ginzburg had compiled the 'White Book' of documents on the Sinyavsky–Daniel affair. These arrests sparked off more demonstrations, more arrests and a widening, if still small, circle of people who were affected by dissident ideas and their official repression. Andrei Amalrik saw the trial as the origin of what he called the 'democratic movement', a 'political opposition in embryo' because 738 people signed petitions protesting against violations of legality at the trial of Ginzburg and Galanskov.[25]

Amalrik was expelled from the USSR in 1976 after serving a five-year sentence for the publication abroad of his essay 'Will the Soviet Union Survive Until 1984?' in which he identified three broad trends within the 'democratic movement': genuine Marxist–Leninism; Christian/moral; and liberal. Although simplistic, these categories remain useful in describing groups which received much attention in the West, less in the USSR, and never numbered more than a few thousand at most.

The first group believed that the Revolution had been perverted and that the USSR needed to return to pure Marxist–Leninism. Included in this category were General Piotr Grigorenko and the brothers Medvedev; Roy who felt that communist ideology had ossified under the ruling bureaucratic oligarchy, and Zhores, a geneticist, who was exiled to Britain in January 1973. At the other extreme were those who wanted to return to traditional values, Great Russian nationalism, the Russian Orthodox Church and, retaining authoritarianism but eschewing Marxism, to cut loose from the satellites and turn their backs on the decadent West. The high priest of this philosophy was Alexander Solzhenitsyn described by the Spanish Communist leader Santiago Carrillo as like:

> one of those priests of the Russian Orthodox Church, half mystical prophets, half rogues, who centuries ago used to set out on the roads of Russia to announce the end of the human race . . . this man, . . . may be the extreme expression of disappointment and despair carried to the pitch of the most ungovernable hatred, brought about by the fact that the dream is out of phase with the reality.[26]

With a fine literary reputation that was later to become worldwide, Solzhenitsyn launched his protest at the fourth Congress of Soviet Writers in May 1967 when he demanded an end to censorship and criticized the Writers' Union for siding with the authorities. Thereafter, until his enforced exile in February 1974, Solzhenitsyn was a nuisance to the authorities and became an embarrassment to other dissidents who were less strident, self-confident or messianic than him. His open 'Letter to the Supreme Leaders' on 3 September 1973 indicted Soviet and Western systems and 'offered not a model of an open urban scientific society joining the modern world, but a mystic vision of a future-past, a dream of Holy Russia resurrected by turning inward into itself and pulling away from the 20th century'.[27] Solzhenitsyn was sent abroad. The very fact of exile weakened his domestic moral standing as the spokesman for Mother Russia.

Amalrik's third category included those like Andrei Sakharov, whose 1968 memorandum, 'Progress, Peaceful Coexistence and Intellectual Freedom', spelt out his belief that capitalism and communism had certain virtues and ought to 'converge', and that unless the return of Stalinism could be prevented, the arms race halted and Moscow's more aggressive instincts checked by Western resolve, then the human race faced annihilation. Solzhenitsyn's moral authority had derived from his acknowledged literary genius and his eleven years in labour camps and exile: Sakharov's came from his scientific achievements and his access to the Soviet leadership. Until his exile to the closed city of Gorky in January 1980, Sakharov continued to speak out against the Soviet state, but his voice became increasingly lonely as others were exiled or silenced. In 1975 he was refused permission to leave the USSR to receive the Nobel Peace Prize, but news of the prize heartened Soviet dissidents as did continued Western interest in him. Evidence of this is the letter of support written to him in February 1977 by President Carter of the USA. When Sakharov was exiled in 1980, Soviet foreign relations had been so damaged by the Afghan adventure that the Kremlin incurred with equanimity the Western outcry. Sakharov was one of the last of a generation of dissidents who had reacted to the Brezhnev regime in similar ways and who had been allowed so to react because Stalinist terror had been dismantled a decade previously.

Dissident ideas circulated underground in the form of *samizdat* ('self-publishing') reproduced literature and *magnitizdat* ('magnetic self-publishing' by the use of the *magnitofon* or cassette recorder). The *samizdat* heyday in 1969–70 saw the publication of a large amount of unofficial literature; some of it not overtly political, but simply serious literature. One *émigré* dissident estimated that he had a 'lending library' of 200 works at that time and circulated a catalogue.[28]

Obviously it was in the interests of the authorities to eradicate dissidence not only because of its foreign and domestic resonance but because there was the possibility that it might change its nature. On 22 January 1969 a 22-year-old Army Lieutenant Ilyin attempted unsuccessfully to assassinate Brezhnev.[29] In 1970 five men were sentenced for attempting to hijack an Aeroflot airliner in Leningrad.[30] Both incidents were the work of 'dissidents'. With the expansion of *détente*, repression of dissidence mounted, as many dissidents looked to the West for support and inspiration, and the authorities sought to prevent the spread of contaminating ideas.

The USSR is an orderly society and most people therefore accept the material goals of their society. It was simple, then, for the state to portray dissidents as disaffected wastrels, tools of the West, and potential or actual traitors. Dissidents received little public support and were subject to official displeasure, including an economic blacklist, loss of jobs and penury. Selective arrests, imprisonment, interrogations, confessions and unexpected early release of prisoners were all used by the KGB to sow doubt and demoralization in dissident groups.

In June 1972, the KGB arrested Viktor Krasin and Piotr Yakir, founders in 1969 of the Action Group for the Defence of Human Rights in the USSR. They were also both involved in the important *samizdat Chronicle*. They eventually 'confessed' and implicated many others: 200 more people were arrested. The effect on dissident morale was deadening. When Sinyavsky and Daniel returned from Siberia they stayed out of politics. By 1975 dissent in the USSR was demoralized. Some, like Grigorenko, had been confined to mental hospitals, others had simply gone into exile. Writers Valeri Tarsis and Joseph Brodsky, cellist Mstislav Rostropovich, Andrei Sinyavsky and Pavel Litvinov (the son of the Foreign Minister in the 1930s, Maxim Litvinov) departed, among many others. This was probably the most effective technique used against dissidents. It removed the chance that they might contaminate their neighbours. It was quick and allowed them to be portrayed as defectors. Ultimately, it must have lessened the commitment to an enduring struggle on the part of some who were left behind.

The Soviet signature to the 1975 Helsinki Agreement, with its promise of human rights for all, regenerated opposition in the USSR, as it did in Poland, Czechoslovakia and East Germany. In May 1976 an eleven-member group was established in Moscow to monitor the USSR's compliance with the Helsinki provisions on human rights. The group was led by Dr Yuri Orlov, a physicist; Alexander Ginzburg, a former custodian of a fund established by Solzhenitsyn to help political prisoners and their families; and Anatoly Shcharansky who linked the dissident group to Jewish 'refuseniks' (those who had been refused exit visas) and was a go-between with the Western press. The Moscow Helsinki group became an immediate target of the KGB, not only because it drew attention to the USSR's failure to implement Helsinki's human rights provisions, but also because it represented a banner under which the disaffected of all political, artistic and religious interests could gather.

The monitoring group was broken up by arrest and exile in early 1977. Orlov was arrested for 'anti-constitutional activity' and 'his attempt to question in the eyes of the international public, the sincerity of the Soviet

Union's efforts to implement undeviatingly the international obligations it has assumed'.[31] Ginzburg was arrested as a 'sponger' and 'profiteer', but Shcharansky faced the capital charge of spying for the USA – which President Carter personally denied. The threat posed to the system by the dissidents was emphasized in September 1977 by the televised speech of KGB chief Yuri Andropov, who described the dissidents as 'an isolated band of renegades' who were the result of 'political or ideological aberrations, religious fanaticism, nationalistic quirks, personality failures and resentments and in many cases psychological instability'.[32]

In breach of the USSR's own law, the three were only brought to trial in May and July 1978 and all received heavy prison sentences, although Ginzburg was 'swapped' to the USA in 1979 and another member of the group, General Grigorenko, was sent into exile in April 1978.

The dissident issue gave other countries political ammunition to use against the USSR, created problems at home and even caused difficulties with friendly parties. When Vladimir Bukovsky was exchanged in December 1976 for Chilean communist leader Luis Corvalàn, the tacit acceptance that such a dissident was as dangerous to Moscow as a communist leader was to Pinochet's rule in Chile, and that there were political prisoners in the USSR, angered the Eurocommunists.

At the beginning of the 1980s, the quietened dissident voice was hushed even further with the internal exile to Gorky of Andrei Sakharov, leaving historian Roy Medvedev as the last major dissident still at large. Nevertheless, the dissident issue continued to focus critical Western attention on the USSR and to stimulate Western doubts about Moscow's intentions. Furthermore, dissidence which attracted Western attention was no longer the preserve of the intellectual. In January 1978 Vladimir Klebanov, an ex-miner, who had spent the previous twenty years in detention or unemployed, set up the Free Trade Union Association of the Soviet Working People and on 27 January 1978, 200 Soviet workers signed an appeal to the West for recognition of the FTUA.

The FTUA had such an initial foreign impact that, over the objection of the USSR, its largest financial contributor, the UN's International Labour Organization, investigated FTUA allegations that forty-three of its members had been arrested or hospitalized without trial.

Creating an impact abroad was not the same as creating one at home. The authorities successfully isolated dissidents from society at large, and dissidence was reduced to insignificant proportions by 1980 by the patient, deliberate application of effectively unanswerable, implacable and arbitrary force. The dissidents disposed of the pen and courage in a sea of indifference, ignorance or hostility. The authorities deployed the dungeon, labour camp, exile or strait-jacket.

# PART II

Foreign Affairs

# Seven

# STALIN: FROM ALLIANCE TO COLD WAR

The Second World War was a triumph for the Soviet Union, for Mother Russia, for communism and for Stalin's personal rule. The victories over the Axis were cruelly bought and bitterly expensive (see pages 7–8), but they carried the Red Army in a tide across eastern Europe and brought relations between Moscow and her Western allies to a pitch of mutual respect and cordiality that would have been unimaginable before the war.

Things had changed since the early summer of 1939 when Britain and France felt that a military alliance with Moscow would be of doubtful value. Certainly the Soviet Union's previous military adventures were undistinguished. She lost territory to Poland after the war of 1920 and although she defeated Japanese forces in Manchuria in August 1939, the West paid more attention to Soviet reverses by tiny Finland in the winter war of 1939–40.[1] Red Army losses at the hands of the Germans were enormous (about 10 million had died), but despite this the USSR had 11,365,000 men under arms in May 1945. In 1945 her armies were well equipped, well-led and morale was high.

When Japan surrendered on 15 August 1945, the USSR was left supreme in the heartland of Eurasia, her new-found strength reflected in the sway she extended over Eastern Europe. Soviet strength in 1945 masked terrible domestic weakness, but her military power was palpable. It enabled her to reabsorb the three Baltic states which she had annexed in 1940. She annexed territory from Japan, Finland, East Prussia, Romania, Poland and Czechoslovakia (see Map 10 on page 150), and occupied Poland, east Germany, Czechoslovakia, Hungary, Romania, Bulgaria, northern Iran, northern Korea and Manchuria. Albania and Yugoslavia fell within the Soviet sphere of influence and Finland had to accept subservience to Moscow's interests as the price of autonomy. Elsewhere, Soviet pressure was felt in Greece and Turkey.

With no oceans or mountain ranges to protect her, Russia has been invaded and overrun again and again throughout her history. The

American diplomat George Kennan wrote that Russia had no tradition of 'good neighbourliness or stable political demarcation lines'.[2] 'The natural enmity of neighbours is a precept for Russians that stems very directly from long historical experience.'[3]

Between the middle of the sixteenth century and the end of the seventeenth century, Russia conquered territory the size of Holland every year for 150 years running. The West failed to understand that the USSR expected the hostility of her neighbours (as did tsarist Russia). Furthermore, territorial expansion was 'the Soviet way' just as it had been 'the Russian way'.[4] It must also be said that if Stalin was a crusading ideologist then it was his duty to carry the Marxist gospel to the East Europeans once he had the opportunity.

By 1945 the Soviet Union was accepted as one of the 'Big Three' – soon to be one of the Big Two – arbiters of the world. Stalin had been courted by Churchill of Britain and Roosevelt of America at the conferences of Teheran in 1943 and Yalta in January 1945. Churchill had even visited Moscow for talks in October 1944.

Formal alliances had been signed with Britain in 1942 and France in 1944. Although the USSR played no part in the Bretton Woods Conference of 1944 when forty-four states set up a new monetary system and created the International Monetary Fund (IMF), she did play one of the major roles in the establishment in June 1945 of the United Nations Organization. With America, Britain, France and China, she became one of the five permanent members of the UN Security Council, with all that implied in terms of status. Stalin won agreement for the permanent members of the Security Council to have the power of veto and for the two most war-damaged Soviet republics – Belorussia and the Ukraine – to have General Assembly seats as well as the USSR herself.

Even so, Moscow could only ever rely on the UN votes of her satellites and Stalin never trusted the UN where the USSR could be outvoted on any issue. Indeed, by 1948 the Soviet veto had been used forty times. The USSR had joined the UNO's precursor, the League of Nations, in 1934 in the hope that this would protect Russia from a war which Stalin saw coming. It did not, and Stalin was determined thereafter that the USSR should ensure her own security, without dependence upon an international order based upon principles that were largely alien to the experience of Russian governments. In Moscow's view America and Britain could afford to trust the rest of the world because they owned much of it and were protected by the oceans.

At the major wartime conferences Stalin and his allies sought agreements which would ensure security for their respective countries. The Big Three met in Teheran in Iran in November and December 1943 and agreed on plans for the defeat of the German forces. In February 1945 Stalin, Roosevelt and Churchill met at Yalta in the Crimea. They agreed on free elections in Eastern Europe; Russia's entry into the war against Japan; the principle of territorial adjustment to Poland; reparations from and the administration of Germany; and the structure of the UNO. Yalta was a high point of allied co-operation: Roosevelt declared that never before had 'the major allies been more closely united not only in their war aims but also in their peace aims'.[5] However, Yalta was staged by allies who still needed each other to defeat their tenacious enemy. The conference produced agreements on principles and generalities to which all could agree, but by the time of the Potsdam Conference there was no avoiding detail, on which agreement was more difficult.

The Potsdam Conference delegates assembled in Berlin from 17 July to 2 August 1945. The conference was fundamental to postwar East–West relations.[6] It brought together the Big Three when the *raison d'être* of their collaboration, Nazi Germany, was gone. Prior to Potsdam, Stalin had dealt on equal terms with two elder statesmen for whom he had a genuine respect if not affection. At the end of Yalta Stalin had said that as long as the three of them remained at the helm, there would be peace, although it would not be easy. As leaders of war governments, Churchill and Roosevelt had had exceptional powers to make quick decisions. But by July 1945 any personal bond was gone. Roosevelt was dead and replaced by Harry Truman, a man without Roosevelt's stature, strength of vision, or natural patrician charm, but with all of his iron will, and who owed Stalin nothing. At Potsdam Churchill was not the man he had been and was worsted by Stalin in the sessions he attended until electoral defeat replaced him as British Premier by Clement Attlee who, as a socialist, was the heir of those who had rejected the Russian Bolsheviks' revolutionary path to the Marxist utopia and so was guilty of heresy in Soviet eyes.

Despite a slight heart attack just before the conference, Stalin was the dominant personality at Potsdam, even if Truman represented the dominant power. With a clearer grasp of detail and intricate argument and better briefed than the others, he remained, as British General Brooke had described him at Teheran, 'a military brain of the very highest calibre'.[7] Churchill's doctor wrote: 'Stalin's tenacity and obstinacy have no counterpart on our side. He knows exactly what he wants and he does not mind how he gets it. He is very patient too and never loses his temper.'[8]

What did Stalin want from Potsdam? Some things had already been decided; the zones of Germany and Austria and the sectors of Berlin and Vienna (Map 2). Some issues were ducked; the peace treaties and reparations; and some like Poland, world peace and the UNO idea had been partially resolved. Above all else, he wanted his allies to recognize that by occupying Eastern Europe he had already taken the steps he saw as necessary to assure the future security of the USSR: there was no

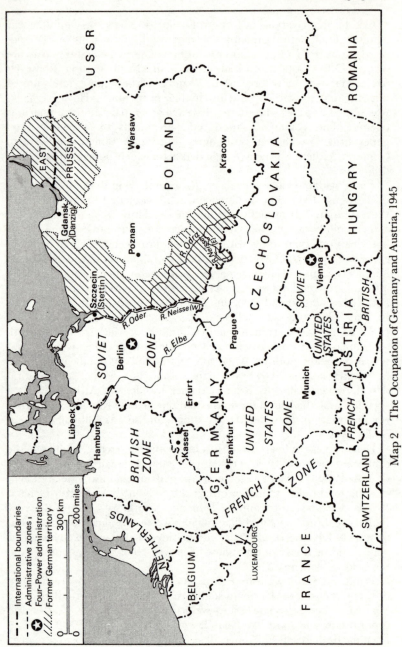

Map 2   The Occupation of Germany and Austria, 1945

prospect of him letting go of Eastern Europe. Having no natural frontiers to deter an aggressor from the west, Russia had only her size. By pushing her frontiers westwards and occupying her neighbours, she increased her space and created a vast glacis, a buffer zone or killing ground, between herself and potential aggressors from the west. Stalin had made sure that if Russia was attacked again, then the frightful civilian and material losses of Leningrad and Stalingrad and the enormously destructive battles of Vyazma–Bryansk, Kharkov and Kursk would all happen in someone else's country. The East Europeans were later to be converted to communism, but Stalin's original use for them had been quite simply as barricades.

On Germany, however, the conference made progress. It was to remain one economic unit with a standard of living equal to the prewar average for other European countries. This was estimated at 74 per cent of Germany's 1936 GNP. There would be no central government, but central departments for finance, trade and industry, under the direction of the zonal commanders, the Allied Control Council of four 'viceroys' who were charged with the implementation of Potsdam. Stalin was disappointed over reparations, and the US and UK refused to break off relations with Franco's Spain or grant the USSR a trusteeship of Italy's ex-colony of Libya.

Adding to the complexities of Potsdam was the successful test on 16 July 1945, the day after the conference opened, of the world's first nuclear device at Alamagordo, New Mexico. At Yalta, while both European and Asian wars still stretched away into the distance, the Americans were pleased to win Stalin's promise that the Red Army would enter the war against Japan three months after the collapse of the Reich and thus relieve the USA of some of the one million casualties that were expected if Japan had to be taken by storm. After 24 July, when Truman was informed that a bomb could be prepared for use against Japan by 3 August, Russian military help was no longer needed. One author wrote: 'This change in the attitude of the Americans and British at Potsdam gave dramatic confirmation of Stalin's worst fears and suspicions. Moreover, it offended him deeply as an act of ingratitude and rejection.'[9]

The nuclear destruction of Hiroshima on 6 August and Nagasaki on 9 August had their impact in Moscow also, as the Americans intended.[10] Japan capitulated on 15 August, but not before the USSR had fulfilled to the letter her Yalta promises and 1.6 million Soviet troops had burst into Manchuria, northern Korea and northern China. In the one-week war the Red Army lost 8,219 dead and 22,264 wounded, but inflicted 80,000 casualties upon the Japanese, took 594,000 prisoners, huge amounts of war *matériel* as booty, the Manchuria railway, southern Sakhalin and the Kurile islands. Although the Soviets (and the British) were denied a place in the military government of Japan, the brief war conferred great benefits upon the Kremlin: it introduced the Red Army into northern China in such numbers and with such surplus captured weaponry as to be able to intervene in the confused communist versus Kuomintang struggle that was going on in China. The Soviets got the use of Port Arthur, the Manchurian railway and revenge for the shame of their defeat by Japan in 1904–5. Of great long term significance, by occupying the whole island of Sakhalin and all the Kurile islands, they gained control of all the entrances to the sea of Okhotsk which became thereafter the safe home waters of the Soviet Fourth Fleet.[11]

Stalin knew of the existence of the bomb even before Truman told him about it on the evening of 24 July. The USSR had been working on the atomic bomb since 1942, but the work accelerated in January 1945 when intelligence reports from the Yakovlev ring at the heart of the US nuclear project showed how near were the Americans to completing the bomb.[12]

Great efforts were made to overhaul the American nuclear lead. Espionage played a part, but in fact, Soviet scientists had independently developed the A-bomb trigger mechanism theory at the same time as the Americans and were then helped considerably by Hiroshima and Nagasaki which demonstrated that the bomb was not just theory, but actually did work.[13] Until the USSR exploded its first A-bomb in 1949, the Americans had a nuclear monopoly which turned out to be of little military value. They made too few bombs; only five in the year up to October 1946. The bombs were big, inaccurate and the bomber delivery vehicles were too vulnerable for the A-bomb to be a credible weapon.[14] The only attempt by the Americans to use nuclear diplomacy against the Soviets in the 1940s was in July 1948 when, at the start of the Berlin Blockade, B-29 atomic bombers – minus bombs – were moved to the UK, although this had no discernible effect upon the crisis. In fact any air-base from which the US could launch a nuclear strike was within range of the Soviet Air Force and anyway, the few A-bombs in existence would have been largely irrelevant to a conventional war. The superiority of even a demobilized Red Army was such that it would have needed only four or five days to reach the English Channel (had Stalin so wished).[15]

Stalin wanted to build his own 'bomb', and he rejected the American Baruch Plan in 1946, by which the USA offered to turn over to a UNO atomic authority its nuclear know-how and destroy its existing weapons stocks if all other nations renounced the 'bomb'. Even then the USA could not have removed that knowledge from the minds of its scientists and military.

Potsdam and the nuclear issue emphasized differences between the Big Three, but the conference itself took place in an atmosphere which had already been strained. Profound strategic and ideological differences between the USSR and the West had been partially obscured by the need for wartime co-operation, but they began to surface again even before Potsdam. Major problems took shape over attitudes towards Eastern Europe, but of more immediate relevance before Potsdam were three issues which Stalin may have regarded as part of an American grand strategy.

The USSR received so much Lend–Lease war *matériel* from the US that Stalin told Roosevelt at Teheran: 'Without American production, the war would have been lost.'[16] Stalin watched the USA disburse $43 billion in Lend–Lease and $3 billion in United Nations Relief and Rehabilitation Agency aid, while none of this prevented the US economy from doubling in size during the war. In January 1945 Foreign Minister Molotov formally requested US credits of $6 billion to help Soviet reconstruction. It is doubtful if the West appreciated the extent to which Stalin had to compromise his nationalist pride to ask for a loan and therefore to indicate economic weakness, but not only was the request not granted, it was ignored until March 1946 and then refused.

The second element of this financial triad concerned the suspension of American Lend–Lease shipments to the UK and USSR on 8 May 1945 by the new President Truman. Stalin felt that Lend–Lease had been ended 'in a scornful and abrupt manner' and as a means of showing American displeasure with the USSR.[17]

But closest to the heart of the problem and least understood by the West was the issue of reparations. Daniel Yergin wrote: 'The Americans could never comprehend the emotional intensity the Russians attached to reparations. Reparations may well have been as much a "test case" for the Russians as Eastern Europe was to become for the Americans.'[18]

Heirs to the Keynsian view that the reparations paid by Germany after the First World War had weakened her economy, soured her politics and created the seedbed in which Nazism could grow, and wishing to avoid any recurrence, the Americans and the British disapproved of all reparations. Moscow, however, was determined that Germany should pay for the damage she had caused, and at Yalta the Allies reluctantly conceded that the USSR should have $10 billion in reparations from Germany, but they did not agree how those reparations should be paid. The Russians could not get from their zone of Germany all $10 billion worth of reparations without so weakening it that they would have had to support the populace. However, they could only have reparations from the Western zones after the 'first charge principle' was met. The Americans and British demanded that all exports from west German production should first be used to pay for goods imported from the West and only afterwards should they be used for reparations deliveries to the USSR. This made economic sense since the Americans and British had to pay $700 million between 1945–7 just to prevent mass starvation in their zones; but the Soviet need was desperate.

With no American loan, reparations formed an important element in Soviet thinking about reconstruction and were even incorporated into the 1945–50 Five-Year Plan. From the Kremlin it looked as though America's first concern was the economic rehabilitation of Germany into the Western economic order, rather than 'justice' for the USSR. Potsdam agreed that Germany must be treated as one economic unit and indeed, the whole of Germany contributed reparations to the USSR. But Britain and America sent aid to their zones, whereas the Soviet Union made her Germans, and their Soviet garrison to a significant extent, live off the eastern zone, while the Red Army dismantled plant and shipped reparations back east. The West resented making indirect payments for reparations deliveries to the Soviet Union in this way. Accordingly, in spring 1946 the US zonal commander, General Clay, halted reparations deliveries to the USSR. He later wrote that this 'led to bitter altercations in the [Allied] Control Council and in the meetings of the foreign ministers and was a major contributing factor in the break-up of quadri-partite government'.[19]

Lend–Lease, the American loan and reparations created suspicion and ill-feeling between the allies and, as the Potsdam Conference approached, Poland and the issue of the administration of Romania and Italy worried away at relations between the Big Three. As the Nazis were driven out of Eastern Europe, tripartite (UK, USA and USSR) Allied Control Commissions were set up to supervise the transition to peace. But two weeks after Yalta the Soviets dismissed the Radescu government in Romania and replaced it with a communist-dominated one without reference to the Allied Control Council. The annoyance of his allies may have struck Stalin as hypocrisy. After all, in his Moscow visit of 1944 Churchill offered and Stalin had accepted postwar spheres of influence in Eastern Europe.[20] Also, despite his efforts, Stalin had been excluded by the Americans and British from any say in the government of Italy, yet he allowed the British free rein in Greece.

At Yalta the Big Three issued the Declaration on Liberated Europe which promised democracy and free elections to the East Europeans, but the words 'democracy' and 'free' meant different things on different sides of the ideological divide. Also, in 1941 Stalin had already revealed his attitudes to such matters as the declaration and the 'Balkan Deal' when he observed to British Foreign Minister Eden: 'A declaration I regard as algebra, but I prefer practical arithmetic.'[21] In April 1945 Stalin offered his own interpretation of the Declaration on Liberated Europe to the Yugoslav communist Milovan Djilas when he said: 'This war is not as in the past; whoever occupies a territory also imposes on it his own social system. . . . '[22]

Poland exemplified this basic conflict of interest between the allies. In 1939 Britain and France had gone to war over Poland and the USSR had 'liberated' eastern Poland. To the West, Poland was a matter of honour, but as Stalin said at Yalta: 'For the Russian people, the question of Poland is not only a question of honour but also a question of security . . . Twice in the past 30 years our enemies, the Germans, have passed into Russia [through Poland].'[23] Poland was crucial to the USSR and Stalin went to great lengths to secure it. After the occupation of eastern Poland in 1939 some 10,000 officers and NCOs of the Polish armed forces were murdered by the NKVD and buried in a mass grave at Katyn.[24] On 1 August 1944 the expectation of help from General Rokossovsky's (himself a Pole) First Belorussian Front across the Vistula had spurred the Polish partisan Home Army to rise against the Germans in Warsaw. Rokossovsky did not move,[25] and Stalin delayed until too late the granting of landing rights to allied aircraft flying supplies to the Poles from bases in Italy.[26] Both these episodes, when linked with the purges of the bourgeoisie carried out in eastern Poland by the Red Army in 1939 and again in 1944–5, may or may not have been part of a Kremlin plan to behead the Polish nation by destroying those elements of the Polish population which the Germans had missed and which could provide nationalist and non-communist leadership after the war. Whether or not, the effects were the same.

Moscow severed relations with the provisional Polish government (the London Poles) in 1943 after the Katyn Woods story broke. In 1944 Stalin set up his own Polish communist government, the Lublin Committee, in liberated Polish territory. On 5 January 1945 Moscow recognized the Lublin Committee as the legal Polish government, ignoring the claim of the London Poles and sparking off a major row with the allies which only calmed down when the Soviets agreed to accept Mikolajczyk, the leader of the London Poles, as Vice-President of the new Polish government.

Stalin got the government he wanted in Poland. He unilaterally shifted the country westwards by seizing eastern Poland and handed over to the Poles the former German territory east of the Oder and western Neisse rivers: he confirmed this in an agreement on 2 April 1945 with the Warsaw government, which President Truman later called a 'high-handed outrage'. Sixteen surviving leaders of the Polish non-communist partisans were arrested by the Russians.[27] Potsdam agreed that 'the final delimination of the western frontier of Poland should await the peace settlement'.[28] But the point cannot be overemphasized: once the Teheran Conference agreed to a westward shift of Poland's frontiers, then apart from the trifling concession over Mikolajczyk, Stalin was not deflected from the single-minded pursuit of a vital Soviet interest: the creation of a Poland which was pro-Soviet and therefore – probably inevitably – communist, irrespective of the consequences for his Anglo–American alliance.

From Potsdam onwards, widening circles in the West portrayed Moscow's ambitions as warlike. Truman wrote that he had realized at Potsdam that 'the Russians were planning world conquest'.[29] If Truman believed this then his actions indicated that he did not believe they were planning it soon. Nevertheless, a succession of American actions in the late 1940s, namely, the Truman Doctrine, the European Recovery Programme and NATO, were all designed to thwart a threat described as emanating from or at least exacerbated by the Kremlin. Yet, neither Stalin nor any of his lieutenants publicly advocated world conquest. Indeed, Stalin's actions were not those of a man courting war. The Red Army was demobilized rapidly from a peak of 11,365,000 in May 1945 to 2,874,000 by early 1948. Admittedly, the joint Anglo–American forces at this time numbered only about 2 million and this may have helped create a feeling in the West of being heavily outnumbered on the ground, especially as about half the Anglo–American servicemen manned the navies and a large proportion of the British (and French) armies were in the colonies.

As the Anglo–American armies melted away, the sixty Red Army divisions in Eastern Europe appeared ominous to some, but this was a case of deliberate misrepresentation or of confusing intentions with capabilities. The USSR returned to a peacetime basis after hostilities ceased. Demobilization began. On 4 September 1945 the State Committee for Defence was dissolved. Martial law was ended, except in the newly-conquered territories, and huge quantities of railway track were ripped up in eastern Germany and sent back to Russia as reparations. Also, Stalin instructed the large, powerful and confident French and Italian communist parties to acquiesce in their expulsion from government in 1946 and eschew violent revolution or any other measure which might antagonize the USA and embroil the USSR in a conflict for which she was not prepared. Singly, these moves would have complicated an invasion of western Europe. Together, they rendered it impossible. Furthermore, this argument fails to take into account either the ability of the Soviet economy (in 1948 Soviet GNP was estimated to be less than 30 per cent of America's) to sustain a war against the enormously wealthy, confident, powerful nuclear United States and her allies;[30] or the *matériel* and morale available to the Red Army which, although efficient and confident, in invading western Europe would not have been defending Holy Russia as it had been against the Nazis. Also, the sixty Red Army divisions in Eastern Europe were performing police roles and were not deployed as spearheads against the West. At the beginning of 1946 US Naval Intelligence reported: 'Maintenance of large [Soviet] occupational forces in Europe is dictated to a certain extent by the necessity of "farming out" millions of men for whom living accommodation and food cannot be spared in the USSR . . . . Economically the USSR is exhausted.'[31] Not until 1948 was the reduction in size of the Soviet armed forces halted, when both the USSR and USA began simultaneously to rearm.

The Western allies publicly defined the fruits of victory in terms of international peace from which, it was assumed, their national security would flow. Stalin's definition involved the territorial aggrandizement, traditional for military conquerors. But when he exerted pressure on Iran, Greece and Turkey (Map 3), Western chancelleries assumed that this was part of a package that included the takeover of Eastern Europe, the formation of Cominform and the anti-colonial unrest in the empires of the European powers; that is, a coherent Soviet plan to probe and expose Western weakness prior to the world-wide export of communism.

For a century past, the Russian and British empires had feinted at each other between the Caucasus and the Himalayas. When Stalin selected Iran for his first postwar anti-Western move outside Europe, he re-opened the 'Great Game' of nineteenth-century imperialism. In September 1941 Iran had been occupied by Soviet troops in the north and British in the south in order to deny the country to German influence and secure a safe route for Lend–Lease supplies to the USSR. An Anglo–Soviet agreement of January 1942, restated at Teheran in 1943, pledged both countries to withdraw from Iran within six months of the end of hostilities: the British did, the Russians, only after eight months and a number of official Iranian protests later. The Russians stayed to support the communist Tudeh Party government of the separatist puppet state of Azerbaijan, the Iranian province which bordered the Soviet republic of Azerbaijan with which it shared the same cultural, linguistic and ethnic characteristics. Possibly Stalin was simply playing the Great Game, reintroducing Russian ambition into a traditional sphere of influence, trying to outflank the British in the area. He may even have been aiming at the warm-water port on the Indian Ocean which was a distant goal of Nicholas I and Alexander II and which might have looked a distinct possibility to Stalin in view of the imminent departure of the British from the subcontinent. Also, it should be remembered that at this time the other great powers were all flexing their military and economic muscles. The USA was paymaster to the West. The French were re-establishing their control over Indo-China and north Africa, and the British were reasserting themselves in Malaya. Even the Dutch had retaken Indonesia. Possibly Stalin assumed that great-power status allowed or required the USSR to interfere in the affairs of those whom it could be claimed were inside her sphere of influence.

When the Iranian question was at its most tense, Stalin probably admitted no more than the truth when he said to the US Ambassador Bedell Smith: 'You don't understand our situation as regards oil and Iran. The Baku oilfields are our major source of supply. They are close to the Iranian border and they are very vulnerable . . . We are not going to risk our oil supply.'[32] However, the massing of Soviet troops on the Iranian border to try to deter Teheran from putting down the separatist revolt was shown to be a bluff when the Anglo–Americans lined up the UN in support of Iran and America supported the British who moved a brigade to Basra in Iraq in support of Teheran. Soviet support for an

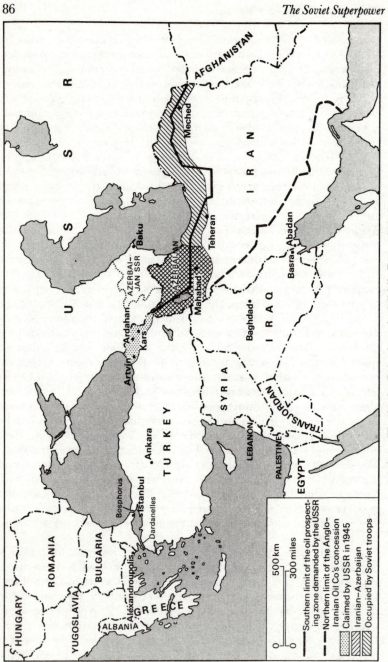

Map 3   The Soviet Drive into the Middle East, 1945–7

independent Azerbaijan was withdrawn. Although Stalin may have been surprised at the strength of the Western reaction, he was well aware how sensitive were the British to interference in – or near – their empire, and he was beginning to learn how sensitive were the Americans to anything which could be interpreted as Soviet expansionism. However, Stalin was a true heir of Lenin – the author of the pamphlet on tactics *One Step Forward, Two Steps Back*. His foreign policy was usually cautious and pragmatic, and he was prepared to give way to superior force and try again elsewhere.

A by-product of the Iranian affair which Stalin may not have expected was that Truman attached more significance to it that he did. Truman was furious and wrote to Secretary of State Byrnes: 'Iran was Russia's ally in the war . . . Yet now Russia stirs up rebellion and keeps troops on the soil of her friend and ally Iran. There isn't a doubt in my mind that Russia intends an invasion of Turkey and the Black Sea Straits to the Mediterranean. Unless Russia is faced with an iron fist and strong language war is in the making.'[33]

Stalin had no intention of starting a war against the West which an invasion of Turkey would probably have involved, but the rest of Truman's analysis rings true. Unless Stalin was faced with a determined response he probed grey areas between spheres of influence. This was the case in Iran and was to be the case in Greece and Turkey.

At Teheran Churchill had accepted that Russia's access to the oceans was inadequate for such a great power. Stalin apparently concluded that the West might accept a revision of the 1936 Montreux Convention which controlled the Straits and allow them to pass under joint Turkish–Soviet control. Moscow exerted a great deal of diplomatic leverage against Ankara, demanding also the cession to the USSR of the three Armenian vilayets of Kars, Ardahan and Artvin which had been seized by Turkey in 1921. Firm diplomatic backing by Britain and America, together with British economic aid and the despatch by the US of a carrier task force to Turkish waters, helped the Turks to stand off Stalin.

Stalin had ambitions on the other side of the Aegean too. He demanded the use of Alexandroupolis in Greek Thrace as a Soviet naval base. Meanwhile, 60,000 British troops were needed to prop up the Greek monarchy which had to fight off communist insurgents who received help from Albania, Yugoslavia and Bulgaria, and indirectly from the USSR. In helping the Greek communists, Stalin was not going back on his 'Balkan Deal' with Churchill (see page 82). Rather he was pushing the British to see if they still wanted to cling to the deal. When the exhausted British were replaced by the Americans in 1947 as the buttress of the eastern Mediterranean, following the announcement of the Truman Doctrine, Stalin did not allow the Greek adventure to interfere with his other plans. He told Yugoslav and Bulgarian leaders in February 1948: 'Do you think that Great Britain and the United States –

the United States, the most powerful state in the world – will permit you
to break their line of communication in the Mediterranean? Nonsense.
[and then the remark of the man for whom the ideological importance of
carrying the Marxist word to the benighted Greeks was of less importance
than the *realpolitik* practicalities involved] And we have no navy. The
uprising in Greece must be stopped and as quickly as possible.'[34]

Again, Stalin may well have been surprised by the Western response.
Certainly he cannot have expected the Truman Doctrine when it was
proclaimed on 12 March 1947. Truman spoke of the two contending
ways of life between which the world was obliged to choose: 'One way
is based upon the will of the majority . . . and is distinguished by
representative government, free elections . . . The second is based upon
the will of a minority . . . It relies upon terror and oppression.' Of course
Truman was addressing himself to the whole field of East–West relations
and not just Greece and Turkey, but after the rhetoric came the new
forward policy of the US: 'It must be the policy of the United States to
support free peoples who are resisting attempted subjugation by armed
minorities or by outside pressures.'[35]

Stalin learned his lesson: but not the lesson that the US would support
'free peoples' with 'free institutions'. This applied in Western Europe,
but in Greece, Turkey, Iran? No, Stalin learned that the US included
these three countries in her sphere of influence. In return Stalin tacitly
demanded that the West recognize *his* sphere of influence. Although
cloaked in the language of a *guerre à outrance* between hostile dogmas, the
Cold War continued largely as a contest between two territorial powers,
neither of which were exactly sure where their sphere of influence ended
and the other power's began.

As one writer commented: 'The Cold War would tend to be intractable and unlimitable to the extent that each side allowed itself to be
entranced by the nominal and ideological questions at issue,
subordinating the real strategic issues.'[36] But the 'nominal and
ideological questions' only became major issues once agreement had
been reached on all that could be agreed, leaving only the
stark issues of Germany and Austria to be resolved.

After peace treaties were signed on 10 February 1947 with Italy,
Finland, Bulgaria, Hungary and Romania, the usefulness of the Foreign
Ministers Conference was ended. The Moscow Conference of March–
April 1947 failed. The proclamation of the Truman Doctrine on 12
March, two days after the commencement of the conference, had
ensured this failure. Agreement on Germany was impossible, and
discussion was deferred until the November 1947 London Conference.
The failure of the Moscow Conference has been identified as the
beginning of the Cold War.[37]

The Cold War can be defined as the period of tension between East
and West in which each expected the worst from the other and where

neither perceived the real issues lying between them to be susceptible to diplomatic solution and where the tension was exacerbated by mutual misunderstanding, conflicting security interests, 'doomsday' rhetoric and the willingness to support armed forces over and above those needed for defence purposes. Some argue that it began with the Russian Revolution,[38] and some that it originated in nineteenth-century imperial rivalries of Britain and Russia in central Asia and that Russia's security interests remained constant under the old and the new regimes. Possibly, but it is the case that during and immediately after the Second World War, much was achieved by diplomacy between East and West – the zonal boundaries in Germany and Austria, the UNO, the return of personnel and the peace treaties. However, the peak of the Cold War – the Berlin crisis and the Korean War – coincided not just with the absence of diplomatic achievement, but with the absence of expectation that diplomacy could achieve anything of significance.

Rather than the Moscow Conference, the Paris Conference of June 1947 to discuss the proposals of US Secretary of State Marshall for a European Recovery Programme, marked the end of the wartime alliance. The Americans offered massive aid if Europe would draw up and administer a common aid programme. With the USSR and Eastern Europe badly in need of capital, Moscow took the proposal seriously enough to send Foreign Minister Molotov with eighty-nine technical advisers and assistants to the Paris talks on 27 June. But on 2 July, Molotov withdrew. The Czechs, Poles and Romanians had to follow suit and the European Recovery Programme went ahead without them. Molotov attacked it as a 'vicious American scheme for using dollars to buy its way into the internal affairs of European countries'.[39] Certainly Stalin would have found repugnant the degree of disclosure of economic detail that involvement in the programme entailed. More importantly, acceptance of it might have dragged Eastern Europe out of the Soviet and into the Western economic orbit. The American Ambassador in Moscow described Czechoslovakia's forced withdrawal from the programme as a Soviet declaration of war for the control of Europe.[40] The East European states now all had to sign economic treaties with Moscow, join the Cominform, abandon (in favour of outright communist control) the coalition governments they had had since 'liberation' and move towards 'collectivization' as the only appropriate path to socialism.

At the inaugural meeting of the Cominform in September 1947, the Western communist parties were mobilized to obstruct the European Recovery Programme and American influence in Europe. The previous year, on 6 September 1946, US Secretary of State Byrnes had offered the USSR an alliance aimed at neutralizing Germany, the economy of which the Americans proposed to rebuild – at least in their zone. Then on 1 January 1947, the American and British zones had merged into Bizonia.

This American break with Potsdam must have convinced Moscow that the US was taking seriously Churchill's speech at Fulton, Missouri, on 6 March 1946, in which he described Russia's hold on Eastern Europe as an 'iron curtain'.

The West regarded Soviet actions in Eastern Europe as a test case, and Moscow regarded continued Western interest in the area as interference in Russia's own legitimate sphere of influence. One source has suggested: 'The Soviets played an essentially opportunistic non-ideological role in Eastern Europe's initial development. They cared little about the previous policies or the ideology of the men in power in the coalition governments so long as they were not anti-Soviet.'[41] Perhaps, but with the presence in strength of the Red Army and NKVD, the economic exploitation of and later 'partnership' with Eastern Europe, and the military necessity of holding on to the satellites, there was an inexorableness by which Eastern Europe went communist (see Chapter 10). And yet, Finland, which because of Western sympathies avoided occupation by the Red Army at the end of the war, survived as an independent state.[42] Stalin trusted nobody, but at least foreign communists could be expected to become his creatures and could be expected to respond to the interests of Soviet Russia more readily than could nationalist non-communists. As one observer said of Stalin: 'As a result of his ideology and methods, his personal experience and historical heritage, he trusted nothing but what he held in his fist and everyone beyond the control of his police was a potential enemy.'[43]

Of course, as the Cold War developed, Stalin never underestimated the value of a world communist movement which served Moscow's interests and owed fealty to the Kremlin as had the old Comintern between 1919 and 1943. But because it consisted of foreigners who were frequently outside his reach, neither did he ascribe to it much more than propaganda value. When Andrei Zhdanov set up the Communist Information Bureau, Cominform, in September 1947, it may have appeared more significant to the West than it did to Stalin. The Cominform consisted only of European communist parties[44] and was used as an engine of Moscow's control over Eastern Europe and restraint in the West. Zhdanov made it clear to the French and Italian parties that although they should attempt to disrupt the recent American initiatives of the Truman Doctrine and the Marshall Plan, no attempt was to be made at revolution.

When Zhdanov spoke at the inaugural meetings of Cominform, his words and sentiments mirrored those of the Truman Doctrine. Both speeches stressed the impregnable rectitude of their own views and the intransigent malevolence of the other. Zhdanov spoke of the 'aggressive and frankly expansionist course' of 'American imperialism' and added: 'Communists must support all the really patriotic elements who do not want their countries to be imposed upon, who want to resist enthralment of their countries to foreign capital, and to uphold their national sovereignty.'[45] The Cominform presented a show of solidarity, but was ancillary to rather than the chief agent of Stalin's direct control over the satellites. Also, the expulsion of Yugoslavia from the Cominform in 1948 and the subsequent removal of Cominform headquarters from Belgrade to Bucharest damaged the organization. In 1956, after Moscow's partial reconciliation with Belgrade, the Cominform was laid quietly to rest. However, its very creation added to Western fears, out of all proportion to its true function, of an attempt by Moscow to orchestrate a world revolution, especially when Zhdanov called on the colonial peoples 'to expel their aggressors'. Indeed, within a year, communists were heavily involved in disturbances and insurrections in Malaya, Indonesia, Indo-China, the Philippines, Burma and India. But the point must be stressed that the Kremlin had neither the material nor logistical wherewithal, nor the ideological or strategic will to give more than moral support to movements whose inspiration was often nationalist as much as communist.

The establishment of the Cominform, followed closely by the communist *coups* in Eastern Europe (see pages 149–51), gave credence to the Western view of Stalin as a puppet-master. The take-over of Czechoslovakia confirmed this view. Since 1938 the West had had a conscience about Czechoslovakia, and when, in February 1948, Klement Gottwald's CP Action Committee seized power in Prague, followed by the mysterious death on 10 March of Jan Masaryk, the only remaining non-communist in the Czech government, Western hopes of liberal regimes in Eastern Europe were finally confounded.

Important though Eastern Europe was to superpower relations, the West could eventually 'forget' about Romania and the rest, but East and West could not avoid each other in Germany where their troops and diplomats, military and political ambitions ran cheek by jowl. Germany became the early cockpit of the Cold War because the former allies stood next to each other on a frontier which each felt obliged to regard as temporary. Potsdam enjoined the wartime allies to draw up a peace treaty for Germany. But such a treaty would have recognized either: a partitioned Germany which Potsdam had outlawed; or a unified Germany in a world so dominated by the continuing wartime alliance that Germany could not have caused serious trouble had she so wished; or a unified neutral Germany in a world where the alliance had collapsed. Neither side was prepared to allow a neutral Germany in case it fell into the hands of, and therefore augmented the power of, the other.

Not only Moscow, but all the capitals of Europe were concerned that Germany should not threaten them again, but if she were unified and independent, she would recover and *could* threaten them again. Nevertheless, the four-power Allied Control Council in Germany worked reasonably well, until American General Clay suspended reparations to the eastern zone in 1946. Even then, little had been done to erect a nationwide administration in Germany, although it was the French who blocked any such measure initially. From the end of 1945, if not earlier, Moscow apparently assumed that the West hoped to incorporate the eastern zone into a Western-dominated state, or at the very least that the Americans were seriously considering making an ally out of the western zones – which they were. This deep fear of a resurgent, revanchist Germany is crucial to an understanding of Soviet policy after the war. For a thousand years the Germans had pursued their *Drang nach Osten* of constant war and colonization against the Slavs. A. J. P. Taylor wrote: 'From Charlemagne to Hitler, the Germans have been "converting" the Slavs, from paganism, from orthodox Christianity, from Bolshevism, from being Slavs.'[46]

Stalin appeared to hope for a unified Germany under Soviet control, but more realistically, he aimed to divide Germany into occupation zones with as much Soviet say as possible in the affairs of the western zones. Foreign Minister Molotov admitted as much to Secretary of State Byrnes at the Paris Foreign Ministers Conference in 1946 when he said that all the USSR wanted was what she had asked for at Yalta: $10 billion reparations and participation in four-power control of the Ruhr.[47] Agreement on reparations and the Ruhr proved impossible, so Stalin settled back, reluctantly, upon the position that, as he said early in 1948, 'the West will make western Germany their own and we shall turn eastern Germany into our own state'.

Soviet pursuit of a unified communist-controlled Germany was largely limited to diplomatic and propaganda methods. Even before the Potsdam Conference, Marshal Zhukov allowed the re-emergence of 'anti-fascist' political parties and trade unions in the Soviet zone in the apparent hope that once these parties were domiciled in the east they would naturally spread to the west taking with them Soviet political influence. The resurrected German CP tried to distance itself from Moscow in the minds of the German electorate by declaring on 25 June 1945: 'We consider it incorrect for Germany to open the path for implanting the Soviet system because such a path does not correspond with the conditions of the development of Germany at this moment.'[48] However, this failed to convince those Berliners, who, when asked to vote on 31 March 1946 for the fusion of the Communist and Social Democratic parties under one programme, resoundingly rejected the notion.

The attempt to control the political parties was counter-productive. Groups in the western zone set about creating new parties. Nevertheless, the Soviet propaganda message to all Germans continued to be that the USSR proposed a unified and neutral Germany whose frontiers would be guaranteed by Moscow, but that the Western allies wanted to dismember Germany.[49]With the east zone in the hands of the well-drilled unified Socialist Unity Party (SED), under the Moscow-trained communist Wilhelm Pieck and the Social Democrat Otto Grotewohl, the zonal *Volkspolizei* (People's Police or *Vopos*) were armed by the Russians as early as 31 October 1945. By early 1950, East Germany had up to 100,000 trained and disciplined police and paramilitaries. West Germany had nothing similar, and in the event of reunification, East Germany might well have been in a position to take over the whole country.

Over the fusion of political parties and the arming of the eastern zone, the initiative was Stalin's, but this began to slip away from him when no German peace treaty was agreed. The Americans did not withdraw from Europe as Roosevelt had promised, and renewed political and economic confidence in the West began to spill over to the western zones of Germany in 1948 when they began to receive Marshall Aid. Where negotiation and propaganda failed, Stalin launched the Berlin Blockade, ostensibly in protest against the currency reform that the Western allies were to introduce in the areas under their control, but also to try to force the Western allies out of West Berlin. He hoped to remove a major political and propaganda irritant from the heart of east Germany, prevent Western moves to set up an independent west Germany and inflict upon the USA and upon Western democracy itself such a political reverse as to damage the credibility of Western resolve to defend and assert itself.

The blockade began on 20 March 1948 when Soviet Military Governor Marshal Sokolovsky stormed out of the Allied Control Council. Road, rail and canal traffic between Berlin and the western zones were progressively interrupted until on 24 June, Soviet troops severed all land and water routes to West Berlin (Maps 4 and 5). Previous crises over Poland, Iran, Greece, Turkey and Czechoslovakia had not involved direct confrontation between Moscow and Washington, for other governments had been involved. But America and her allies had no Berlin government interposed between themselves and Stalin.

The Western effort to airlift into Berlin the daily minimum 4,500 tons of supplies for the 2,108,000 West Berliners and the western garrison surprised Stalin who, throughout, tried to play down the crisis. Moscow was aware that the sheer proximity of armed forces in Germany coupled with heightened passions were such that the crisis could have got out of control. The Americans ostentatiously moved sixty B-29 atomic bombers to bases in Britain, and old Second World War American air-bases in Europe were strengthened or reopened.

Although the Soviets tried to intimidate, they made no effort to bring down Western airlift aircraft, for Stalin wanted the fruits of war, not war itself. In August 1948 he told Western diplomats: 'We are still allies.' Throughout the blockade Marshal Sokolovsky maintained that it was caused by 'only technical difficulties . . . [of a] temporary nature'[50] which were likely, however, to continue until the West abandoned plans for a west German state.[51]

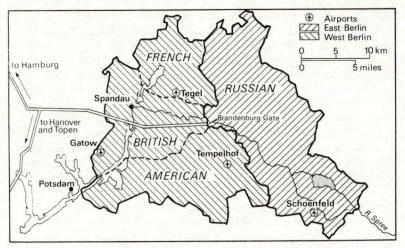

Map 4    Berlin: Sectors of Occupation

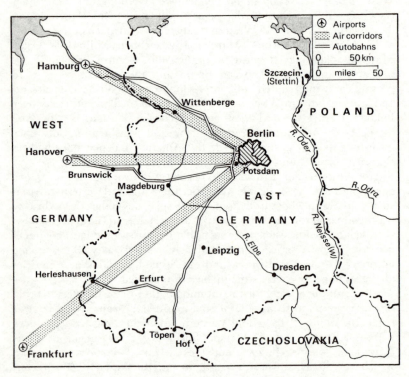

Map 5    Berlin: Air and Road Links with West Berlin

The blockade ended in May 1949. In April the Western allies had approved the new West German constitution, and West Germany came into existence in September 1949. The airlift united the Western allies with the West Germans and Berliners in a common cause. It stimulated the commitment of the USA to the defence of Western Europe in the North Atlantic Treaty, signed on 4 April 1949. It led to a Western counter-blockade of east Germany whose economy had stagnated by 1949. Stalin lifted the blockade in return for minimal concessions – the lifting of the counter-blockade and the calling of a Foreign Ministers council. The USSR recognized realities and there were no more Soviet attempts to halt the appearance of West Germany. Indeed, the Russians went ahead with the proclamation of East Germany on 7 October 1949.

The blockade was a major victory for the West, but only a tactical defeat for Stalin, and it seemed not to affect his authority at home or in the satellites. Still, as one writer argued, the blockade 'along with its demonstration of an implicit Soviet–American understanding that the crisis itself would be contained, effectively divided Germany and a divided Germany was after all, one solution to the German question'.[52]

Some, but not all, of the uncertainty had gone. Moscow and her satellites refused to recognize West Germany, and the West refused to recognize East Germany, but Stalin sought other answers to the German question. In 1949 he proposed a unified Germany which would be neutralized and disarmed. The implementation of such a scheme – if it was not simply a Soviet device to drive a wedge between the Western allies and the German people – would have prevented the re-emergence of a German military threat and would have created a large buffer zone between Soviet and Western territory. The idea was popular in some quarters, but was rejected by the Western allies and the Bonn government.

In the first few years after the war, Stalin held the foreign policy initiative, but from 1948–9 it began to slip away. The economic resurgence of Western Europe and moves towards integration in the European Coal and Steel Community in 1950, coupled with the political confidence of the region brought about by America's newfound commitment to the defence of the West in the North Atlantic Treaty, all marked a reversal of fortune for the USSR. The accession of China to the communist bloc on 1 October 1949 was greeted with less than total enthusiasm in Moscow and anyway only contributed to the restoration of the balance that had tilted with the defection of Yugoslavia the previous year. Even though Moscow broke the American nuclear monopoly and exploded her first atomic bomb on 14 July 1949, she remained well behind in the nuclear race. Besides, NATO provided a framework within which Western military strength could grow under a US nuclear umbrella, and American troops returned in strength to Europe. Moreover, the start of the Korean war stimulated the rearming of the West and created demands for a contribution from Bonn to Western defence. The move to rearm West Germany, enshrined in the European Defence Community idea, first floated in the French National Assembly on 24 October 1950, was anathema to the Russians as it was to many other Europeans. NATO, its Brussels Treaty predecessor, the European Coal and Steel Community and the European Defence Community (EDC), created a momentum which, if sustained (it wasn't) could have led to the creation of a 'United States of Europe'. By virtue of its size this would have been as big as the USSR in terms of population and much bigger in terms of industrial output. The EDC offered a long-term threat to the USSR, but the question of rearming West Germany struck a raw nerve in the Kremlin.

A Soviet propaganda offensive played on deeply-held fears, especially in France, of a rearmed German state, but also tried to weaken German interest. On 10 March 1952 Moscow proposed a draft treaty for a reunified, neutralized, partially armed, independent Germany – although without those east Prussian lands which had been annexed to the USSR. This proposal held much appeal for many Germans, but the West argued, and Chancellor Adenauer accepted, that it was simply a ploy to delay the signing of the EDC treaty. It may well have been, but it was also a serious proposal offered through the correct diplomatic channels, which sought to answer the German problem. The Soviet proposal remained on the table until 1955 when it was replaced by the more realistic recognition that there were to be 'two Germanies'.

Elsewhere, Soviet interests were pursued with the same tenacity as in Europe. The Middle East, covering Russia's soft underbelly and bordering on her own non-Russian, Muslim areas, was Russia's backyard in the same way that the Caribbean was America's. It was in Moscow's interest to speed the departure of Western influence from the region by supporting Syria, Lebanon and Egypt in their calls for France and Britain to leave the area and by approving the appearance of the state of Israel because that put the seal on the departure of the British from Palestine. In 1947, as the European Cold War was getting underway, the USSR joined with the USA, Canada and Guatemala in a Special Committee whose recommendation to the UN General Assembly was accepted – by all except the Arab states – that Palestine be partitioned between Jew and Arab. Moscow irritated the Arabs even further by being the first state to recognize Israel in May 1948 and by supplying arms to the Israelis – via Czechoslovakia – during the first Arab–Israeli war of 1948.[53] Moscow's involvement in the region alienated the Arabs and united the West in their recognition that Moscow had designs on the area and must be repelled. Therefore, in May 1950 the USA, UK and France offered to end their 2-year-old arms embargo on Israel and the Arabs, and guarantee the existing Israeli frontiers. Then on 11 November 1951 the USA, UK, France and Turkey formed a Middle East Command – the forerunner of the Baghdad Pact and

CENTO – in an obvious move to strengthen Turkey and extend the USA's ring of military alliances designed to contain the USSR. Three months later Greece and Turkey joined NATO, and Stalin's venture into the Middle East had failed for the time being.

Stalin made no attempt to profit from Britain's discomfiture in Iran in 1951, when the pro-Western premier was overthrown and British oil interests were nationalized. Nor did he interfere when the American CIA launched a counter-*coup* which restored Western – but American rather than British – influence in the country. In the Far East, the insurgency of the largely Chinese Malayan Communist Party and the Hukbalahaps in the Philippines, the war against the French in Indo-China, the success of Mao Tse-Tung in mainland China and the Northern invasion of South Korea on 25 June 1950, were thought erroneously in the West to be part of a communist conspiracy, but this was not so. The Malayan CP drew moral support from Moscow, but even more from Peking, and even then it was so remote that it had to live off its own resources and was eventually defeated by the British. The Huks were similarly defeated by the Filipino authorities, but the North Vietnamese received some supplies over the land routes from the new People's Republic and from the USSR and they defeated the French in 1954 and forced them to withdraw.

The Iranian, Malayan, Filipino and Indo-Chinese affairs had not been instigated by Moscow, although they formed part of the climate of the Cold War; but Korea was different. When the North Korean forces, armed and trained by the USSR, irrupted into South Korea in June 1950, their plans to unify the 'Hermit Kingdom' in one communist state involved the risky undertaking of attempting to inflict military defeat and humiliation upon American forces in Korea. Until 1950 the Cold War had been basically European, but Korea made it global.

At the end of the Second World War Soviet troops occupied the north and America the south of Korea. The Americans armed their client with defensive weaponry and the Russians armed theirs with offensive weaponry. A communist victory in Korea, followed by one in Indo-China, would have expelled the West from the Asian mainland (apart from the British in Malaya), seriously damaged American prestige and encouraged the Japanese communists only 100 miles (161 km) away.

Possibly the Korean adventure was a miscalculation by Stalin, that nearly embroiled the USSR in war with the USA.[54] But it was China which sent 1 million troops to rescue the North Koreans from the Americans and it was China which was threatened with conventional and nuclear bombardment. Stalin may have thought the North would win, and win quickly, and he may have been taken by surprise by the growth of American defence spending from $14 billion to $50 billion between 1950 and 1953, but both superpowers had already begun expanding their arsenals before Korea. Soviet forces doubled from a postwar low of 2.9 million to nearly 6 million in 1954.

Stalin was a gambler in foreign affairs, but he was not foolhardy. He made a mistake in absenting the USSR from the UN in June 1950 in protest over the exclusion of the People's Republic of China, because this allowed the Americans to ram through a Security Council vote condemning the invasion and promising UN military support for South Korea. But in other respects he was much more careful.[55] Moscow had signed friendship treaties with all her satellites and with China, but the treaty signed on 17 March 1949 with North Korea was remarkable in that, unlike the others, it did not contain a mutual defence pact. Yet North Korea was hurriedly armed by the USSR, although none of the other socialist states were, apart from East Germany's police.

Stalin may have gambled that the USA would allow the loss of South Korea since she had allowed the loss of the infinitely more valuable mainland China. Also, in a speech on 12 January 1950, US Secretary of State Acheson had excluded South Korea from the island chain of America's defence perimeter in Asia. But this argument ignores the fact that North Korea could only have won if American forces in South Korea were defeated and/or evacuated, with the enormous loss of face which would have followed. Perhaps Stalin thought the Americans would accept defeat if it was inflicted quickly enough, or perhaps he simply could not tightly control events 6,000 miles from Moscow. Khrushchev wrote later: 'I must stress that the war wasn't Stalin's idea, but Kim Il Sung's [the North Korean leader] although Stalin did consult Mao who approved the idea and thought that the USA would not intervene.'[56]

Although the Korean war led the USA to strengthen her grip upon Japan and press ahead with rearmament with which the USSR had to try to compete, it also brought benefits to the USSR. It widened even further the chasm between China and America, embroiled the USA in a costly war, held back any assertion of China's independence from Moscow and allowed Stalin to be portrayed – wrongly – as the puppet-master, the grand strategist.

When Stalin died on 4 March 1953 some of the bleak implacability of the Cold War died with him, and his successors introduced into foreign affairs the beginnings of 'the thaw' which also appeared at home. Stalin left the USSR as he found it: a garrisoned state with a siege economy encircled by watchful enemies. Yet its strength had grown enormously. Militarily, a regional power but ideologically, a world power, the Soviet empire was greater than that of the tsars and its voice was listened to more intently.

# Eight

# KHRUSHCHEV: COEXISTENCE AND CRISIS

Stalin left a dangerous world behind him. Truman had given way to the soldier President Eisenhower and his Secretary of State John Foster Dulles who loathed communism and had been preaching the alarming doctrine of 'roll-back' which argued that a forceful American foreign policy might help the East Europeans to 'rollback' the occupying Russians and dismantle the Iron Curtain. It was Dulles who talked of 'brinkmanship' – 'the ability to get to the verge of war without getting into the war' – in his dealings with Moscow and Peking. It was also Dulles who brandished the new strategic doctrine of 'massive retaliation' that threatened to hold Moscow responsible for any act of communist aggression anywhere which would be met by instant American massive nuclear retaliation against a target of her own choice.

The foreign policy initiative was very much in America's hands in March 1953. She was heavily involved in Korea and in paying for the French war in Indo-China. Her 'containment' of communism had built up NATO. The West had rearmed and the diplomacy was already underway to create, by 1955, an arc of allies and alliances around the Eurasian landmass.

In these circumstances the Soviet Union's foreign policy imperatives were quite clear. The tense international situation had to be defused and care taken not to provoke America unnecessarily. Meanwhile the USSR had to build up her nuclear capacity to offset America's strength. The Soviet grip on the satellites had to remain firm and her place at the head of the socialist community asserted. It was in Russia's interests to prevent the rearmament of West Germany if she could or, if she could not, to arrive at some solution to the German and Berlin questions that would settle the frontiers of Eastern and Western spheres of influence in Europe. Furthermore, every effort had to be made to break out of the encirclement of America's 'containment' alliances by driving wedges into the alliances where possible, cultivating neutrals, like Afghanistan and India, and by trying to win support in the Third World, which could bring UN votes to counter the USA's inbuilt majority at the Assembly. Of course, as the exponent of Marxist–Leninism and anti–imperialism, it was the USSR's duty to offer moral and material help and ideological example to the rest of the world, which, since the collapse of capitalism was foretold, was expected ultimately to follow Moscow's road to Marxism.

Actions over Korea set the first tone of the post-Stalin leadership. On 18 March 1953 the British were told that the Russians would attempt to secure the release of British prisoners of war in North Korea. Ten days later the Sino–North Koreans agreed to exchange sick and wounded prisoners with the UN forces. The stalemate was broken and a Korean armistice was signed on 27 July 1953, thus removing one major source of international tension which had threatened to spread to China, which had a mutual defence pact with Moscow. Another problem area was dealt with when the Russians put down an East German uprising in June 1953 with no hint of American intervention. 'Roll-back' was thus shown to be an empty phrase disguising America's recognition, albeit a very reluctant one, of Moscow's suzerainty in Eastern Europe.

With Korea and 'roll-back' behind, and the USSR on the verge of joining the hydrogen bomb club,[1] Premier Malenkov, on 29 August 1953, offered friendship to Iran and Turkey, which were both targets of Dulles's alliance making, renounced Moscow's claim to territory on Turkey's north-east border (see page 87) and reopened diplomatic relations with Yugoslavia, Greece and Israel. He spoke well of the peoples of Japan, India and Britain, but played on French fears that a European Defence Community might encourage German militarism at a time when the bulk of French forces were in Indo-China and Africa.

The recent war and her ideology led the USSR to expect the hostility of the rest of the world. It was idiomatic of the Soviet ideologue and the Russian nationalist that military strength and territorial depth conferred safety. With an economy only one-third the size of America's, the USSR could not outspend the USA in the arms race that began with the Korean war, but it cost much less to pay and feed a Soviet soldier than an American one. Soviet defence policy in the 1950s was based upon mass armies, but as comparable NATO armies failed to appear – despite the rearming of West Germany – effective Soviet ground forces were allowed to decline from a postwar peak of 3.2 million in 1954 to 2.1 million in 1964. Resources were diverted to other areas of the economy and to other military sectors, including the air force, nuclear forces and the navy.

Soviet science was hard on America's heels in producing the H-bomb and was ahead of the USA in producing a bomb of weapon, rather than experiment, size. The first Soviet H-bomb to be test-dropped from an aircraft was in November 1955, six months earlier than the USA. The appearance at the 1955 Moscow May Day Parade of a new long-range Bison bomber, followed at the June 1955 Aviation Day by a show of

Bisons, accompanied by Bear bombers, led the West to believe that a bomber gap had opened up between the USA and the USSR; that Moscow now had the capacity to deliver nuclear weapons against America, and that the day of unchallenged American superiority was over – which it was. But there never was a bomber gap. The West assumed that the 3,500 mile-range (5,632 km) Bear was being built in great numbers either as a bomber or as an inflight tanker for the faster 2,000 mile-range (3,218 km) Bison. In fact, in the mid-1950s the USA outnumbered the USSR by 5:1 in numbers of aircraft which had the round-trip capacity to strike at the other's homeland.[2]

Soviet efforts at nuclear parity with the USA were aimed at the inter-continental ballistic missile. On 26 August 1957 *Tass* announced the first successful test of an ICBM, and on 4 October 1957 the USSR launched Sputnik I, the first orbiting satellite. These events exploded the Western myth about technological superiority. Sputnik, and its successor programme which put the first man, Yuri Gagarin, into space in April 1961, did not lead to the missile gap which so alarmed the American public.[3] Rather it led to the growing public realization in the West that nuclear war was both politically and technically possible. The Soviet leadership had realized this in 1953 and had concluded that compromises would have to be made if war, which they might lose, was to be avoided. But the Malenkov, and later Khrushchev, strategy was to talk to America from a position of military strength and ideological security as the head of the socialist bloc. Military strength was developed by Moscow's own efforts, but socialist unity was less open to direction from the Kremlin.

The Soviet hold on Eastern Europe created many difficulties (see Chapter 10) and world communism paid much less attention to Khrushchev than it had to Stalin. Khrushchev spent much time quarrelling with China, courting Yugoslavia and trying to keep tight hold of the satellites on the one hand and the world communist movement on the other. He failed in this latter aim, and it is probably true of Khrushchev, as of his successor, that he tried to offset the breakdown in cohesion in the communist bloc by taking advantage of the political turbulence in the Third World which followed,or promoted, decolonization. Nevertheless, involvement in the Third World was to result in the Cuban Missile Crisis (see pages 114–19) as Moscow sought to combine ideological and strategic goals by attempting to leap-frog the encirclement of Western alliances and turn America's flank, for at the heart of Soviet foreign policy was the USA.

China, West Germany, European unity, the waywardness of foreign communist parties and the ingratitude and unreconstructed narrow nationalism of some East European allies were all potential and serious dangers to the USSR. But America was omnipresent in Soviet thinking as the awesomely productive, enormously powerful, aggressively confident opponent against which the USSR was matched. The bipolarity of the early Cold War in which states gravitated for protection and leadership either to Moscow or Washington remained intact in 1953 and 1954, and the USSR was outnumbered. Early in 1954 Ho Chi Minh said of his compatriots who wanted to continue fighting in Indo-China: 'They see the French yet do not see the Americans.'[4] The Kremlin, however, saw the Americans everywhere in all their dealings with the West or the Third World.

The post-Stalin leadership proposed to counter the power of the USA by the policy of 'peaceful coexistence', which was enunciated in part by Malenkov on 20 August 1953, extended by Khrushchev in the Secret Speech in 1956, and developed thereafter until in Brezhnev's time it became *détente* (see Chapter 9).

In 1959 Khrushchev declared:

> Our desire for peace and peaceful coexistence is not prompted by any time-serving or tactical considerations. It springs from the very nature of socialist society in which there are no classes or social groups interested in profiting by means of war or by seizing and enslaving foreign territories . . . The main thing is to keep to the sphere of ideological struggle . . . In our day there are only two ways, peaceful coexistence or the most destructive war in history. There is no third way.[5]

In November 1960, eighty-one communist parties issued the World Communist Declaration which announced:

> Peaceful coexistence of countries with different social systems does not mean conciliation of the socialist and bourgeois ideologies. On the contrary, it means intensification of the struggle of the working class, of all the communist parties, for the triumph of socialist ideas. But ideological and political disputes between states must not be settled through war.[6]

This was the essence of peaceful coexistence: no nuclear war with the USA. China, however, rejected the theory as cowardly until she developed her own nuclear weapons and learned their potential.

Khrushchev's belief in the inherent economic and moral superiority of Soviet communism was sincere. He claimed and really thought that the USSR would overhaul the USA by 1980. He was misunderstood on his American trip in 1959 when he told Midwest farmers: 'We will bury you.' In fact he was echoing an anecdote he related in his memoirs to describe the Soviet view of peaceful coexistence which he compared to a young man in the West who married a rich old woman: 'Despite having little in common, they would live peacefully until the woman died and the young man inherited her wealth.'[7] Believing in a Marxist 'pre-destination', why attempt to hurry into a frightfully destructive war when the demise of capitalism was inevitable anyway? Furthermore, the

Soviet leadership and people had been so seared by the Second World War that they saw no purpose in inviting a third world war. This is not to say that Khrushchev – and his successors – would not embark on foreign policy adventures once they had calculated the risks involved and found them acceptable.

The new foreign policy rejected the inevitability of war. It demanded that diplomacy be employed to achieve Moscow's aim and regain the world status she had enjoyed at the end of the Second World War when important international decisions were unthinkable without Soviet participation. Accordingly, for the first time since 1949, a four-power foreign ministers conference met at Soviet request in Berlin early in 1954. Although it made no progress on peace treaties for Germany and Austria, it did agree to reconvene in April 1954 in Geneva to discuss two outstanding East–West issues: Korea and Indo-China.

The Geneva Foreign Ministers Conference made no progress on Korea, and the July 1953 armistice remained (and still remains) in force, but then Moscow had nothing to gain from peace or further war in Korea but much to gain from armistice and stalemate which tied down US forces, kept America and China at loggerheads, enabled Moscow to portray America as a neo-colonialist power occupying an Asian country and allowed the USSR to pose as defender and spokesman of the week. During the conference, the French were defeated at Dien Bien Phu in North Vietnam and their resolve collapsed. Although Russian diplomacy succeeded in getting Ho Chi Minh to agree to a temporary partition of Vietnam, it could not prevent the French role in Indo-China being taken over by the Americans. Nevertheless, Moscow had played a major part in the diplomacy of a region in which she had previously had no material interest.

In December 1953, President Eisenhower upstaged the Soviets with his 'Atoms for Peace' proposal to the UNO which harked back to the Baruch Plan of 1946 and offered if, and only if, the USSR would participate, to put fissionable materials into a common pool to be used for peaceful purposes. Moscow could not accept such a surrender of sovereignty, so all that came out of the proposal was the creation of the International Atomic Energy Agency (IAEA) in Vienna. 'Atoms for Peace' only nibbled at the edge of the nuclear issue, but in preparation for the July 1955 Geneva Summit showcase of the Soviet 'peace offensive' of 1954–5, Moscow made a diplomatic move which went to the heart of the nuclear disarmament issue.

On 10 May 1955, the USSR announced her almost total acceptance of the 'Six Principles on Disarmament' that the Americans had put forward in 1952.[8] Publicly accepting the principle of nuclear and large-scale conventional disarmament, Moscow offered to allow UN 'control posts' on Soviet territory to carry out the surveillance which was necessary if the West was prepared to believe that disarmament was going on. The

Americans were taken aback and at Geneva, in July 1955, Eisenhower countered with his 'Open Skies' offer whereby both the USA and the USSR could overfly each other's territory to photograph ground installations and therefore assure themselves that the other really was keeping his side of the nuclear bargain. The Russians rejected this as Eisenhower knew they would.[9] After all, the American U-2 aircraft were about to begin photographic overflights of the USSR, but Moscow had no comparable aircraft. 'Open Skies' covered American unwillingness to accept the Soviet proposals which were effectively shelved.[10]

Moscow had gone far to establish her peaceful credentials by July 1955. She had formally ended the state of war with Germany on 26 January 1955, formally accepted the non-interventionist declaration of the Third World Bandung Conference, staged a *rapprochement* with Yugoslavia and initiated the four-power Austrian State Treaty which left that country free and neutral. To some extent these had been countered in Western eyes by the establishment of the Warsaw Pact. Despite this, the atmosphere at the Geneva Summit in July 1955 produced talk of 'the spirit of Geneva' – the air of give and take in which East and West might be prepared to compromise in the common interest of peace. In fact, Geneva produced little that was tangible. German reunification was postponed and the West only paid lip-service to Premier Bulganin's proposal for a European security pact in which Canada and the USA might join (this was, in fact, finally signed in Helsinki in 1975).

Nevertheless, the very holding of the Geneva Summit involved tacit Western acceptance of the partition of Europe: one of the principal objects of postwar Soviet foreign policy. Yet 'the spirit of Geneva' did produce some results: in August 1955 Sino–American talks began on the repatriation of each other's nationals; the USSR returned the naval base of Porkkala to Finland, reduced the Red Army by 600,000, attended the International Atomic Energy Agency talks in Vienna on the peaceful use of atomic energy and exchanged agricultural and scientific delegations with the USA. Furthermore, the radio propaganda war had almost stopped. But 'the spirit of Geneva' lasted only until the autumn of 1955.

The October 1955 Big-Four Foreign Ministers Conference failed, for relations had already soured over UN rows about the representation of China and Moscow's anti-French vote for the independence of Algeria. More significant had been the revelation on 27 September 1955 of the deal to supply arms to Egypt by Moscow's proxy, Czechoslovakia. The West regarded this as trespass, but it had always been in the USSR's interest to establish herself in the Middle East and it was not a signal for the general Soviet abandonment of peaceful coexistence as many thought in the West, rather it was an integral part of peaceful co-existence. A more accurate test of Soviet intentions was to be found in the partition of Europe and Germany, focusing eventually on Berlin, the microcosm of East–West relations.

The West recognized the governments of Eastern Europe, but did not recognize Poland's frontiers nor the existence of the DDR. Also, the example of capitalist West Berlin was a constant threat to the Soviet hold over East Germany. Moscow had sought a disarmed neutralized Germany out of a genuine Russian fear of what even a truncated West Germany could do if her economic miracle continued and she was allowed to rearm and give military and political expression to the enormous territorial grievances she now had against her eastern neighbours – grievances which dwarfed those which had contributed to the start of two world wars. Two Germanies were becoming a reality, and Moscow was unable to prevent the West agreeing in October 1954 to rearm West Germany and admit her to NATO. However, the military balance had altered and the development of an effective Soviet nuclear capability reduced Soviet fears of a West German non-nuclear army.

The final effort to prevent Bonn acceding to NATO was the sudden Soviet action to negotiate and sign the Austrian State Treaty with the other three occupying powers. The Treaty was signed on 15 May 1955, and all occupying troops departed within three months, leaving Austria to be free and neutral.[11] On 18 April Radio Moscow offered an 'Austrian Solution' to West Germany but neither the Western allies nor Bonn were interested. In fact, Austria had a unified freely-elected government before the treaty so the Austrian solution did not apply directly to Germany; neither did the Russians pursue the issue with any tenacity. Even though the West refused to recognize the DDR, West German Chancellor Adenauer was received in Moscow in September 1955 and Moscow exchanged ambassadors with Bonn, opened trade talks and promised to release thousands of prisoners of war.

It remained Moscow's ambition, which was only finally realized in the early 1970s, to have the DDR internationally recognized, and Khrushchev apparently determined to enforce recognition upon the West using as a lever, and at the same time solving the problem of, Berlin. But by finally endorsing, in practice as well as in theory, the principle of separate, independent German states, Khrushchev laid himself open to new pressures. East German independence was not as absolute as Moscow claimed. Nevertheless, there was an East German government with interests of its own to which Moscow had to listen. Walter Ulbricht the East German leader wanted recognition for his state but also survival, for the DDR was under grave pressure. Between 1949 and the end of 1958 2,188,000 East Germans out of a population of 17.5 million people fled to the West.[12] A disproportionate number of these were young, trained or professionals and no country could survive indefinitely such a haemorrhage of talent. By the end of 1958 the East Germans had fenced and fortified their frontier with West Germany leaving just the bolt-hole of West Berlin.

Berlin was and is legally distinct from East and West Germany. In the 1950s the West poured investment into West Berlin which was a beacon for capitalism and a yardstick by which East Germans judged the economic performance claimed by their own government. Ulbricht wanted the Berlin problem solved for immediate reasons but Moscow also recognized that removal of the West from Berlin would be a huge propaganda defeat for the Americans which would call into question the strength of the American commitment to defend her allies. Furthermore, with East–West tensions increased by the American fear of a missile gap and their moves to deploy medium-range ballistic missiles in Europe, the Kremlin feared that West Germany might gain access to nuclear weapons. Khrushchev, therefore, wanted to minimize Western power in central Europe and obtain Western guarantees that Bonn would never be allowed nuclear weapons.[13] Also, relations between Moscow and Peking were turning sour. Moscow had signally failed to back up the Chinese over the August–October 1958 Formosa Straits crisis and needed to refurbish her credentials as a supporter of the interests of her allies.

In a speech on 10 November 1958 and then in official notes to the three Western occupying powers, Khrushchev announced the imminent change of status of Berlin. The note claimed that Berlin 'may be compared to a smouldering fuse that has been connected to a powder keg. Incidents arising here, if they seem to be of local significance, may, in an atmosphere of heated passions, suspicions and mutual apprehensions, cause a conflagration which will be difficult to extinguish.'[14] Khrushchev offered the West a six-month deadline after which he threatened to surrender to the East Germans control of their own frontiers and of access from West Germany to West Berlin. Thereafter, the West would have had to deal directly with the East Germans at the transit points and, therefore, effectively recognize the DDR or try and ignore it, with incalculable consequences.

The West closed ranks and Khrushchev realized that he could not bully them, so in March 1959 he accepted British Premier Macmillan's idea of a summit meeting on Berlin and the issues of European disengagement and disarmament. He withdrew his six-month ultimatum and cooled off the issue by declaring: 'I believe that the US, Britain and France do have lawful rights for their stay in Berlin.'[15] The four foreign ministers met unsuccessfully in Geneva from May–August 1959, but the accepted presence of a DDR delegation was a kind of recognition and may have encouraged Khrushchev to keep up the pressure in the hope that more compromises would follow. However, agreement was reached that Khrushchev should go to the USA in September 1959.

The trip to America, culminating in the Camp David meeting with Eisenhower, was a public relations success for Khrushchev. At the

United Nations in New York he proposed a four-year plan for total disarmament. This caught the Americans by surprise as had his unilateral suspension of nuclear tests in March 1958, but the proposal was not taken seriously, if it was meant seriously. The trip indicated Khrushchev's faith in peaceful coexistence and taught him much about the USA. On his return to Moscow he declared that the American President 'enjoys the complete confidence of his people' and 'sincerely wants like us, to end the Cold War'.[16] Of course, he had to justify his trip in some such terms, but he must have known that such a declaration of common interest could only further damage his relations with China. However, he had returned with something that he thought tangible. Eisenhower had agreed that a solution to Berlin must be found, thus implying that the *status quo* could be changed, and that a summit should be held in Paris in May 1960.[17]

When a diplomatic solution to Berlin appeared no nearer, Khrushchev's heavy personal investment in peaceful coexistence and the path of diplomacy came under fire from both domestic and foreign critics. On 27 November 1959 he proposed that Berlin become a free city. In a speech to the Supreme Soviet on 14 January 1960 he warned the West: 'If all our efforts to conclude a peace treaty with the two German states fail . . . the Soviet Union . . . will sign a peace treaty [with DDR] with all the consequences proceeding from this.'[18] He also announced that the USSR was producing a weapon so 'fantastic' that there was no solution other than peaceful coexistence,[19] and he balanced this with a 33 per cent cut in the size of Soviet forces and no resumption of nuclear tests as long as the West did not resume theirs.

As the Paris Summit approached however, it began to look as though it would not provide solutions to Berlin or anything else, and opposition to the policy of co-operation with the USA was causing real trouble with the Chinese, in the Praesidium and throughout the socialist bloc. Khrushchev wanted a Berlin deal at Paris, but he may also have wanted an agreement to prohibit nuclear weapons in the Pacific area, balanced by a ban on such weapons in Germany.[20] Such a scheme reflected a deep fear of a German or a Chinese 'bomb', but one-half of the plan had already foundered. At a Warsaw Pact meeting on 4 February 1960, Chinese observers warned that Peking 'would not consider itself bound by any international disarmament agreement' to which it had not been a party.[21]

Possibly the U-2 incident provided Khrushchev with the pretext to call off the Summit, to be seen to be tough with the Americans, and to fend off his Chinese and domestic doubters. On the other hand, the affair may simply have infuriated Khrushchev as an example of American duplicity and his own gullibility. Since the winter of 1956–7, American high-altitude U-2 reconnaissance aircraft had frequently flown from bases in Turkey or Pakistan to Norway across the Soviet Union, photographing missile sites and military installations. The Russians knew about these flights but only on 1 May 1960 could they bring down their first U-2.[22] The pilot was captured and shown to the world press to contradict American protestations of innocence. Khrushchev demanded an apology for the violation of Soviet airspace, punishment of the culprits and the cessation of U-2 flights. He offered Eisenhower the opportunity to deny personal involvement in the affair, but this attempt to salvage the investment of both leaders in their relationship failed when Eisenhower accepted full responsibility and refused to ban further U-2 flights.

The Paris Summit collapsed after acrimonious exchanges on the U-2 affair, but it did not mark the end of Khrushchev's efforts towards diplomatic solutions, merely the end of his efforts towards diplomatic solutions with Eisenhower. He proposed that the summit be postponed for eight months[23] and he then awaited Eisenhower's successor. In the eyes of Khrushchev's critics the U-2 affair discredited his diplomatic efforts. By the time Kennedy became President in January 1961, Khrushchev needed a triumph 'and he would pursue it in an increasingly reckless manner, as with the passage of time and the accumulation of failures he felt his own weakening position in the Kremlin at stake'.[24] The failure of his Virgin Lands scheme (see Chapter 5), falling industrial expansion, the split with China and Albania, and involvement in the affairs of Indo-China, Cuba and the Congo, all limited his ability to master any one problem and made him vulnerable in the Kremlin infighting of the time.

From his accession to power, Khrushchev had dealt directly and indirectly with the major political figures of the day: with Mao and Eisenhower, Tito and Adenauer, Eden and Nasser. With all of them, Khrushchev had been the acknowledged new boy. A past master at domestic politics, he had been unschooled in international affairs and diplomacy, but learned quickly. With the arrival of Kennedy, the situation was reversed and Khrushchev may have felt he could turn Kennedy's inexperience to his advantage. If this was the case, then the Bay of Pigs affair[25] can only have hardened Khrushchev's attitude, just as the Soviet success on 12 April 1961 of Yuri Gagarin, the first man in space, boosted Soviet prestige and Khrushchev's confidence prior to his summit with Kennedy in Vienna in June 1961.

Khrushchev behaved towards Kennedy with a directness that had been lacking in his dealings with other statesmen. He demanded that the office of UN Secretary-General be transformed into a troika with one Eastern, one Western and one Third World nominee;[26] that a nuclear test ban be agreed on Soviet conditions; and, most importantly, that a German peace treaty be signed by December 1961, otherwise he would sign a separate peace with the DDR. Since Kennedy's inauguration the Soviet propaganda machine had been relatively conciliatory towards him and restrictions on travel to and from West Berlin had been eased, but after the Vienna 'ultimatum' things changed. On 25 June Kennedy asked Congress to increase defence spending, call up reservists and increase the draft. On 8 July 1961 Khrushchev announced that Western intransigence had forced the USSR to increase defence spending by one-third and abandon plans to cut military manpower by one-third. Threat and counter-threat: on 25 July Kennedy called for a build-up of NATO forces.

The closing of the East–West German frontiers in 1958 allowed the population of the DDR to stabilize and the economy to expand, but numbers escaping to West Berlin increased in 1961. In the first six months of that year 103,000 fled, 30,000 left in July and 20,000 in the first twelve days of August. The very survival of the DDR was at stake. A peace treaty and international recognition were not enough; indeed they were irrelevant to the immediate problems. Twice in early August 1961 Ulbricht tried to seal off West Berlin and twice Soviet troops turned back the DDR *Vopos* (*Volkspolizei*).[27]

Khrushchev must have been deeply concerned about the possible consequences of revoking the Potsdam agreement and denying Western rights in Berlin. Although Berlin was divided *de facto*, *de jure* it remained under four-power control, and the military authorities had (and have) rights of access to each other's sectors of the city. Perhaps Khrushchev's dilemma was eased when on 30 July the influential Senator Fulbright, Chairman of the US Senate Foreign Relations Committee, said on television: 'I don't understand why the East Germans don't close their border, because I think they have a right to close it.'[28] Damaging though West Berlin was to Soviet interests, there was never any question of its being overrun by Soviet troops. The 11,000 man Western garrison was inadequate to defend the city, but quite big enough to set off the nuclear trip wire if the Red Army attacked it. Besides, Khrushchev did not want war, he wanted a solution to a serious problem.

In the early hours of Sunday 13 August 1961, while skeleton staffs manned Western embassies, unarmed East German police supported by Soviet troops, sealed off East Berlin from West Berlin and began building the Berlin Wall. They left only four crossing points. The Wall was a desperate expedient. The human cost was high. It cut people off from their families, friends and livelihoods and divided what had been one city. But the political cost was marginal. The Western powers proclaimed outrage, and there were incidents at the crossing points. An American military convoy was sent down the autobahn from West Germany to 'probe' Soviet intentions. The USSR resumed nuclear tests on 29 August, followed by the US in February 1962. But even before 13 August the situation had been critical. Tension and a crisis atmosphere lasted for the next 18 months, but Khrushchev saved both the West and himself some embarrassment by not pushing too far his demand that Western flights to West Berlin come under East German control. He also allowed the December 1961 peace treaty deadline to lapse. On 19 September 1961 he said to the Belgian Foreign Minister Paul-Henri Spaak: 'Berlin is not such a big problem for me. What are two million people among a billion communists.'[29]

The Berlin Wall was a defeat for East and West, but it was also a failure on the part of Khrushchev that he did not deliver the peace treaty that his East German client had demanded and he had promised. It must have been obvious to many in the Soviet bloc that no matter what Khrushchev and Ulbricht said about the attractions of socialism and how the Wall was designed to keep criminal elements out of the DDR, they had actually had to build a wall to keep the East Germans *in*. Nevertheless, the long-term benefits were worth it. Until 13 August 1961, of all Moscow's client states, the one with the strongest pull to the West was the one whose people could exercise a degree of choice about communism. It had been difficult and dangerous, but over 2 million East Germans had fled to the West. After the Wall, the East Germans had to get on with the business of building a loyal successful communist state. After the crisis came to a head in Cuba, Berlin subsided in status from time bomb to irritant.[30]

Western passivity in the face of the building of the Wall may have encouraged Khrushchev to believe that the West would not fight and that he could, slowly but surely, drive a wedge into NATO, push the West out of Berlin and seize the initiative elsewhere.[31] If this is the case, then it is a view which may have been reinforced by Khrushchev's encounters with the West as he attempted to vault the ring of alliances around the Soviet Union's frontiers and establish Soviet diplomatic, economic and military interests in the Third World.

There was much scope in the Khrushchev era for an extension of Soviet influence and ideology into the Third World, not least in the Middle East where Moscow regarded any Western military or diplomatic presence as a potential threat to her vulnerable southern border with its non-Russian peoples. The departure of the French from Syria and Lebanon in 1946 and of Britain from Palestine in 1948, the nationalization of British oil interests in Iran in 1951, and the unilateral abrogation by Egypt of her 1951 treaty with Britain, all showed the extent to which Western power was diminishing in the area. Nevertheless, in setting up the Baghdad Pact (later CENTO) in February 1955 and in attempting to divert the defensive attentions of Arabs away from Israel towards the Soviet Union, the West actually invited Soviet intervention in the region, if only in attempts to subvert the Pact.

The major Arab opponent of the Baghdad Pact was Egypt, so this country became the focus of Soviet diplomacy despite the deeply religious and anti-communist sentiments of the Egyptian leader, Gamel Abdel Nasser. But until 1956 the limit of Soviet success was the September 1955 Czech deal to supply to Egypt the arms she could not obtain in the West. However, Arab nationalism shredded Western interests in 1956. The British commander of Jordan's Arab Legion was sacked in February and in May Cairo recognized China. In July the promise of Western aid for the construction of the Aswan Dam was withdrawn and Nasser nationalized the Suez Canal. Moscow's offer to finance the dam was accepted by Nasser, but the Russians did not want war to break out in the region. An unsuccessful Arab war against Israel might have destroyed Arab faith in Soviet professions of help and friendship, and Western intervention might have re-established Britain and France in force in the region. Besides, the USSR only had a small navy. In the summer of 1956, Soviet Foreign Minister Shepilev declared in Egypt: 'The Soviet Union does not intend to encourage the hostility of Arab peoples against any of the Western powers.' Nasser reported Shepilev as having said: 'The USSR does not want to come between the West and Egypt.'[32]

When war did come however, it served Moscow's purpose. When on 5 November 1956, Anglo–French forces attacked Egypt in collusion with the Israelis it served to stifle some of the Western outrage at Moscow's treatment of Hungary. It also allowed the USSR to be seen as a champion of the Arabs: Premier Bulganin sent letters threatening France and Britain: 'What would have been the position of Britain if she had been attacked by one of the stronger powers, with all kinds of modern offensive weapons? And remember that such countries . . . could use . . . rocket techniques . . . . The war in Egypt can spread to other countries and grow into a Third World War.'[33] American outrage at the Anglo–French action was so great and their economic leverage against London and Paris so effective that the Russian threats were irrelevant to a crisis, the end of which was predetermined in Washington, not Moscow. Furthermore, having voted with the USA against Britain, France and Israel in the UN on 30 October, and having proposed joint Soviet–American military aid for Cairo, it would have been madness to attack Britain and France, for the Americans made it quite plain that the NATO guarantees still stood. In fact, Moscow's threats were only made after the American position had become clear.[34]

Still, the USSR had committed herself to the Arab cause by threatening nuclear war against a great power. She condemned the Eisenhower Doctrine of January 1957 which opposed the extension of Soviet influence into the region. Through the Eisenhower Doctrine and the Baghdad Pact, the US sought to promote anti-Soviet commitment. Moscow sought to promote the reverse, but in a form which appeared more disinterested than the American approach. On 11 February 1957 Moscow proposed the complete neutralization of the Middle East, but the commercial and strategic interests of East and West in the region were too great for neutrality to have a chance of success. Besides which, it remained Moscow's interest to disrupt the Baghdad Pact and respond positively to requests for help if she was to remain the Arab champion.

Accordingly, Soviet arms were supplied to Egypt and Syria, but when Soviet instructors were sent to train the Syrian forces this touched the core of Western interests. Nasser's flirtation with Moscow angered the West. But his anti-communism was profound and the West did not, therefore, fear a communist take-over in Cairo.[35]

However, the West did fear that Syria, with its radical Ba'ath Party, could become communist. This might well have driven a wedge between Turkey and Iraq and undermined the Baghdad Pact. Two serious crises shook the region, heightened tensions, and resulted in Moscow uttering apocalyptic threats before the West fully came to accept that Soviet presence and influence were going to remain in the region. In September–October 1957, the Russians apparently thought that Turkish mobilization and exercises on the Syrian frontier presaged a Turkish–American assault on Syria to prevent it from becoming communist. On 9 October 1957 Khrushchev told the USA: 'If war breaks out, we are near Turkey and you are not. When the guns begin to fire, the rockets can begin flying and then it will be too late to think about it.'[36] The crisis faded when bluster failed to remove the Russians from Syria and Saudi Arabia accepted that Syria was not about to embrace communism.

Crisis flared up again in 1958 when a revolution in Iraq overthrew the monarchy. Fearing that the Iraqi revolution might destabilize Lebanon and Jordan, American marines were sent to Lebanon and British paratroops to Jordan. Moscow deplored the Anglo–American actions as neo-colonialist, but both Lebanon and Jordan were in the Western sphere of influence and the Western forces made no move to threaten Syria. This crisis ebbed away when Iraq was seen to keep East and West at arm's length and in 1959 she withdrew from the Baghdad Pact.

As one writer commented:

> The crisis of 1957 offered a seductive example of how in the Middle East more than in any other area of the world the Soviet Union . . . could wait for the next turbulent development in Arab nationalism, the almost equally inevitable American reaction against it, and then issue warnings and threats that did not have to be acted on but that earned her even higher repute in the Arab world and brought even greater discredit to the United States and her friends.[37]

The Soviet presence remained precarious and Arab attitudes towards the USSR remained ambivalent, clouded by the latter's opportunism and her atheism. Nevertheless, despite the failure of Arab communist parties to thrive, Moscow secured footholds in Syria and Egypt. Her warships were able to use harbour facilities and the Aswan High Dam became the showpiece of Soviet assistance to the Third World.

The logic which carried the Russians into the Middle East also led them to practise a windfall foreign policy elsewhere. When the French abandoned Guinea in 1958 the Soviets attempted to fill at least part of the resultant economic and administrative vacuum. In the Congo affair in 1960 and 1961 Moscow airlifted help to the government of Patrice Lumumba against the intervening Belgians and the Katangan secessionists. When Lumumba was overthrown by General Mobutu in a Western backed *coup* and later assassinated, Moscow blamed this on UN Secretary-General Hammarskjöld, and for a time there was a prospect that America and Russia might support on the ground their respective Congo protégés, but Mobutu restored order of a kind and expelled all Soviet and Czech personnel.

No doubt the Soviet leadership believed as Khrushchev later wrote that: 'Our foreign policy is rooted in our conviction that the way pointed out to us by Lenin is the way of the future not only for the Soviet Union but for all countries and peoples of the world.'[38] That was for the future however. Khrushchev recognized that not only was Soviet ideology inapplicable to much of the undeveloped world, it was also unwelcome in traditionalist religious societies. Soviet aid was another matter. Khrushchev expressed with characteristic lack of tact his ideological certainty in 1962 when he snapped: 'Certainly we are supporting Nehru; but we support him as the rope supports a man to be hung.'[39]

Afghanistan and India occupied gaps in the American alliance ring and received the full weight of a Soviet friendship broadside from the 1950s onwards. Northern Afghanistan had been subjected to Russian penetration since the late nineteenth century and the country received Russian military aid from the early 1950s. Moscow also supported Afghan calls, in 1955, for the creation of an independent Pakhtunistan which would have given statehood to the Pathans of western West Pakistan and, incidentally, dismembered India's western neighbour and greatest enemy.

India was drawn towards the USSR because of a wish to balance between East and West and as a result of the 1954 military pact between Pakistan and the USA by which Pakistan received American arms and America gained the use of Pakistan's Gilgit airbase for U-2 flights over the USSR. It was in Moscow's interests to stop America's use of the Gilgit field and this added to the Russian support for India in her dispute with Pakistan over Kashmir. India received economic aid from the USSR from 1955 and also received an official visit from Khrushchev and Bulganin in the same year. Friendship with India had a further value for Moscow however. It helped Soviet standing in the Non-Aligned Movement,[40] of which Premier Nehru was a founder member, and helped balance China. Indeed, India was one of the sources of Sino–Soviet friction for Moscow extended to Delhi an uncritical support that was never forthcoming for China. On 12 September 1959, Moscow approved a 1.5 billion rouble loan to India. This was more than China had ever received and was agreed within a month of armed clashes between Chinese and Indian troops, during which the Chinese had reasonably demanded, but failed to get, the support of their fellow communists. They also failed to receive Soviet support during much more serious clashes with India in October 1962, at which time the Praesidium was heavily engaged with Cuba.

The USSR had co-chaired with Britain the Geneva Conference on Vietnam in 1954. Her interest in the region thereafter grew in proportion to her material ability to influence this area, the gathering difficulties with China, the growing military involvement of the USA in South Vietnam and the Soviet need to be seen to be giving aid and comfort to fellow communists. Moscow extended aid to the large Indonesian Communist Party and supplied the North Vietnamese and Vietcong, and the Pathet Lao in Laos. Until a *coup* in August 1960 overthrew the American-backed regime, Laos was a Western preserve. But a Soviet airlift of supplies to the nationalist Pathet Lao guerrillas gave Moscow such a stake in the country that America considered a limited intervention. Instead, a great-power conference in July 1962 proclaimed Laos neutral. In the tension of the time the Laos agreement represented not just Soviet–American ability to compartmentalize their relations, but a joint recognition that the situation in Laos could have become uncontrollable. The USSR recognized that the USA had 11,000 'advisers' in South Vietnam in 1962 together with airbases in Thailand and that Moscow could not match that level of commitment. Anyway, in the summer of 1962 Khrushchev had other irons in the fire.

Cuba provided Khrushchev with his greatest opportunity, greatest risk and greatest humiliation, and brought the world closer to nuclear war than it had ever been before. Yet the USSR only became involved in Cuba by default. On 1 January 1959 Fidel Castro's guerrillas overthrew the Batista dictatorship in Havana. Committed to economic and social reform, Castro expropriated the American companies which had a stranglehold on the Cuban economy, but made no approach to Moscow until his request for a $30 million loan was refused by the USA, which in July 1960 cut the import quota of Cuban sugar.

In February 1960 Deputy Premier Anastas Mikoyan visited Havana to sign an economic agreement whereby the USSR gave Cuba $100 million in low-interest credits and bought Cuba's sugar, but at a lower price than the USA had been paying. So the relationship was established. The deal with Russia further convinced Washington of Castro's communism. Early in 1961 Washington severed diplomatic relations with Havana and in April the CIA-backed Bay of Pigs landing put 1,400 Cuban *émigrés* ashore in Cuba where they were quickly dealt with by Castro's forces.

Khrushchev may have been surprised at the strength of American revulsion at the happenings in an insignificant country. Moreover,

Castro, not yet a communist, was a long way away and difficult to control. Ignorant of the region, the Kremlin had largely to accept at face value Castro's own assessment of the situation. Soviet involvement in Cuba was costly in terms of difficulty in controlling the situation, the size of loan granted to Cuba, which was in hard currency, not roubles, and the requirement to be seen to defend the island against her neighbour, who, as evidenced by the Bay of Pigs affair, had a blind spot about Cuba.[41] But this was outweighed by the ideological and military value of Cuba to the Soviets. The USSR could not refuse help to a country which asked for it in the name of revolutionary solidarity. This was especially true at the time of the defection of China and Albania. Besides, the potential extension of communism to Cuba[42] allowed the Russians to argue triumphantly that their ideology was the wave of the future and was applicable to Third World countries despite what the Chinese said.

In July 1960 Khrushchev announced that Soviet missiles would protect Cuba from attack by the USA, an attack that Castro legitimately feared. By the summer of 1962 Soviet surface-to-air missile sites were under construction in the island and plans were announced on 25 September for a port to be built to accommodate a Soviet fishing fleet. On 2 September 1962 *Tass* announced a Soviet–Cuban arms deal and America, alarmed at the pace and quality of Soviet involvement and the 5,000 Soviet 'technicians' on the island, warned Cuba against exporting her revolution. Then on 7 September Congress approved President Kennedy's call-up of 150,000 reservists who were moved to bases in Florida prior to a possible invasion of the island.

Much more serious, however, was the decision to send by freighter, forty-two Ilyushin bombers, forty-eight MRBMs and twenty-four IRBMs to Cuba. Situated only 90 miles from the American coast, intermediate and medium-range nuclear missiles[43] and nuclear-capable bombers could have escaped American radar, which guarded against attack from over the Arctic, and would have reduced American warning time from 30 minutes to virtually nothing. Moscow received solemn warnings that America would not tolerate offensive missiles on Cuban soil but Khrushchev still went ahead (Map 6).

On Monday 15 October 1962 President Kennedy received photographic evidence from U-2 aircraft that the USSR was emplacing nuclear missiles on Cuba. Kennedy reacted decisively. Latin America, NATO and world opinion were canvassed and on Monday 22 October Kennedy announced his 'quarantine', threatening to board vessels voyaging to Cuba. Unable to match the American conventional presence in the region, Soviet ships turned back and on 28 October Khrushchev agreed to dismantle and remove the missiles. Khrushchev gained some credit from the episode. Kennedy promised not to invade Cuba and when the following year America withdrew her obsolescent missiles from Turkey, Moscow was able to claim this as part of a *quid pro quo*. Khrushchev said

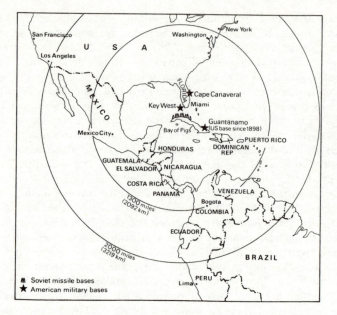

Map 6    The Cuban Missile Crisis, 1962

his decision to withdraw the missiles was in the interests of world peace (which of course, it was) but he could not conceal – especially from the Cubans and Chinese – the scale of his failure over Cuba.

It seems that the Praesidium were surprised by Kennedy's 'quarantine'.[44] Certainly they had no military answer to it. On 26 October Khrushchev wrote offering to dismantle the Cuban missiles in return for an American promise not to invade Cuba. This was followed the next day by another letter, very different in tone, which offered to trade off missiles in Cuba for missiles in Turkey. The Americans ignored the second letter and responded positively to the first. It may be that the sudden defusing of the crisis saved Khrushchev, for the government newspaper *Izvestia*, on 27 October, was critical of the conciliatory line in his letter of 26 October.[45]

It was an accident that the Cuban missile crisis coincided with Chinese clashes with India, but it appeared as concerted communist expansion to some 'cold warriors' in the West, who were ignorant of the true state of Sino–Soviet relations. This coincidence was but one example of the unexpected which complicated a situation that threatened to get out of hand. The crisis-management techniques of Moscow and Washington were shown to be deficient. On 28 October at the height of the crisis, when Soviet and American forces were on full alert and an armed clash was only hours away, a U-2 went astray over the USSR, but the Soviets took no action even though, as Khrushchev warned: 'Is it not a fact that an intruding American plane could be easily taken for a nuclear bomber, which might push us to a fateful step . . . ?'[46] The previous day, a U-2 was brought down by a SAM over Cuba, 'fulfilling previously decided (US) conditions for a retaliatory strike against a single SAM site'[47] which could have killed Soviet personnel and invited a Soviet reaction . . . . Also, contrary to Kennedy's orders, some Soviet submarines were forced to the surface by US vessels.[48] Khrushchev would probably have agreed with Kennedy when he said: 'There is always a son-of-a-bitch who doesn't get the word.'[49]

So why did Khrushchev invite potential disaster: because he was desperate for success after a string of domestic and foreign failures or to ward off the increasingly barbed criticism of the Chinese? Both were valid reasons. Khrushchev wrote later: 'The main thing was that the installation of our missiles in Cuba would, I thought, restrain the United States from precipitous military action against Castro's government.' More to the heart of the matter, Khrushchev went on: 'In addition to protecting Cuba, our missiles would have equalized what the West likes to call "the balance of power". The Americans had surrounded our country with military bases and threatened us with nuclear weapons and now they would learn just what it feels like to have enemy missiles pointing at you.'[50] He then explained that he backed down from the Americans to save Cuba from invasion: 'We received information from Cuban comrades and from other sources on the morning of 27 October directly stating that this attack [by America on Cuba] would be carried out in the next 2 or 3 days.'[51]

Kennedy was prepared to invade Cuba if necessary, and Khrushchev recognized that he could not defend the island with strategic missiles. It might have made more military sense to send to Cuba a garrison which could then have served as hostages as did Western troops in Berlin.[52] It is the case that if all the Soviet missiles had been emplaced they would have doubled the Soviet capacity to strike at America and would, to a large extent, have equalized the strategic balance between America and Russia which was then running in America's favour.

Perhaps Khrushchev misunderstood Americans in general and Kennedy in particular and did not believe that they would fight to protect their vital interests. According to this argument the American failure to eliminate Castro, to intervene in Laos and to prevent the Berlin Wall convinced Khrushchev that he could place missiles in Cuba with impunity.[53] However, this analysis does not explain why such a risk was taken at such short notice when the Soviets could do little materially to support their initiatives so far away from their shores.

And what a risk: it depended for its success on the Russians being able to send, unobserved by the Americans, an unprecedented quantity of Soviet bloc shipping to Cuba carrying seventy-two missiles, dismantled bombers and the materials and personnel for the construction of the launching sites and airfields. Success depended upon having the missile sites operational before the Americans could do anything about them, but although the weather grounded U-2 flights over the USSR for some weeks, the Americans found out what was happening on 14 October.

It has been argued that the risk was taken to force the West out of Berlin, but Berlin was not a major issue by 1962. However, Adam B. Ulam argued that Soviet priorities in 1962 were to prevent China and West Germany from becoming nuclear powers[34] and to sign a German peace treaty which would have perpetuated the division of Germany. Ulam suggested that the Cuban crisis may have been designed to solve Khrushchev's foreign problems at a stroke: 'Once in Cuba, the missiles would become negotiable, their removal conditional upon the United States' meeting Soviet conditions on the German peace treaty.' Khrushchev planned a speech to be given to the UNO in November 1962 when his missile sites would be complete at which, according to Ulam, 'he would present the world a dramatic package deal resolving the world's most momentous problems: the German peace treaty containing an absolute prohibition against nuclear weapons for Bonn and a similar proposal in reference to the Far East.'[35]

All explanations are more or less speculative and based upon less than full information about the factors which informed the Soviet decision. All impute to Khrushchev a greater or lesser degree of shortsightedness which borders on crassness and stupidity. Khrushchev was many things, but stupid he was not. All explanations are worth consideration, but it may simply have been that Khrushchev the politician made a politician's mistake and misjudged his opponent as he was to misjudge Brezhnev, Kosygin and Podgorny two years later.

At the very least, the Cuban crisis put flesh on the bones of the argument for peaceful coexistence. Khrushchev had been convinced of Kennedy's determination to risk all over Cuba, and Kennedy similarly felt: 'If we had invaded Cuba I am sure the Soviets would have acted.'[36] The 'hot line' was installed as a proof of both sides' desire that future crises would not be exacerbated by poor communications between them. Both sides moved towards a Partial Test-Ban Treaty and agreed to demilitarize outer space. Both sides tacitly accepted that the U-2 'spy plane' which had played such a role in recent Soviet–American crises performed a function necessary for peaceful coexistence. It allowed one side to obtain an accurate picture of the other's capabilities. Thereafter, both overflew each other's territory with spy satellites.

Having been treated as a mere pawn in the superpower game, Castro's prestige fell in Latin America, and although Moscow continued to subsidize Havana, relations between the two were poor until 1969.[37] At home the Cuban adventure was one of the charges laid up by opponents against the day of Khrushchev's fall. It has been suggested that the

USSR learned from the Cuban episode that superpower status required a superpower navy and that Russia 'lost' the crisis because of American military preponderance. However, that lesson was reinforced rather than learned in the USSR. Stalin had known it and had begun to construct a 'blue water' navy. His programme was partially interrupted by Khrushchev, but only until 1958 when events in the Middle East showed what the Anglo–Americans could do with navies and foreign bases. The major expansion of the Soviet navy, which became significant in the 1970s, resulted from decisions taken in the late 1950s.[58]

Khrushchev left a mixed legacy behind him. Albania and China had departed from the Soviet bloc. Yugoslavia had not re-entered, and Romania behaved embarrassingly at times, but Moscow's hold over the Warsaw Pact was firm. The American alliance systems remained intact and a prosperous uniting Europe must have worried Khrushchev. The Third World, apart from Cuba and parts of Indo-China, appeared unreceptive to communism, but receptive to links with the USSR. More importantly, German unity was as far off as ever, and Berlin and Cuba had cleared the air between East and West. A new and deeper understanding of each other's fundamental interests had been achieved – the prerequisite for the extension of Khrushchev's peaceful coexistence (peace, but competition) to Brezhnev's *détente* (peace, but competition and sometimes co-operation).

# Nine

# BREZHNEV: *DÉTENTE* AND INTERVENTION

Discontent with Khrushchev's foreign policy contributed to his fall, but it was discontent with the style and not the substance of policy, and it was style and not substance which now changed. The triumvirate of President Podgorny, Premier Kosygin and First Secretary Brezhnev accepted the decisions of the Twentieth Congress of the CPSU but they proceeded with caution.

In 1971 the official *History of Soviet Foreign Policy* declared that foreign policy was designed to:

> secure together with the other socialist countries, favourable conditions for the building of socialism and communism; strengthen the unity and solidarity of the socialist countries, their friendship and brotherhood; support the national-liberation movement and to effect all-round co-operation with the young developing countries; consistently to uphold the principle of peaceful coexistence of states with different social systems, to offer decisive resistance to the aggressive forces of imperialism and to save mankind from a new world war.[1]

In practice this policy involved: the consolidation of the socialist bloc – and its expansion if any attendant risk was 'acceptable'; the reassertion of Moscow's primacy in world communism; an understanding with the USA and the West that would recognize the division of Europe and lessen any risk of war; the search for diplomatic and military parity with the USA.

In Eastern Europe the lessons of 1956 were fading and although the Warsaw Pact and Comecon sought to co-ordinate defence and economic policies, Romanian foreign policy and Hungarian domestic policy both departed from the Soviet model. Elsewhere, the new leadership attempted unsuccessfully to reverse the slide in Sino–Soviet relations (see Chapter 11). Communist unity, or a semblance of it, was a major goal of party boss Leonid Brezhnev and the Politburo's ideologue,

Mikhail Suslov and when the Moscow meeting of nineteen communist parties – twenty-six had in fact been invited – failed to produce it in March 1965, much energy was spent in mounting a full-scale world communist conference. This conference finally met in Moscow in June 1969, one year after the Czech crisis and at the height of the Sino–Soviet dispute. Representatives of sixty-seven out of eighty-one invited CPs attended but did not endorse Moscow's authority or condemn China.

In the Third World the Khrushchev heritage included economic commitments to Cuba, Egypt, Syria, Afghanistan, India and North Vietnam: the USSR was owed approximately $6 billion in aid. But the main thrust of policy was directed at America and the West with which Moscow was determined to deal from a position of strength.

Although Khrushchev's successors inherited a cut of 4 per cent in the defence budget for 1965, they raised it each subsequent year to reach a figure of $42 billion in 1969,[2] against a US figure of $39.7 billion.[3] Spending on scientific research, much of which was defence-orientated, doubled in this period. By 1969, America's strategic nuclear lead had been overhauled (see Table 9.1).

Table 9.1 The Growth of Strategic Missile Strength 1959–69[4]

|  | 1959 | 1960 | 1961 | 1962 | 1963 | 1964 | 1965 | 1966 | 1967 | 1968 | 1969 |
|---|---|---|---|---|---|---|---|---|---|---|---|
| USA: ICBM | — | 18 | 63 | 294 | 424 | 834 | 854 | 904 | 1,054 | 1,054 | 1,054 |
| SLBM | — | 32 | 96 | 144 | 224 | 416 | 496 | 592 | 656 | 656 | 656 |
| USSR: ICBM | some | 35 | 50 | 75 | 100 | 200 | 270 | 300 | 460 | 800 | 1,050 |
| SLBM | — | — | some | some | 100 | 120 | 120 | 125 | 130 | 130 | 160 |

By 1969 the present phase of deployment of American land-based and sea-based strategic missiles was complete, and Soviet preponderance in IRBMs and MRBMs partly countered America's superiority in SLBMs. It is not known whether nuclear parity or superiority was the Soviet objective. When Khrushchev's doctrine of minimum nuclear deterrence[5] was abandoned by his successors, the muted strategic debate that followed advanced arguments for both parity and superiority.[6] By 1969 Moscow possessed a capacity for Mutual Assured Destruction (MAD) similar to Washington's.[7] This has been variously estimated as the capacity to destroy between 20 and 25 per cent of the enemy's population and between 50 and 75 per cent of his industry.[8] However, the USSR always assumed that nuclear deterrence could fail and war could result which *might not* involve a thermonuclear exchange. Therefore, the post-Khrushchev leadership re-emphasized the role of conventional forces and their superior 'war-fighting' capability, which would allow them not just to survive but to *win* a nuclear war[9] and which, in the absence of war, gave the USSR 'equal security' with America.

In 1969 Warsaw Pact forces outnumbered NATO in the crucial northern and central European theatres; in men by 925,000 to 600,000; in tanks by 12,500 to 5,250 and in tactical aircraft by 3,795 to 2,050. Furthermore, the 7,000 tactical nuclear warheads in NATO's arsenals were partly offset by Soviet preponderance in IRBMs and MRBMs – 700 to none, and medium bombers – 1,050 to 150. Stabilized at about 2 million men in 148 divisions, the Red Army's conventional role at the centre of Soviet military planning was re-emphasized, after having a back seat in the Khrushchev years, by the recreation in 1967 of the separate Ground Forces Command which had been disbanded in 1964. The satellite forces were slimmed down, re-equipped and assigned responsible roles in the alliance for the first time. In 1967 military service was cut to two years in the Red Army and pre-conscription military training was made compulsory as part of the curriculum in schools. More strikingly, earlier reforms bore fruit so that by 1969, 80 per cent of officers in the Strategic Missile Forces were graduate engineers[10] with incalculable results for the competence and status of the officer corps. Strategic parity coupled with conventional military confidence, reinforced no doubt by the smoothness of the Czechoslovakia operation in 1968, provided the backcloth to and one of the reasons for the launching by the USSR at the end of the decade of the policy of *détente*.[11]

On 20 January 1969, the same day as President Nixon's inauguration in America, the USSR announced her willingness to negotiate the 'mutual limitation and subsequent reduction of strategic delivery vehicles, including defensive systems'.[12] A positive response from Nixon on 27 January 1969 was accompanied by America's public acceptance of nuclear 'sufficiency' rather than superiority, and therefore an acceptance of Soviet parity. Moscow acceded to Nixon's demand that superpower arms talks must be paralleled in other fields.

The year 1969 was a turning point in Soviet foreign policy, as 1956 had been, and it can have been no accident that it coincided with the emergence of First Secretary Leonid Brezhnev as *primus inter pares* in the Politburo. There was still a collective leadership and major policy decisions were taken by the Politburo oligarchy, but enthusiasm for *détente* was less than total in the Kremlin. Unprecedently, the 1969 May Day Parade was cancelled amid speculation that Brezhnev may not have been able to control the speech of Defence Minister, Marshal Grechko.[13] But there were pressing reasons for this shift in Soviet policy.

Relations with America were poor during Johnson's Presidency. A confident aggressive America had taken little account of Moscow in pursuing policies which were seen in Moscow and in some other capitals as designed not to preserve 'peaceful coexistence', but to mount a co-ordinated offensive against Soviet and radical nationalist positions all over the world.[14] America massively escalated the war in 1965 against

North Vietnam. She put down a radical *coup* in Dominica in the same year. The overthrow of President Sukarno and the massacre of the Indonesian CP; the overthrow of the radical-leaning President Goulart in Brazil; the fall of Nkrumah in Ghana and Ben Bella in Algeria; the take-over by the Colonels in Greece, and the Israeli attack on Egypt in 1967, may all have appeared to the Russians as part of an American orchestration even more worrying when viewed alongside Johnson's attempts at 'bridge-building' in Eastern Europe. American Senator Fulbright was right when he said in 1967: 'The Russians are frightened of us, not only because of our enormous power but also because of our erratic behaviour in such places as Vietnam and Dominica.'[15] In the autumn of 1966, Brezhnev said of Johnson to UN Secretary-General U Thant: 'He's more dangerous than Dulles.'[16]

The Six-Day War and the Soviet invasion of Czechoslovakia exacerbated the poor relations with the USA. By 1969 China was no longer just an alienated ally, but a hostile neighbour, and Moscow could not afford continued hostility with both. Although there was a crude parity in strategic weapons, American weapons were more sophisticated and more accurate, and a programme was underway to equip them with 'multiple independently targetable re-entry vehicles' (MIRVs) which would give the USA an enormous qualitative lead over the USSR. Furthermore, on 14 March 1969 Nixon proposed to develop the 'Safeguard' Anti-Ballistic Missile (ABM) system which, if deployed, could have rendered enough of America's missiles invulnerable to a Soviet first-strike as to destroy Moscow's nuclear parity and make *her* vulnerable to American nuclear power. Russia was developing her own unsophisticated 'Galosh' ABMs, but knew that she would lose a new arms race in the face of the technological and financial strength demonstrated in July 1969 when America put astronauts on the moon and then brought them back safely.

The nuclear issue forced Moscow and Washington to acknowledge a common interest in avoiding mutual destruction, but there had been examples of co-operation and conciliation upon which Brezhnev and his colleagues could build. Both superpowers had stayed out of the Malaysia–Indonesia confrontation and the Sudanese civil war. They had supported the same side in the upheavals in Ceylon and the Nigerian civil war. American diplomacy had supported Soviet efforts to mediate between India and Pakistan in 1965. Neither East nor West had allowed the invasion of Czechoslovakia to cause a crisis in relations. And there had already been substantial agreements. In 1967 the USSR, USA, UK and France signed a treaty banning nuclear weapons from outer space and on 2 July 1968, the USSR, USA and UK signed the Non-Proliferation Treaty (NPT) which outlawed the passing of nuclear know-how or materials for the making of weapons to non-nuclear countries. The three powers also declared that in the event of the use or threat of use of nuclear weapons against a non-nuclear state: 'The nuclear weapons states which are Permanent Members of the United Nations Security Council would have to act immediately through the Security Council to take the measures necessary to counter such aggression.'[17] Moscow's fears of the nuclear future were calmed even further when on 28 November 1969 West Germany signed the NPT, for a constant fear over the previous decade had been that West Germany might go nuclear.

Furthermore, blind accident played its part in the origins of *détente*. There came to power in America a President who recognized the limits of US power, who in July 1969 proclaimed the Guam or Nixon Doctrine and began to withdraw US troops from Vietnam,[18] and whose National Security Adviser, Henry Kissinger, was committed to a managed *détente*. Elsewhere a new reality was taking shape in Europe.

After *les événements* of May 1968 and the fall of de Gaulle in 1969, Moscow could no longer be sure of a European policy hinged upon a French maverick keeping NATO off-balance. The new President Pompidou was less Gaullist and acceded to demands from his EEC partners that Britain be allowed to enter the Community.

Since becoming Foreign Minister in Bonn in 1966, Willy Brandt had pursued a cautious *Ostpolitik* of attempting to normalize relations with Eastern Europe by acknowledging the postwar territorial division of the continent. In September 1969 he became Chancellor and the pace of *Ostpolitik* speeded up. In January 1967 Bonn had established diplomatic relations with Bucharest and there was the prospect of other states responding to the blandishments of trade links with and access to the capital markets of Bonn and her allies. This could have undermined the Soviet hold on Eastern Europe. However, in April 1967 a conference of East European CPs at Karlovy Vary in Czechoslovakia agreed that no more countries would open relations with Bonn unless East Germany agreed, and called for a European security conference.

Moscow, too, was vulnerable to the economic sirens of the West. The economy could no longer satisfy defence needs *and* the rising tide of consumer demands unless it either abandoned the command economy and allowed a free market to operate, or achieved a short cut by massive imports of Western technology, capital and management skills. The latter course carried risks of infection by Western liberal ideas. The crushing of Czechoslovakia in 1968 (see Chapter 10) set the scene in Eastern Europe and in the USSR itself a policy of repression coincided with *détente*. Indeed, repression 'becomes all the more necessary in the eyes of Brezhnev when threats from outside recede', because then 'the penetration of alien ideas can be more dangerous'.[19]

The introduction of *détente* must have created political difficulties for the Soviet leadership. They had to explain, to themselves at least, why they were abandoning autarky. It must have seemed contradictory to some that while Moscow was talking peace with the American arch-enemy of communism, small but furious battles were going on with communist Chinese troops along the Sino–Soviet border. However, Moscow argued that *détente* was forced on the West by Russia's new-found military strength. But there was also a neat ideological argument: Soviet ideology calls for the abolition of all arms and armies; if this happened then the economic basis of capitalism would collapse because military spending is an important stabilizer of the capitalist economy, whereas the socialist states, having no internal contradictions and no external political objectives do not need a permanent arms economy;[20] therefore, peace would bring about the ultimate triumph of communism as capitalism was destroyed by its own internal contradictions, just as Marx had said.

What then was *détente*? It involved Soviet moves towards the control of the arms race, but there was never any intention to disarm. The USSR continued to build a 'blue water' navy and strengthen her armed forces to counter potential hostilities from China and the West and to control Eastern Europe.

*Détente* certainly involved a big step back from the 'high ambition . . . unlimited cost policy' of Cold War[21] and a step on from peaceful co-existence which was characterized by no war, but all-out competition. To paraphrase Clausewitz, *détente* was the continuation of peaceful coexistence by other means. It followed logically, given the needs of the time, that the Soviet Union should seek to co-operate with the West in certain narrow material fields, but the ideological struggle continued.

There is no word for *détente* in Russian[22] (just as there is not in English). It derives from the French *détendre*, the archer's action in releasing the tension of his bowstring as the arrow flies on its way. In diplomatic usage, *détente* meant simply the reduction of tension, however limited in scope. At the June 1969 meeting of communist parties in Moscow, Brezhnev disclosed that 'peaceful coexistence does not extend to the ideological struggle'.[23] This remained the Soviet view of *détente*. On the eve of his departure for the USA in 1973, Brezhnev said: 'The class struggle of the two systems . . . in the sphere of economics, politics, and . . . ideology will be continued . . . . But we shall ensure that this inevitable struggle is transferred to a channel which does not threaten wars, dangerous conflicts and an uncontrolled arms race.'[24] To the Party Congress in February 1976, Brezhnev reported: '*Détente* does not in the slightest abolish, nor can it alter the laws of the class struggle . . . . we see *détente* as the way to create more favourable conditions for peaceful socialist and communist construction.'[25]

The American government understood this minimalist Soviet inter-pretation of *détente*. In 1974 Secretary of State Kissinger noted: '*Détente* is not rooted in agreement on values: it becomes above all necessary because each side recognizes that the other is a potential adversary in a nuclear war. To us, *détente* is a process of managing relations with a potentially hostile country in order to preserve peace while maintaining our vital interests.'[26] Brezhnev and Nixon understood each other clearly, but public opinion in the West soon assumed that *détente* meant peace, but it was never that. For the USSR *détente* was a tactic, not a strategy, not an end in itself. Against the bitter criticism of the Chinese, who accused Moscow of revisionism and worse, the Russians claimed that they were merely following Lenin's policy of dealing with the capitalists, while exploiting their internal differences, and that in a relaxed international climate a socialist world strengthened by its trade with the West would be better able to help 'progressive' forces and communist parties. This is not to minimize the fundamental importance of *détente* to the Russians, merely to point out that they were not governed by the short-term electoral cycle that dominated Western politicians. They could afford to look forward to a millennium which, though distant, would surely come. Brezhnev was committed to the policy. In a speech in Alma Ata in August 1973 he declared that the objective of Soviet foreign policy was 'to render irreversible the phenomenon of *détente*'.[27]

Moscow and Washington had agreed to discuss the control of nuclear weapons when Premier Kosygin met President Johnson at Glasboro, New Jersey in July 1967. But when the Strategic Arms Limitation Talks (SALT) began on 16 April 1970 they paralleled talks on other bilateral or European matters. Both sides were aware that increased missile accuracy together with the deployment of MIRVs and ABMs would destroy the existing nuclear equation and its accompanying mutual predictability unless they could jointly control these new and potentially destabilizing developments. Both sides, too, were concerned to deal bilaterally with each other on matters of mutual interest, but there was a spin-off for Moscow here. In leaving the West Europeans out of negotiations which were of vital importance to them, NATO cohesion was damaged by the European fear that the superpowers might ignore European interests.

Early in 1972 Nixon spelt out his thesis on the 'pentagonal balance of power' which, he suggested, had replaced the old bipolar system in which Washington and Moscow were supreme in the only two power blocs: 'I think it will be a safer world and a better world if we have a strong healthy United States, Europe, Soviet Union, China and Japan; each balancing the other, not playing one against the other, an even balance.'[28] Such a view must have looked naïve to the Kremlin but nevertheless, it was preferable to what had existed in the past and could emerge in the future. After all, in the past, Europe, the United States and Japan had all been on one side of the balance, outweighing the USSR, and there was the prospect of them being joined by China. But if Nixon wanted to engage in the kind of bilateral negotiations which might arouse suspicions of his intentions in Europe and Japan and if he wanted to weaken the bonds which tied Europe and Japan to the USA then it was in Moscow's interests to smooth his path.

There was a note of urgency in Moscow's diplomacy in the early 1970s. Nixon might talk of pentapolarity, but his reversal of America's China policy and his February 1972 visit to Peking opened the possibility of him completing the encirclement of Russia with a Sino–American alliance. So important was a deal with Nixon that his visit to the USSR – the first by an American President – went ahead in May 1972 despite his earlier visit to China and despite the American mining of seven North Vietnamese harbours on 11 May which actually resulted in Soviet casualties and damage to Soviet ships.

In February 1971 the USSR, USA and UK signed the Sea-bed Treaty, which banned the emplacement of nuclear devices on the sea-bed. On 30 September 1971 the USSR and the USA agreed to convert the hot line to a satellite communications system and to reduce the risk of accidental nuclear war by undertaking to keep each other fully informed about accidental launches and to provide each other with the help and information necessary to destroy a missile which had been launched by mistake. But the high spot of this phase of *détente* came on 26 May 1972 when Nixon and Brezhnev signed a battery of agreements on: Co-operation on Environmental Protection; Medical Science and Public Health; the Exploration and Use of Outer Space; Science and Technology; Prevention of Incidents over the Sea; and Basic Principles of Mutual Relations in which they agreed to observe the principle of peaceful coexistence[29] and to work towards three common goals – prevention of war and crisis, limitation of offensive armaments, and the development of cultural, economic and technical links.

The Nixon visit also produced an American agreement to provide credit to finance Soviet purchases of $750 million worth of American grain over three years; a five-year deal by the Soviet government with the Occidental Petroleum Company for the joint development of Soviet oil and gas reserves; and the acquisition by Moscow of a licence to brew Pepsi-Cola. Overshadowing all this however, was the centrepiece of the visit, the three agreements which made up the SALT Treaty. The ABM agreement limited both the USSR and the US to only two ABM sites, each containing 100 defensive missiles, one around the capital and one around an ICBM site. The rationale was that if the enemy could protect his command and control centre and a significant proportion of his land-based ICBMs, then no matter how successful a surprise attack upon the rest of his inventory, he would still retain the capacity to retaliate in kind.

An interim agreement of five years' duration placed a ceiling on the numbers of land-based strategic missiles that either side could deploy. The agreement mentioned no numbers, but effectively limited the USA to the 1,054 she already had. The USSR was allowed to increase its existing 1,530 ICBMs to 1,618. Soviet superiority here was offset by the number of American MIRVs and the Treaty made no mention of bombers or numbers of warheads, in both of which the USA had a predominance, or IRBMs and MRBMs in which the Soviets were superior.

The third element limited the USA to 710 SLBMs and 44 up-to-date ballistic missile submarines (in fact, she remained at 656 SLBMs and 41 submarines) and the USSR to 950 SLBMs and 62 modern submarines. The extremely complicated details of the Treaty[30] allowed trading-off between retiring old systems and new ones so that at the end of 1979, when the USSR deployed only 1,398 ICBMs, she had offset this by an increase of SLBM strength to 1,028. This was still within the terms of the treaty.[31]

In June 1973 Brezhnev went to the USA and agreements were reached on agriculture, transport and the peaceful use of atomic energy. An 'Agreement on the Prevention of Nuclear War' declared an intention to conclude a permanent treaty on the limitation of offensive missiles in 1974, but by then the world was changing. Moscow's China problem was still extremely serious, but not as acute as it had been in 1969. Besides, Nixon's visit to China had created in Japan the trauma of the 'Nixon *shokku*' when Tokyo had not been forewarned about America's Chinese *volte face* and naturally began to look more favourably upon an accommodation with either or both of its huge neighbours. The Americans had withdrawn from Vietnam in 1973, and the October 1973 Arab-Israeli war and the resultant embargo on oil deliveries to the West by OPEC introduced new elements into the international balance.

SALT I had been enormously complicated to negotiate, but SALT II was even more complex. Weapons were more sophisticated. The West Europeans were more uneasy at what America was trying to achieve, and Nixon became a broken-backed President who could not deliver on anything of substance in the wake of the Watergate affair which the Russians failed to understand and publicly dismissed as the work of American enemies of *détente*. An American observer in Moscow in 1974 wrote: 'Russians . . . were mystified – even horrified – that the American Congress, judiciary and press could – and deliberately would – shake the foundations of American leadership. It went against the grain of their own political habits. Their history had given them no way of comprehending the legal, moral and constitutional issues about the limits of presidential power.'[32]

SALT I was a personal triumph for Brezhnev, but he also won *détente* agreements in Europe where the Russians set about securing a general European settlement. *Détente* in Europe was governed by similar considerations to those which operated in the case of the USA, but although the West tended to see them all as parts of a whole and the US tried to impose 'linkage' on the USSR (no progress on a Security

Conference until progress in other areas) the Kremlin kept its relations with Western Europe and the USA compartmentalized. The West Europeans did not pose a major nuclear threat to the USSR, but they were militarily and economically strong and Moscow had no desire for trouble on its western borders. All the significant diplomatic initiatives which characterized *détente* began in 1969, and they can be traced back to one stimulus. At a Warsaw Pact Summit meeting in Budapest on 17 March – two days after the second big Sino–Soviet clash on the Ussuri river – one observer noted: 'Brezhnev's face was red and he did not look well. He was nervous and impatient. His temper flared and he pounded on the table. He had only one thing on his mind – and that was China.'[33] This was where Moscow's *'Westpolitik'* appears to have been born.

A new range of diplomatic and commercial overtures were made to the West Europeans, with the exception of Britain with whom relations remained strained between 1968 and 1973 for a variety of reasons, including the issue of Soviet espionage for which 105 Soviet diplomats were expelled from Britain in September 1971. After an apparently successful visit to Britain by Premier Kosygin in 1967, negotiations on a new friendship treaty proved fruitless and as the UK's economic and diplomatic weight in the world lessened the Soviet Union paid less attention to the country that had been Russia's major Western trading partner until 1968. Elsewhere, in July 1970 the USSR and Finland extended their treaty of friendship, co-operation and mutual assistance, to 1990, and in December 1972 Moscow even signed a trade agreement with Franco's Spain. This was Moscow's first formal agreement with Spain in thirty-five years. But the main thrusts of the policy were towards France and West Germany.

The USSR had a 'special relationship' with France since President de Gaulle's visit to the Soviet Union in 1966 when he had been honoured as the first Westerner to visit the secret space-launching site at Baikonur in Kazakhstan. Moscow had encouraged the French to keep NATO at arm's length and in March 1971, in an unprecedented display of favour, the Russians agreed to enrich uranium for a French nuclear power station. After the enlargement of the EEC by the entry of Britain, Denmark and Ireland in January 1973, France's voice as the self-appointed spokesman of Western Europe was an important one and she had to be handled carefully. Discreet encouragement of French *amour propre* was one way of preventing the emergence from an enlarged EEC of a true federation, of which some of its members still dreamed. The Russians saw the enlargement of the EEC, and also its increased unity, as a serious threat to their ambitions in Europe. Although nothing came of the talk at the time of a possible 'European nuclear force' consisting of an Anglo–French combined deterrent force and targeting strategy, the idea must have looked ominous to the Kremlin while it was in circulation. Moreover, the *rapprochement* between Moscow and Bonn was of such a degree that it could have disturbed Franco–Soviet relations if Soviet diplomacy had not been so skilful.

On 12 August 1970, exactly thirty-one years to the day after the signing of the Nazi–Soviet Non-Aggression Pact, West German Chancellor Willy Brandt and Soviet Premier Alexei Kosygin signed in Moscow a Soviet–West German Non-Aggression Treaty in which they recognized frontiers in Eastern Europe and agreed never to use force against each other. Moscow had won *de facto* West German recognition of the permanent division of Germany and Europe – the central issue left unresolved in 1945 – prompting one serious Western newspaper to ask the question: 'Did the War End Last Friday?'[34] In return for the Soviet seal of approval on Bonn's *Ostpolitik*, which then produced treaties with Poland in December 1970, Czechoslovakia in December 1973 and the opening of diplomatic relations with Eastern Europe, the Russians obtained access to West German trade, capital and technology and a favourable European climate of opinion.

The Moscow treaty marked the take-over by Brezhnev from Kosygin of control of foreign policy. The First Secretary's ambition was to expand the Moscow treaty into a European Security Conference. For this he was prepared to pay a price. Thus America, Britain and France refused further steps towards *détente* and West Germany delayed the ratification of the Moscow treaty until May 1972, until after the Four-Power Agreement on Berlin had been reached in September 1971. In its turn Moscow delayed full acceptance of the Four-Power Agreement on Berlin until after Bonn had ratified its Moscow and Polish treaties, and the agreements on transit between West Germany and West Berlin, and West Berlin and the DDR, which had been signed in December 1971 by East and West Germany.

The East German party leader Walter Ulbricht resisted Brezhnev's efforts to push him into the Berlin accommodations and the Basic Treaty between the two Germanies which was eventually signed in December 1972. The Berlin deal fell short of the total East German control of access routes to Berlin that Ulbricht and Khrushchev had tried to win between 1958 and 1961. In fact, Ulbricht proved so intractable that Brezhnev engineered his retirement and replacement in May 1971 by the more responsive Erich Hoenecker.

The new cordiality between Moscow and Bonn showed itself in Brandt's visit to the Crimea in September 1971 and Brezhnev's to Bonn in May 1973 at which a 10-year agreement was signed on technical co-operation. But at another level Moscow's policy had not changed. In 1971 the West German Ministry of the Interior estimated that there had been 35,000 known attempts to recruit spies in the Federal Republic and that Moscow was spending up to £800 million per annum on subversion of West Germany.[35] Two incidents illustrated the continuing degree of the Soviet-backed effort. On 6 May 1974 Chancellor Brandt resigned after revelations that his assistant, Gunter Guillaume, was an East German spy. Then in December 1977 Bonn revealed the arrest of another East German spy, Renata Lutze, who had been passing military and NATO secrets of an 'extremely serious' nature to the East Germans until her arrest in June 1976. Such episodes served to jaundice Western opinion against Soviet protestations of *détente*, but in fact they were fully a part of Moscow's policy towards the West, and anyway, the West was trying to spy on the East.

On 15 January 1973 preparatory talks for a European Security Conference (CSCE) opened in Helsinki. The CSCE was first proposed by Molotov in 1954 and was seen by Moscow as the web which would draw together all the threads of its European *Westpolitik*. All participants accepted the American and Canadian presence; the West Europeans as a guarantee against the Russians and the Soviets because American presence could help guarantee the *status quo*. Moscow wanted the CSCE to yield common recognition of the division of Europe, the Soviet hold over East Germany and the legitimization of East Germany which had already been partially achieved by the Basic Treaty between the two Germanies.

In return for the European Security Conference, the Russians conceded a parallel conference on Mutual and Balanced Force Reductions (MBFR), which opened in Vienna on 30 October 1973. This was supposed to proceed at the same pace as CSCE in its attempts to reduce troop and weapon commitments in central Europe while preserving the military balance. These talks were extremely complicated for they proceeded from different assumptions of the benefits to be gained by East and West from reductions in force levels, qualitatively and quantitatively different weapons systems and different 'war-fighting' doctrines based upon different views of how and why a European war might start and how it might develop. MBFR talks dragged on for the rest of the decade but they were always more important to the West than to the East and they achieved nothing of substance beyond a closer understanding of each other's military preoccupations.

There were urgent reasons why Moscow attempted to create a climate in which she could switch some economic emphasis away from the defence sector. Although the Kremlin feared the effects upon Soviet society of the introduction of Western materialism, it also feared the effects of not producing a higher standard of living for the population. The Polish riots in December 1970 against price increases, brought down party boss Gomulka, and gave the authorities throughout Eastern Europe cause to cast anxious glances over their own shoulders at populations that were becoming aware of the economic good life in the West and wanted some for themselves. Added to which, in 1972 there were expressions of Ukrainian, Baltic and Jewish nationalism and discontent. Brezhnev apparently felt these could be cured by access to consumer goods. This, however, required the diversion of resources within the economy and, therefore, good relations with the West.

On 1 August 1975, in a blaze of publicity in Helsinki, the thirty-three representatives of all the European states, except Albania, plus the USA and Canada signed the Helsinki Final Act of the CSCE and thus allowed Brezhnev to land that for which the Kremlin had been angling for twenty-one years. The Final Act covered four areas. It recognized the inviolability of frontiers and included 'confidence building measures', which involved giving twenty-one days' notice of military manoeuvres of more than 25,000 men taking place within 155 miles (250 kilometres) of national frontiers; and the exchange of observers at such manoeuvres. Section Two involved economic, technological and environmental co-operation. Section Four promised a follow-up conference at Belgrade two years hence, but the section that involved Moscow making concessions in return for the first two sections, was the so-called 'basket three'.

Basket three guaranteed respect for 'human rights' and fundamental freedoms including the freedoms of thought, conscience, religion and belief. It guaranteed the rights of national minorities and all states agreed not to interfere in each other's internal affairs. It guaranteed wide-ranging cultural and educational exchange and co-operation and created the possibility of such a level of individual travel between East and West that all countries would be able to observe each other's implementation of the Helsinki provisions. The fact that Moscow agreed basket three is a measure of how much the Soviets were prepared to sacrifice to win general approval of baskets one and two.

Certainly the 'human rights' issue rebounded upon the Kremlin. Helsinki monitoring groups appeared throughout Eastern Europe and were encouraged by the West. In 1977 the emphasis placed upon human rights by the incoming American President Carter harmed relations with the Russians. They resented Carter's public letter to the dissident Andrei Sakharov in February 1977 which they saw as an interference in their domestic affairs. The Helsinki Review Conference at Belgrade lasted six months throughout the winter of 1977–8, but it achieved little. In acrimonious exchanges East and West accused each other of breaches of the Helsinki accords. Carter's stand on human rights had soured the atmosphere, not only with the USSR, but with his European allies who echoed Soviet concern that the USA was introducing a new element into *détente*. When the Belgrade Conference ended, Soviet delegate Yuli Vorontsov spoke of the West's 'specific political campaign [over human rights] conducted for specific political reasons. Like other such campaigns it will not work.'[36]

Brezhnev must have expected difficulties at the Belgrade Conference, but cannot have expected that a new American President would take it all so literally. Carter's emphasis on human rights, involved a change of American policy towards the USSR, but Moscow's policy towards the

West had not changed. Especially towards Western Europe, the USSR played a 'good neighbour' role before and after Helsinki. Brezhnev took no apparent advantage of the disarray in NATO and the EEC in 1973 and 1974 brought on by the Arab–Israeli war and the oil crisis. Although the USSR was naturally very interested in the Portuguese revolution in 1974, claims that she and East Germany gave £50 million inside a year to the Portuguese Communist Party were exaggerated.[37] Recognizing NATO's legitimate interest in the fate of its Portuguese member, Russia's interest appears to have been not so much in Portugal itself but in the severing from Portugal of its African colonies.

The mid-1970s saw the fully-fledged emergence of Eurocommunism as the Italian and Spanish Communist Parties, joined not totally whole-heartedly by the French CP, questioned the historic inevitability of Marxist–Leninism by saying that, once in power, they would relinquish office if voted out again. Eurocommunism worried Moscow where there was no enthusiasm for mass communist parties which were different from the Soviet party and which were ostensibly willing to be voted out of office, but which did not accept unquestioningly Soviet leadership. Anyway, a communist government in Italy or France would have changed the geopolitical balance and destroyed the *status quo* so carefully advocated by Moscow ever since the Second World War. A communist country in Western Europe would have introduced such a random destabilizing element into the East–West balance that 'predictability', the essence of East–West *détente*, would have been lost, with unforeseen and therefore dangerous consequences. So Moscow's relations with Western Europe remained not just correct, but even cordial. Brezhnev continued to encourage France's independent stance within NATO and in June 1976 he even went so far as to approve a hot line with France to prevent accidental nuclear war between the two countries. Co-operation in peaceful nuclear energy continued. The two countries agreed on 3 October 1978 to collaborate on developing a fast-breeder reactor, and France was invited to join the Soviet space programme.

Elsewhere, the Soviet Union's territorial dispute with Norway over the Barents Sea was settled on 16 November 1977 when Moscow and Oslo agreed to partition the disputed area. Earlier, beyond proposing a UN sponsored peace conference in August 1974, Moscow made no attempt to fish in the troubled waters of the NATO crisis that resulted from the Turkish invasion of Cyprus in July 1974. Relations between Greece and Turkey remained bad for the rest of the decade, but the Russians were circumspect in their approach to both countries. The Greek Premier Karamanlis was welcomed in Moscow and trade agreements were concluded in October 1977, but the major Soviet interest was with Turkey. This was reasonable since Turkey controlled the airspace through which Soviet aircraft sometimes had to fly to reach the Middle East and also controlled the entrance to the Mediterranean for the Black

Sea Fleet and to the Black Sea for the American Sixth Fleet, which had
sent warships into the Black Sea up to January 1966.[38] In June 1978 the
Russians signed an agreement on friendly relations and trade co-
operation with Turkey which, however, fell short of the non-aggression
pact that Brezhnev had wanted.

Throughout the 1970s the Soviet Union and her satellites increased
their trade with the West. This followed an analysis by the USSR that
the crisis of capitalism was not about to happen. On 29 October 1974,
even while Western economies were badly hit by the oil price rise after
the 1973 Arab–Israeli war, the Army newspaper *Red Star* asserted that
capitalism would recover from its present crisis. During the visit to
Moscow of British Premier Wilson, Brezhnev spelled out what the
Russians saw as the West's advantage in trade with Moscow which
could provide 'new job opportunities for thousands and thousands of
workers in your country and a new impetus for the economy.'[39] This
Soviet rationale for trade with the West led to the growth of the idea of
'convergence' in the West – the notion that the more the USSR traded
with the West, the more the two systems would 'converge' and the USSR
would inevitably begin to adopt Western values. Yet Russia traditionally
imported technology and skills while excluding the liberalism that
produced them. Leonid Brezhnev has been jokingly compared with
Peter the Great because like Peter, and other tsars, he imported technology and technocrats, but ruled with an iron hand. While the volume
of trade with the West was at its height in 1979, the campaign against
dissidents was so successful that their voice was muted compared with
five years earlier.

Moreover, although in the search for investment capital and technology the USSR moved gradually closer to diplomatic recognition of
the EEC and an accommodation with Japan, she was unable to open
wide the door to the major source of capital and technology. The 1975
grain deal allowed Moscow to buy up to 8 million ton(ne)s of American
grain each year before negotiating directly with the government. But
Brezhnev failed to win most favoured nation trading status with the
USA. The 1972 American Trade Bill which would have liberalized
Soviet trade became saddled with the Jackson Amendment which demanded that the Russians allow 60,000 Jews to emigrate each year.
The Politburo was so eager for this agreement that they swallowed the
humiliation of the principle involved and beat Kissinger down to 45,000
Jews per year, but when Senator Jackson would not accept this figure the
USSR rejected the deal in January 1975.

Brezhnev believed that *détente* was a process that needed 'constant
movement forward' otherwise it might fall into disuse. For this reason he
pursued a SALT II treaty which, though very important in itself, was
not the sole answer to the Soviet Union's military problems: these were
in the course of being solved by the development of new armaments.

SALT II had a symbolic as well as a real politico–military value to the Russians, for its achievement would serve to maintain Western commitment to *détente*. However, the best that the unelected President Ford could achieve was the Interim Agreement reached with Brezhnev in Vladivostok on 24 November 1974 to act as the guidelines for a later SALT II Treaty. They agreed to limit strategic vehicles, including missiles and bombers, to 2,400 each: up to 1,320 of these could be MIRVs. The USSR conceded superiority to the USA's existing 850 MIRVed missiles – Moscow had none as yet – but in return the Americans agreed to include bombers, in which they had superiority in numbers, in the reckoning.

Thereafter the talks bogged down and the arms race changed in nature from the quantitative search for new weapons to the qualitative search for more accurate MIRVs. The technical difficulties were also increased by the American development for the 1980s of the MX 'racetrack' missile which could be deployed along underground rail tracks and launched at any one of 23 sites. This made the missile almost invulnerable to nuclear strike. The development of the extremely accurate, relatively cheap ($500,000 each), small ground-hugging Cruise missile threatened Moscow's defences because it could creep underneath radar. The Russians were also concerned at the new US Trident SLBM, the B1 bomber – cancelled by President Carter – and the 'neutron bomb'. In their turn the Western powers were concerned about the Soviet Backfire bomber which Moscow claimed was medium and not inter-continental range and therefore outside the purview of SALT. The USA claimed that the Backfire could, in fact, be stretched to reach the USA and that both it and the new Soviet SS20 missile threatened Western Europe and upset the theatre balance.

Progress on SALT II was slow during the Carter Presidency; held up not just by technicalities, but by Soviet reaction to Carter's pronouncements on human rights, his attempts to rearm NATO and his recognition of China in January 1979, as well as by American perceptions of Soviet 'adventurism' in the Third World. Nevertheless, on 18 June 1979 Carter and Brezhnev signed the SALT II Treaty in Vienna. This complicated treaty limited strategic missiles to 2,250 each, and MIRVed vehicles (including Cruise missile-carrying bombers) to 1,320 each. But SALT II was signed in a different atmosphere from SALT I. Mutual suspicion and hostility was such that the very next month, Carter decided to set up a 110,000 man Rapid Deployment Corps to be used outside the NATO area,[10] and in early September 1979 the Combat Brigade in Cuba Affair broke where the US accused Russia of stationing in Cuba – besides the 6,000 Soviet troops there as trainers and instructors – a 'combat brigade' of 3,000 men.

There was little prospect of Moscow using only 3,000 troops in the western hemisphere for anything other than training. The Russians and

Cubans claimed that the troops had been there since 1964. Carter demanded their withdrawal and Brezhnev refused. Relations between the two were embittered and the prospects for American ratification of SALT II dimmed. Soviet suspicions that it was a gambit by Carter in his tussle with Congress must have been reinforced by America dropping the issue at the end of October 1979 even though the 'brigade' remained in Cuba.

By then Brezhnev was trying to pressure the West Europeans into encouraging Washington to ratify the treaty, at the same time as trying to persuade them to resist American offers of a new generation of medium-range American nuclear missiles to be based in Europe in order to offset the Backfire bomber and the mobile 2,500 mile-range (about 4,000 km) SS20 missile which brought the whole of Europe within reach. Brezhnev offered to and then started to withdraw 20,000 Soviet troops and 1,000 tanks from the DDR by the end of 1980, but this was not enough to deflect the NATO Council, which in December 1979 agreed to deploy 464 2,300 mile-range (about 3,700 km) Tomahawk Cruise missiles and 108 1,300 mile-range (about 2,100 km) Pershing II MRBMs in Europe. The NATO decision in itself did not alter the theatre balance significantly, but it was indicative of the failure of Moscow (and the West) to maintain the atmosphere in which *détente* could grow.

Indeed, the Cold War pot had been kept boiling by a number of incidents: the return to the USSR in examined pieces of a MiG 25 'Foxbat' which had been flown to Japan in September 1976; the Norwegian refusal to hand over the 'black box' flight recorder of a Badger bomber which crashed on a Norwegian island in October 1978; the CIA's raising for examination in 1974 of a sunken Soviet submarine; the revelation in 1976 that Brigadier Jeanmaire, former head of Swiss air defence, was a Soviet spy; another spy ring uncovered in West Germany in 1978; the defection to the US of Arkady Shevchenko, a high-ranking UN official in September 1979, and a rash of sporting and artistic defectors the same year, including three members of the touring Bolshoi Ballet. These incidents, among many others, illustrated the continued willingness to believe the worst on the part of East and West. The premises upon which *détente* was built were already undermined before the Soviets moved into Afghanistan at Christmas 1979 and this was due, in large part, to Western reactions to Soviet policy towards the Third World and Soviet arms spending.

Brezhnev continued Khrushchev's policy of support for socialist regimes, revolutionary movements and nationalist governments in the Third World, but Moscow was unable to match the economic aid of the West. With no food, energy or industrial surpluses, the bulk of Soviet aid was arms. This led to the views expressed by Kissinger: 'All the Russians can give you is arms; we Americans can give you peace' and Chou En-lai: 'What has happened to the first socialist country in the world? It's become nothing but an armaments dealer.'[41] Much Soviet effort was aimed at Islamic countries, upon which Soviet atheism jarred, and additionally, the Soviets frequently had language and cultural problems in trying to establish rapport with Third World states.

Two hundred thousand Arabs went to the USSR to train, study or negotiate up to 1977, but less than 100 married Soviet girls and they found their marriages unwelcome in the USSR, whereas of the 15,000 Arabs who went to study in the USA in the late 1950s and early 1960s, nearly half married American girls. Arabs were not allowed to mix in Russia and the 120,000 Russians who travelled to Arab lands also kept themselves apart.[42] Of course, Soviet ideology and arms *were* welcome in some quarters, but Moscow learned that influence was not always commensurate with the amounts of aid offered. By acknowledging ideological links, the Russians often entered into relationships over which they had little control and from which, ultimately, others were likely to gain rather than themselves. The $1 billion of arms and aid received by Indonesia in the early 1960s did not stop President Sukarno supporting China in the Sino–Soviet dispute, nor did it prevent the suppression by the Indonesian army of the Indonesian CP in September 1965 when 100,000 party members were killed and the party was virtually wiped out.

Khrushchev had been chary of building up Soviet influence in South-East Asia, feeling that although this could turn China's flank, it would infuriate the Americans. Accordingly, Soviet aid to North Vietnam fell in 1963 and 1964, but after Khrushchev this changed, although only in reaction to events. After the Tongking Gulf incident led to increased American involvement in the Vietnam war, the USSR was obliged to support its co-ideologist which, in turn, escalated the war. The Vietcong's guerrilla war turned into a conventional war, which meant that the Vietcong needed arms and supplies from Hanoi and had to accept the political and strategic control that went with it. But Hanoi could only give aid because she was herself now receiving help from the Russians. This merely invited the American air attacks which Hanoi's obvious control of the war would bring. In November 1964 Moscow promised to protect North Vietnam and began to install SAM batteries around Hanoi and Haiphong. In February 1965 Premier Kosygin went to Hanoi and made the first public offer of Soviet military aid to North Vietnam (at the precise moment when the Americans began bombing the North). Thereafter, the Russians gave North Vietnam aid which totalled $1,660 million between 1965–71, but although they urged moderation upon Hanoi they were unable to exert decisive influence upon a regime which was only dragged reluctantly into the Sino–Soviet dispute.

There were benefits for the USSR, however. Vietnam absorbed $100 billion of American wealth up to 1972, damaged America's reputation, confidence and resolve and strengthened Moscow's claim as defender of the weak against imperialism. Nevertheless, the Russians did not let Vietnam get in the way of their *détente* with America, and they pressed Hanoi to compromise and accept the Paris Peace of 1973, by which time the Americans had withdrawn from South Vietnam. In the next two years Moscow poured war *matériel* into North Vietnam. Hanoi's victory by 30 April 1975, the communist successes in Cambodia on 17 April and in Laos on 23 August 1975, followed by the reunification of Vietnam in 1976 and Vietnam's hegemony over South-East Asia vindicated Soviet policy.

America's *débâcle* in Indo-China prompted SEATO to disband itself in September 1975, a Soviet aim since its inception, led all of southern Asia to make some sort of accommodation with Moscow, and gave the Russians a Vietnamese counterweight to China. As the Chinese played the European card against Russia, so did Moscow play the Vietnam card against China. On 29 June 1978 Vietnam became a full member of Comecon, and on 3 November 1978 signed a treaty of friendship and co-operation with the USSR. However, Moscow did not control Vietnam and had to support Hanoi both when she invaded Cambodia and ousted the Pol Pot regime in December 1978 and when her provocative action invited a Chinese attack in February 1979. Neither did the USSR take over the huge ex-American base at Cam Ranh Bay.[43] Although far from becoming a satellite, Vietnam had become an ally as had Cuba.

Soviet–Cuban relations remained strained after the missile crisis until Castro supported Brezhnev over Czechoslovakia in 1968. Thereafter, Cuba became more 'responsible' and stopped advocating so strongly armed revolution in Latin America which had so antagonized the Americans. A biddable Cuba received enormous Soviet help. She joined Comecon in 1972, received military supplies and her economy was subsidized by up to $1,500,000 per day. She was a base for a Soviet fishing fleet, a foothold in the western hemisphere and an example to the Third World of what could be achieved with communism and Soviet help.

Described erroneously by American Senator Moynihan as the 'Gurkhas of the Russian Empire', the Cubans were not puppets. Castro's and Brezhnev's policies coincided: the USSR had developed the airlift and sealift capabilities to deliver and supply Cubans in Africa in support of the ambitions of Fidel Castro for whom Cuba was too small and Latin America too unproductive.[44] Cuba became a stalking-horse for the USSR, and the charismatic Castro as Chairman of the Non-Aligned Summit in Havana in summer 1979 helped deflect some of the odium that might otherwise have attached to Russia as patron of Vietnam, the invader of Cambodia and instigator of the flight and death of hundreds of thousands of 'boat people' refugees.

Cuba received large-scale Soviet support partly because of its accessibility. When the Marxist Salvador Allende was elected President of Chile in 1970, the treatment he received from Moscow was much less favourable. Chile was too far away for decisive help. When an increasingly desperate Allende went to Moscow in December 1972 to ask for $500 million in hard currency loans, all he got was $30 million credit and the Lenin Peace Prize. Although the Soviets condemned the USA when Chile was destabilized and Allende overthrown and killed in September 1973, they had not given him the help that could have turned Chile communist since this would have jeopardized *détente* with the USA.

In 1974 Soviet opportunities in Africa were increased by the collapse of the Portuguese empire, the fall of Emperor Haile Selassie of Ethiopia, the establishment of radical regimes in Benin, Somalia and Madagascar and the USSR's new found military 'reach' which equipped her to intervene far from her own frontiers. Soviet difficulties in Africa were typical of her difficulties elsewhere in the Third World, but were accentuated by the poverty, poor educational standards, tribalism and rural nature of much of Africa to which the USSR could not serve as a model for development.

National liberation movements fighting against white rule found a natural ally in Moscow, but Soviet help was limited in the 1960s. In 1960 the Patrice Lumumba University was established in Moscow to train Third World students. Guinea, Ghana, Mali, Algeria, Egypt, Somalia and Tanzania all received aid. Help was given to Agostino Neto's Popular Movement for the Liberation of Angola (MPLA) guerrillas in Angola, Joshua Nkomo's Zimbabwe African People's Union (ZAPU) guerrillas in Zimbabwe and South-West African People's Organization (SWAPO) in Namibia, but only in 1968 was a special African Department established in the Soviet Foreign Ministry. Until then, Soviet efforts in black Africa reflected their unfamiliarity with the continent and their appreciation of the risks involved. In October 1965, after Rhodesia's (now Zimbabwe) Unilateral Declaration of Independence (UDI) from Britain, *Pravda* warned 'the young nation states' [of Africa] that the USSR could not solve their national liberation problems for them, for any such Soviet action would carry the risk of "world thermonuclear war".'[45]

Africa was a theatre of competition with China, but with China's introspection over the Cultural Revolution Moscow had the communist field relatively clear. Between 1971–5 she gave over $1,500 million in arms to African countries, excluding Egypt. This policy changed in substance between April and October 1975 when she sent twenty-eight shiploads and up to forty Antonov 22 airfreighter loads of arms, some Soviet 'technicians' and 13,000 Cuban troops, all of which allowed Agostino Neto to establish a government in Angola. American involvement was trivial: the CIA furnished Neto's enemies with approximately $300,000. Meanwhile, South African intervention served only to provide the Cubans with a pretext for intervention, and the Soviet Union with the claim that it was not intervening in a civil war but helping to repel an aggressor.[46] By 1980 20,000 Cuban troops were engaged with the Angolan army in fighting the pro-Western Jonas Savimbi's National Union for the Total Independence of Angola (UNITA) forces. The USSR failed to get the naval facilities in Angola or Guinea that she had asked for, and her arrival alarmed some states. On 28 January 1976 President Kaunda of Zambia said of Angola: 'A plundering tiger with its deadly cubs is coming through the back door.'[47] Angola was cited in the West as the chief example of Soviet bad faith over *détente*. In March 1976 American Secretary of State Kissinger warned: 'We are not the world's policeman but we cannot permit the Soviet Union or its surrogates to become the world's policeman either [Map 7].'[48]

In Angola Moscow gave decisive aid to a cause she had supported for a decade, but in the Horn of Africa she displayed an unusual degree of opportunism. In the early 1970s the USSR acquired naval facilities at Berbera on the Somali coast which allowed the Soviet navy to direct operations into the Red Sea, Persian Gulf and Indian Ocean. The USSR trained and equipped the 20,000 strong Somali army, but when this army was turned on crumbling Ethiopia in 1977, Moscow responded to Ethiopian leader Haile Mengistu's plea for help, by airlifting and sea-lifting arms and 20,000 Cuban troops to his aid. For a short while, until President Siad Barre of Somalia threw the Russians and Cubans out of his country, Russia enjoyed the novel experience of arming, training and advising both sides in the same war. The Somalis were defeated by early 1978. The USA did not intervene despite the deep concern of Egypt, Sudan, Saudi Arabia and Iran; and the Cuban and Soviet advisers then helped Mengistu against the Eritrean separatists in north-east Ethiopia who had previously received help from the USSR.

Moscow lost the Berbera naval base and risked the opposition of Somalia's African and Arab neighbours, the further antagonism of the West and the condemnation of her *realpolitik* by those with ideals: for the Soviet action was pure *realpolitik*. If she won in Ethiopia she stood to gain a naval base there, opposite her base in South Yemen. Help for Mengistu displaced the Americans. Ethiopia, with 30 million people, was more of a catch than Somalia with 3.5 million, and from Ethiopia the USSR could wield influence further up the Red Sea, towards the Sudan and Egypt; for the Middle East was the real focus of Soviet interest in the region. Black Africa remained a side-show.

Immediately after the Arab–Israeli war of 1973, Brezhnev reiterated the claim that the Middle East and eastern Mediterranean were areas 'in the immediate vicinity of the USSR' and were regarded by Moscow as Washington regarded the Caribbean.[49] Already by 1965 the USSR had links with Algeria, Iraq and Syria, but Egypt was the pivot of a Soviet policy that appeared soundly based after the advent of a Ba'athist government in Syria with two communist ministers. Moscow saw the prospect of a block of 'progressive' Arab states linked to the 'socialist

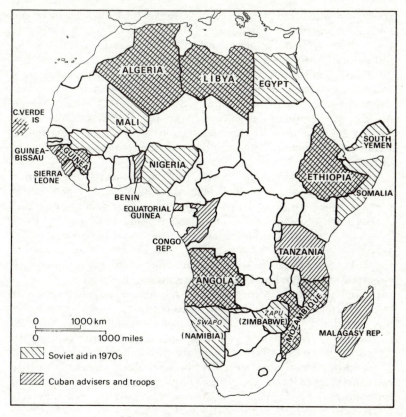

Map 7   The USSR and Cuba in Africa

commonwealth'. Egypt was receptive for in 1965 the US cut off aid and President Nasser had turned to the USSR which agreed to reschedule and cut Egypt's debts and supply her with arms. Soviet influence in Arab states stemmed from the Arab–Israeli dispute which, once solved, might have removed the need for Soviet help on the part of some states which, despite radical governments, remained religious, conservative and hostile to Marxism. It was beyond Moscow's power, nor was it in her interest, to solve the Arab–Israeli deadlock, especially if such a solution involved the destruction of Israel for the Kremlin remained convinced of America's determination to protect the existence of Israel.

When the Arabs lost the June war of 1967 against Israel, Algerian President Boumedienne publicly blamed the Russians, and the Russians blamed the superiority of Israeli equipment (or their handling of it) and Nasser's betrayal by the 'military bourgeoisie'. Indeed, in warning Egypt that ten Israeli brigades were massing on the Syrian border, the USSR gave Nasser the stimulus to mobilize and set in train the events that led to war before the Arabs were ready for it and which caused such superpower tension that the hot line was used for the first time. Only the rapid replacement by Moscow of the Arab *matériel* losses helped restore some of Moscow's standing, but her credibility as a reliable and effective ally was damaged and her clients had been humiliated and had lost territory. For the next five years the diplomatic initiative escaped the USSR. Britain's Resolution 242 was accepted as a basis for peace at the UN and the American Rogers Plan brought about a ceasefire in 1970 after two years of 'canal war'. Russia provided arms and won little credit for doing so, for as President Sadat wrote of his predecessor at the end of 1967: 'Nasser now asked the Soviets for more assistance . . . without the least sign of response. The Soviet Union had planned to provide us with just enough to meet our most immediate needs and at the same time maintain its role as our guardian and ensure its presence in the region – a more important goal from the Soviet point of view.'[50]

The arms supplied to Egypt after 1967 were not enough to allow Egypt to stand-off Israel in the 'canal war', so in 1971 the Russians agreed to provide over 300 modern SAM-3s and up to 20,000 'technicians' to train the Egyptian forces. But they were then obliged to provide the fighter cover for the SAM batteries, therefore 150 MiG-21 aircraft and their pilots were sent to Egypt. These planes stopped Israeli deep-penetration raids over Egypt at the cost of four Soviet pilots, and were an earnest of the USSR's recognition of Egypt's problem, but were unmatched by any diplomatic initiatives.[51] The Soviet military presence gave Moscow some control over Egypt's defence and foreign policies, but although Moscow had leverage in Cairo she had none in Tel Aviv. The essential barrenness of Soviet policy became clear to Nasser's successor, President Sadat, who on 18 July 1972 ordered almost all the Soviet 'technicians' to leave Egypt only 16 months after having signed a 15-year treaty of friendship with the USSR.

The break in relations was healed over by September 1972, but Egypt was free of Soviet control and when Sadat requested the battlefield weapons to allow him to wage an offensive, rather than a defensive, war the Soviets had no option but to agree or risk losing all they had invested in *matériel* and prestige. Between 1967 and 1972 Soviet influence was great in the Middle East and she was able to limit Syrian intervention in the Jordanian civil war of 1970, supply arms to Lebanon and buy oil from Iraq, but she had had to pay a price. In May 1971 Sadat liquidated the pro-Moscow faction in Egypt and in July 1971 a *coup* by communists in the Sudan was foiled and its leaders executed. After 1972, Moscow's influence was on the wane. She was only informed of the Arab attack on Israel in October 1973, a matter of hours before it happened.

With no control over her Egyptian and Syrian clients, the USSR was obliged to respond to Arab pleas for arms with huge airlifts of equipment during the 1973 war, for she could not allow them to lose too heavily.[32] When Sadat invited both superpowers into Egyptian territory to separate the belligerents, the USSR moved naval and ground forces into the Mediterranean, and the USA publicly proclaimed a nuclear alert. Although Moscow's links with Syria and Iraq remained and her foothold in South Yemen strengthened after 1973,[33] the hold over Egypt was gone and relations with Cairo became acrimonious. Sadat could only be satisfied by the huge supply of arms which would enable him militarily to threaten Israel again, but Moscow had no wish to have another threat of nuclear war over the Middle East. The Soviets resupplied Syria lavishly since Syria could not upset the *status quo* on her own. But they did not resupply Egypt for Sadat would not accept the strings attached to resupply and anyway, he was moving towards the Americans for a peace that Moscow could not provide, but which she did not actively try to prevent. It was the USA which arranged the Israeli withdrawal from the Suez Canal and the abortive Geneva peace talks. It was her citizens who manned the Sinai watching posts between the Egyptians and Israelis and who got President Sadat and Israeli Premier Begin to produce the Camp David 'framework for peace in the Midde East' in September 1978.

Moscow urged a solution to the Palestinian problem and made political capital out of the exclusiveness of the Egyptian–Israeli treaty, but nevertheless, Moscow behaved with great restraint and this can only have been because she recognized the importance of the region to America. She wanted no repetition of October 1973 when she had become unwillingly involved in an uncontrolled crisis; Nixon's nuclear alert had shown that keeping the Russians out of the Middle East was more important to the Americans than *détente*. On 5 May 1976 Sadat abrogated the treaty with Moscow and it was argued that apart from the benefits of naval access to the Indian Ocean through the cleared Suez Canal, the USSR had gained little from the Middle East, but there is an alternative view.

According to this hypothesis, Moscow was not interested in bilateral relations with individual non-communist states so much as 'permanent' military relations between 'security subsystems' around the rimlands of Eurasia. The Cubans in Africa and East Germans in South Yemen were cases in point, but in October 1974 300 North Koreans arrived in Damascus to help man the air defences.[34] In 1975 some 200 Cubans and North Vietnamese troops helped train Polisario guerrillas in the ex-Spanish Sahara.[35] Therefore the USSR attempted to create more Egypts:

> The success or failure criteria which the Soviets . . . have adopted may be quite different from the ones we have been ascribing them for years . . . there is little doubt that from the Soviet security system perspective, it [Egypt] has profited Moscow immensely. Egypt has contributed to the Soviet design as no other single non-communist country has; it opened the entire Arab Middle East to Moscow, actively assisting the Soviets in other Middle Eastern and North African countries and . . . contributing for several years to Russia's own security by allowing it air and naval facilities on its territory.[36]

It is the case also that the USSR successfully broke out of the containment cordon erected by the USA in the late 1940s and 1950s (Map 8).

The Sino–Soviet split made good relations with India even more important than they had been in the 1950s, both as a counterweight to China and as an avenue into the Non-Aligned Movement. Soviet diplomatic stock stood high in India following Kosygin's successful mediation between India and Pakistan at Tashkent in January 1966 after their war in 1965. Thereafter the USSR became India's major arms supplier. The Soviet navy was rewarded with port facilities at Vishakhapatnam and in the Andaman Islands (see Map 13 on page 185). In 1971 India and the USSR signed a treaty of friendship and co-operation which was renewed in 1976 and which was the other cornerstone with Vietnam, upon which the USSR built its policy of containing China in Asia.

India gave Moscow firm diplomatic support during the 1970s, but Moscow had to support India too, over her war with Pakistan and the creation of Bangladesh in 1971 and her explosion in 1974 of a 'peaceful' nuclear device. Relations between Moscow and New Delhi depended upon a common perception of a threat from China, for economic links were limited by the fact that the USSR could not export food and was only able to export 5 million ton(ne)s of oil to India between 1977–80. Neither could she buy many of India's industrial products. However, Sino–Indian relations recovered after the death of Mao, and when Premier Kosygin visited India in March 1979 he failed to obtain Indian

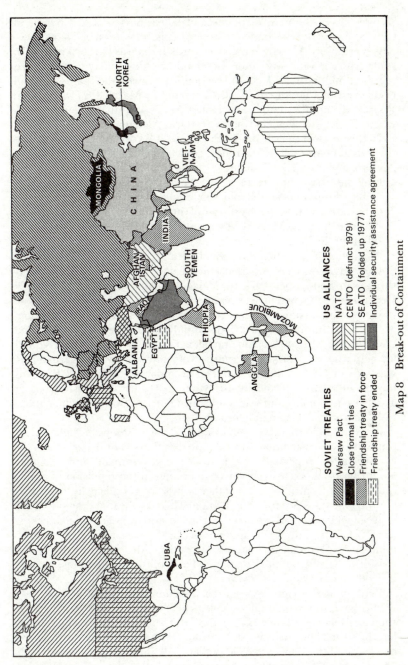

Map 8   Break-out of Containment

recognition of the new Vietnamese-installed, Soviet-backed regime in Cambodia, or Indian condemnation of China's invasion of Vietnam.

Nevertheless, Moscow's policy towards India was part of a pattern in southern Asia of co-operation and good neighbourliness that included regular diplomatic contacts and economic links with the Shah's Iran and even overtures to America's ally Thailand in March 1977 when Thai Premier General Chamanand visited Moscow. But the country with which Soviet involvement was greatest was Afghanistan.

In the nineteenth century the Russian and British empires had played the 'Great Game' across the roof of the world competing for influence in Afghanistan. After 1945, feudal Islamic, monarchist Afghanistan was one of the first countries to receive Soviet aid. In effect, Afghanistan became a Finland from the mid-1950s onwards. Western interest in the country faded so that the overthrow of the king in 1973 and then the *coup* in April 1978 by the Marxist Mohammed Taraki aroused worries but no passions in the West.

A Muslim insurrection threatened Taraki's revolution and up to 1,000 Soviet 'advisers' were reported killed before Taraki himself was overthrown in September 1979 by Hafizollah Amin who lasted until 26 December 1979 when he was reportedly killed by the Soviet troops who invaded Afghanistan over the Christmas period. In a smooth operation, armoured columns and paratroops rapidly seized the roads, towns and government. Moscow's claim that her action was in response to a request for help from the Kabul government (of Amin? or Babrak Karmal who was still in Eastern Europe on 24 December when the first Russians moved in?) was rejected by 104 votes to 18, with 30 abstentions or absences, in the UN and was condemned outright by 35 Muslim nations in Islamabad, Pakistan in February 1980.

By April 1980 there were up to 100,000 Soviet troops in Afghanistan, but Moscow insisted that only 'a limited military contingent' was in the country after 'repeated appeals from the government' and that they would be used 'exclusively for co-operation in the repulsion of armed interference from abroad', in other words, rebels allegedly helped by China, Pakistan, America and Britain. This was the first time since 1945 that Soviet troops had crossed the Iron Curtain frontier, and in breaking the UN Charter, the 1955 Bandung Declaration and the Helsinki Agreement principle on the inviolability of frontiers, Moscow ran an enormous risk of suffering political damage. The Politburo knew this: so why invade Afghanistan?

Perhaps the Soviets invoked the Brezhnev Doctrine. Certainly they would have suffered a major ideological reverse if a Marxist regime on their borders was allowed to collapse. But although Amin only controlled the towns and roads in Afghanistan and insurgents controlled much of the rest of the country, by December 1979, the insurgents were largely Muslim bandits who were fighting for loot rather than power. Besides,

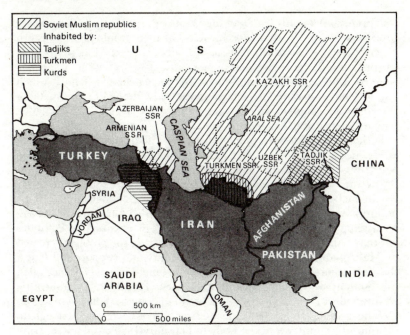

Map 9   The Arc of Crisis: Upsurge of Muslim Fundamentalism

Kabul has seldom exercised much real control over the countryside. Perhaps Moscow was afraid of the upsurge of Muslim fundamentalism in the 'Arc of Crisis' spilling over the border and infecting her own Muslims (Map 9). If so, then Iran was in fact the country to invade. Logically, if Russia had wanted to seal off her Muslims from religious and rebellious contamination then she would not have used troops mobilized for the invasion mostly from the Muslim citizenry of the central Asian republics.[57]

'Perhaps the move was part of a long term tsarist/Soviet interest to seek a vantage point in southern Asia from which Russia might eventually move towards a 'warm water port' on the Indian Ocean and might exert leverage against Iran and further the 'encirclement' of China. Perhaps it was because, as a deeply conservative regime, the USSR abhorred disorder where it was in a position to introduce discipline. In this sense Iran was too big, too disorderly and America's interest too obvious. Perhaps it was part of the new 'adventurous' Soviet policy, obvious in Africa, which resulted partly from the change in relative military strength between East and West and partly from the rise in influence in foreign and defence policy decision-making of the Soviet military.[58] Perhaps the Soviets simply seized an opportunity as it presented itself because the US was preoccupied with Iran and the West with its energy and economic problems. It may be that Moscow felt that there would be no Western outcry or, if there was, that *détente* had already reached its limits. The Europeans had decided to accept new nuclear weapons; the Americans were building the MX missile and were moving closer to China, which had won most-favoured trading nation status with the EEC – something the USSR had signally failed to get; and the SALT II Treaty had failed to win Congressional support.

Perhaps the Soviets felt that any outcry would be shortlived and that a Soviet peace offensive later in 1980 and the *bonhomie* generated by the Moscow Olympics in the summer of 1980 would lead the world to accept the new reality in Afghanistan. Brezhnev may have reckoned that Carter would not be able to carry the Western alliance with him in any sanctions he employed against Russia. The *détente*-minded Brezhnev may have been temporarily outvoted in the Politburo[59] or possibly the Politburo felt that Babrak Karmal would be welcomed after the problems created by Hafizollah Amin, that Karmal had ability and support and that a show of Soviet strength might be enough to quieten the rebels and stiffen the Afghan army into backing their new President. Inhabited by traditionalist, fiercely independent, warlike peoples, Afghanistan was no Czechoslovakia and 100,000 second-rate troops were not enough to conquer the country quickly. Only in February 1980 did the Red Army in Afghanistan begin to replace its reservists with regulars and only then were efforts made to curb Western journalists who had had free rein until then, something the Russians would never have allowed if they had envisaged a bloodbath.

The reaction by the West and the Third World was apparently stronger than Moscow expected. Criticized by the Muslim world, in the UN, by Yugoslavia and failing to win support from Romania, she also suffered an embargo of US grain and restricted access to American fishing waters. The United States cut technology exports and her boycott of the Moscow Olympics was supported by West Germany and Japan among others. The reaction of America's allies was varied but they all demonstrated concern over the Soviet action. Western countries and the EEC moved to suspend, not renew or raise, the interest rates of government-backed credits to the USSR. Afghanistan created a new perception of the USSR. For a time at least, the Soviet image of Misha, the smiling teddy bear symbol of the Moscow Olympics, was over-shadowed by the older vision of the Russian bear: 'The he-bear in his pride.'[60]

# Ten

# THE SOVIET UNION AND EASTERN EUROPE

In 1945 the annexed and occupied areas of Eastern Europe represented a huge potential accretion of power to the USSR. Much of this area was devastated by war and was inhabited by people who were homeless, demoralized and disoriented, and who moreover, had little affection for the USSR. Only in Czechoslovakia had Soviet troops been welcomed with any great enthusiasm. The Red Army portrayed itself as the great liberator, which of course it was, but to Romania, Hungary, Bulgaria, East Germany, the Baltic states and parts of Poland and Karelia it came and behaved as a conqueror.[1]

In all the occupied countries, coalition governments were set up in which local communists played prominent parts until, in 1947 and 1948, they took over the governments. Albania was 'liberated' by the Yugoslavs and adopted a communist government as did Yugoslavia. Elsewhere, the patterns of communist take-over were so similar as to prompt the idea that not only was Stalin intent on using Eastern Europe as a buffer, but that he always had intended to communize his satellites (Map 10).

In Hungary, early in 1947, the CP accused its major coalition partner, the Smallholders' Party, of treason. Arrests were made and on 29 May 1947 the government of Imre Nagy resigned. In the ensuing elections the CP emerged as the largest, but not the controlling, party. However, on 1 November 1947, the communists formed a government and dissolved the other parties. Much the same happened in Bulgaria. On 26 August the Peasant Party was dissolved as Fascist and on 23 September 1947 Nicolai Petkov, leader of the Agrarian Party, was hanged for 'plotting a *coup*'. On 11 December 1947 Georgi Dimitrov assumed the leadership of a predominantly communist cabinet. In Romania the communists dissolved the Peasant Party on 10 October 1947. Its leader Iliu Maniu was sentenced to 'life' on 29 October. King Michael abdicated and went into exile on 1 January 1948. In Poland the leader of the 'London Poles' Mikolajczyk fled the country, and his Peasant Party was dissolved on 21

The Iron Curtain (1948)
Germany after 1945
1937 frontiers
Allied control zones of Germany and Austria
Ceded to USSR by Britain and USA
Annexed by USSR in 1945
States which became Communist 1945–48
Yugoslav gains from Italy 1945

FINLAND

Porkkala

Leningrad

SWEDEN

North Sea

*Baltic Sea*

ESTONIA

LATVIA

LITHUANIA

DENMARK

USSR

AMERICAN

EAST PRUSSIA
*Ann. byPoland*

Szczecin (Stettin)

Bremen    Berlin

BRITISH

ANNEXED BY POLAND

Warsaw

POLAND

NETHERLANDS

BELGIUM

FRENCH

AMERICAN

Prague

CZECHOSLOVAKIA

FRANCE

FRENCH

USSR

Vienna

Budapest

USA BR

AUSTRIA

HUNGARY

SWITZERLAND

FR

Trieste

ROMANIA

Bucharest

Belgrade

ITALY

*Adriatic Sea*

YUGOSLAVIA

BULGARIA

Sofia

ALBANIA

COMMUNIST ACTIVITY 1946–49

*Aegean Sea*

TURKEY

GREECE

0        km        500
0        miles      300

Map 10     Eastern Europe, 1945–8

November 1947. Only in Czechoslovakia did it take longer. On 25 February 1948 the communist Klement Gottwald formed a government, and on 10 March its only non-communist, Foreign Minister Jan Masaryk died in mysterious circumstances.[2] When President Beneš resigned, the communists were supreme in Prague, and an Eastern European process, which began with the Bulgarian, Hungarian and Romanian peace treaties on 10 February 1947, the rejection of Marshall Aid, and included the signing of bilateral trade treaties with the USSR,[3] was completed by the establishment of the Cominform on 5 October 1947.[4] But, although the Russians were prominent in the Romanian affair, nowhere else did it appear that Soviet troops or personnel played direct parts in the communist take-overs. Indeed, the USA estimated that there were only 500 Soviet troops in Czechoslovakia in June 1948.[5]

Of course, Soviet action did not need to be overt, for the 'Soviet presence' and the perceptions by cowed populations of the power and intentions of the Russians could have been enough to encourage local communists who could call on Soviet troops if needed. It is the case also, that huge numbers of East and West Europeans had been radicalized by the war. The old order was swept away and there was widespread support for the reforms that were very quickly introduced and not just by communists.

All the East Europeans either nationalized or shared among the peasants the large land holdings, and only in Hungary was this done at the behest of the Red Army. Banks, mines, insurance companies and large-scale industry were also nationalized.[6] From the start, the East Europeans were not expected slavishly to copy the Soviet economic and political models in all respects although they were expected to toe the foreign policy line. It may be that the turning point in Stalin's attitude to the East Europeans came when, despite his obvious displeasure, Czechoslovakia and Poland wanted to accept Marshall Aid and had to be dissuaded from so doing. Thereafter, Cominform introduced a formal web of control over the bloc parties and a Stalinist reign of terror began in Eastern Europe. Cominform endorsed collectivization as the only appropriate path to socialism, and Polish and East German claims to separate roads to socialism were rejected. However, Yugoslavia's defection from Cominform and her split with the USSR in 1948 (see pages 164–5) prompted a Stalinist purge throughout Eastern Europe of Titoists and those communists who owed their positions not to Stalin, but to their own ability, popularity or records of partisan activity. In Bulgaria, the chief victim was Traicho Kostov, a Deputy Premier; in Hungary, a former Interior Minister, Laszlo Rajk; in Czechoslovakia, ex-Party General Secretary Rudolf Slansky and ex-Foreign Minister Vlado Clementis were, among many others, executed on charges of treason. Others, including Wladyslaw Gomulka in Poland, Gustav Husak in Czechoslovakia and Janos Kadar in Hungary, were merely gaoled in operations which silenced public expressions of nationalist or patriotic sentiment in the bloc for the rest of Stalin's years.[7]

With Stalin gone there was general agreement in the Kremlin on the great potential value to the USSR of Eastern Europe. The stationing of Soviet troops in the bloc allowed the USSR to pursue a forward defence policy against NATO but this defence would be strengthened if the East Europeans contributed to it. The co-ordination of their economies in the Council for Mutual Economic Assistance, Comecon, founded in January 1948, allowed the USSR undisputed access to the raw materials and products within a large 'rouble area' in which hard currency was not needed for trade. Control over their communization and party development allowed the expansion of Soviet-type communism, and therefore supported Moscow's claims that communism was the wave of the future. The East Europeans also represented votes in the UNO and diplomatic support for Soviet foreign policy in a world in which, until the colonial empires were dismantled, the Western powers could always drum up more international support for their actions than could the USSR.

Nevertheless, the Soviet hold over Eastern Europe was frequently resented by the East Europeans on the political grounds that it was communist and on the traditional grounds that it was Russian. With the creation of new east European nation states after the First World War, enthusiasm for the nineteenth-century 'pan-Slav' idea of a united Slavdom under Russian leadership had virtually died, and Moscow was reminded of this four times in the 1950s. The post-Stalin 'thaw' in the USSR did not immediately happen in Eastern Europe where Stalinist regimes remained intact, but a certain restiveness appeared in some areas. Early in June 1953 rioters in Pilsen in Czechoslovakia tore down Soviet and communist symbols and flags and sacked the town hall. The Czech authorities were able to restore order without Soviet help, but on 16 June 1953 about 110 East Berlin building workers struck against wage cuts. By the next day, the strike spread throughout the DDR and tens of thousands of people rose up in East Berlin in an attempt to throw off Soviet and communist domination and reunify Germany. Better than any other East Europeans, the East Berliners, with their ease of access to West Berlin, were able to contrast the Eastern with the Western ways of life. The revolt was quickly crushed by the Red Army and its occurrence was blamed upon Beria who had advocated a relaxation of control in the satellites.

The Czech and East German incidents confirmed the USSR's free hand in Eastern Europe, for despite America's talk of 'rolling back' the Russians, the West did nothing and implicitly acknowledged Soviet mastery over the region. But Moscow had learned a lesson, and Malenkov's 'new course' was now applied in the Eastern bloc too. Purges ended, their victims were rehabilitated and many political prisoners freed. East German reparations were cancelled. Collectivization of agriculture was halted in the DDR and Hungary, and partially reversed in Poland. These measures were designed to strengthen the Soviet hold over the bloc by removing potential causes of trouble, but whereas national sentiment in the USSR could be used to support the state and communism, in Eastern Europe national feeling inevitably focused on opposition of Soviet communist control.

A further complication was introduced when Khrushchev went to Yugoslavia in mid-1955, apologized to Tito for the Soviet–Yugoslav estrangement and acknowledged that even though Yugoslavia was outside the Soviet bloc, it remained a socialist state. Many in Eastern Europe interpreted this as an admission of Soviet political defeat and a vindication of national communists like Rajk and Slansky who had been executed on Soviet wishes because of their 'Titoism'.

However, the USSR had already prepared in part for the possible effects upon the satellites of the apology to Yugoslavia, by the creation on 14 May 1955 of the Warsaw Pact which bound all the bloc countries in a military alliance under joint, in other words Soviet, command. The Pact formalized Soviet control over bloc forces but it also provided a legal basis for the USSR to keep troops in bloc countries and to intervene if they were deemed to be subject to external threat. Of course, the Warsaw Pact was regarded as militarily necessary to counter the strengthening of NATO when West Germany joined on 9 May 1955.

Pressure mounted for the opportunity to follow the Yugoslav road to communism with its greater freedom of expression, worker participation and direction, and some elements of market forces. This pressure increased when Khrushchev's 'Secret Speech' (see pages 23–6) shattered the myth of Soviet and communist infallibility, exposed Stalin as a mass-murderer and led to a revulsion of feeling by Poles and Hungarians against the Stalinist systems they still had to endure.

On 28 June 1956, 15,000 workers in Poznan, Poland, rioted, demanding freedom, bread and the throwing out of communism and the Russians. Some Polish troops fraternized with the rioters, but the riot was eventually put down at the cost of forty-four demonstrators and eleven troops killed. The problem remained, and during the summer Poland seethed as the rioters' demands were debated in the media. Counter-revolution threatened and the leadership turned to Wladyslaw Gomulka, a communist who had been imprisoned for his nationalist views and only released in 1955. The Russians were furious at Gomulka's emergence as Polish leader. Soviet troops ringed Warsaw. Khrushchev flew to Poland, but the Poles stood firm and threatened war if they did not get their own way.

Gomulka was elected First Secretary of the Polish CP in October 1956, and the Russians acknowledged defeat. Soviet citizens like Polish born Defence Minister Marshal Rokossovsky were withdrawn and the 'Polish October' of limited reforms began. But Khrushchev had recognized, albeit reluctantly, that Gomulka, though a nationalist, was also a communist, and with him in charge Poland might be temperamental but she would remain in the Soviet bloc. Hungary was different. Khrushchev later remarked: 'We would have accepted another Finland but the Hungarians were in the process of bringing back Fascism'.[8]

Nationalist sentiment, some of which was communist, had been growing in Hungary since the death of Stalin, but was fanned by the Secret Speech, the Polish example and the efforts of groups like the Petofi circle which denounced communist rule. Moscow sought to ease tension by ousting Matyas Rakosi and replacing him as party boss by Erno Gerö, with Janos Kadar as his deputy. However, events in Hungary overtook Gerö, a hard-liner, and the man with whom the Russians replaced him on 25 October, Imre Nagy. The strength of feeling was shown on 6 October 1956 when hundreds of thousands of Hungarians joined in a memorial to the memory of the executed communist Laszlo Rajk.

The 'uprising' began when demonstrations on 23 October declared solidarity with Poland. Gerö condemned the demonstrations, and violence erupted between police and crowds. Centres of communist control were attacked and the few Soviet units that were called in were fought off. The Russians withdrew their troops from Budapest and replaced Gerö with Nagy, but concessions merely stimulated more popular demands. On 27 October Nagy formed a new government with non-communist members, including Béla Kovács of the Smallholders' Party and ex-President Zoltán Tildy. On 28 October there was a ceasefire in Budapest, but just as Poland had fuelled Hungary, so too Moscow was aware that the Hungarian example could be contagious. Also, the USSR regarded as provocative Western demands to discuss Hungary in the UN Security Council and the continuing incitement of the Hungarian populace by the American-financed Radio Free Europe.

Political prisoners were released, including Cardinal Mindszenty, the long-imprisoned head of the Hungarian Catholic Church. Workers' councils were introduced in industry, and the remaining collective farms disbanded. But although the USSR declared, on 30 October, her adherence to the principles of non-intervention in the internal affairs of other states and offered to negotiate the withdrawal of Soviet troops from the socialist states, events had probably gone too far. The very next day, Britain and France began their attack on Egypt and so drew down a smokescreen to cloud Soviet actions from the world's eye. The Soviet offer of 30 October may well have been genuine, but it was inadequate. Hungarian public opinion outstripped Nagy's efforts to keep control, buy off the insurgents, satisfy the people and remain in the Soviet bloc. On 1 November the Nagy government prepared to declare a multi-party democracy, leave the Warsaw Pact and become neutral. On 4 November Soviet forces attacked Budapest and other cities, and by 9 November it was over. Janos Kadar was installed as party leader, Nagy was eventually executed and order was restored, but at a cost of 7,000 Soviet and 30,000 Hungarian lives and a legacy of bitterness.

Gomulka, Tito and Mao all condemned the Soviet intervention on 24 October but they all approved the Red Army's action on 4 November. Hungary pointed a lesson to Eastern Europe and the world, that Moscow would allow domestic deviation from the Soviet model, but she would not allow the ideological and military glacis, upon which her conventional defences in the west were based, to be dismantled. However, Moscow did acquiesce in the loss of Albania when the Tirana leadership took China's part in the Sino–Soviet split. In 1961 the USSR was forced to withdraw from the submarine base at Valona and in December 1961 Tirana severed relations with Moscow. The Albanians did not leave the Warsaw Pact formally until 1968, but their participation in the Pact ended in 1961 and was allowed to end because to have attempted to bring Albania to heel would have destroyed Khrushchev's continued attempts at *rapprochement* with Yugoslavia and would have harmed Moscow's name at a delicate time in world communist affairs when the Sino–Soviet split had come into the open and Moscow wanted support from her allies. Besides, Albania did not share a border with a Pact state and a military operation against her would have had to have been seaborne and the Soviet navy was not yet equipped to mount and resupply amphibious operations.

In Stalin's time Eastern Europe was a wasting asset, 'a secret policeman's paradise', but the events of 1956 and the trouble with China encouraged Moscow to rethink its attitude to the East Europeans. Khrushchev tried to develop Comecon which had been rather inactive until it was used to handle economic aid to Kadar's Hungary in 1957. The East Europeans wanted to develop balanced economies but Comecon tried to create one East European economy where Czechoslovakia and the DDR would concentrate on heavy industry; Romania, Bulgaria and Hungary would produce food and raw materials; and Poland would do both. The USSR planned to stand outside, but co-ordinate Comecon, and act as the dynamo and supplier of technology, just as the USA had been the power base behind the West's economic recovery. None of the bloc countries approved this Soviet scheme, and Georghiu Dej of Romania led the opposition by skilfully exploiting the Sino–Soviet split to free Romania from Comecon control. Nevertheless, Comecon was given a constitution in 1960 and an international executive in 1962 and its deployment of technical skills and investment resources did play a part in the economies of the region.

More significant was the role ascribed to the Warsaw Pact. In the late 1950s it began to co-ordinate the training of the East European armed forces and re-equip them to deal with their new military tasks of maintaining in power their own communist governments, contributing to their own defence and being prepared to participate in offence if necessary. Through its Political Consultative Committee, the Pact transmitted Soviet policy, co-ordinated its implementation and prepared a solid Eastern bloc front.[9] It had a joint military command, based in Moscow, the commander of which was always a Russian (as the Commander-in-Chief of NATO was always an American), but the Pact high command was an integral part of the Soviet Ministry of Defence and the Pact's air defences were fully integrated into the Soviet air defence system. As part of Pact co-ordination, senior Soviet officers were based in bloc capitals, but there were no comparable East European missions in Moscow.

The Pact forces were reorganized between 1956–60. They were slimmed down by 2.5 million men, given more modern, although often obsolescent, equipment and made more mobile. Privileges enjoyed by Soviet troops in Eastern Europe were withdrawn, as were those Soviet officers in the higher ranks of the Pact forces, such as Minister of Defence, Marshal Rokossovsky in Poland and General Panchevski in Bulgaria. East European forces were 're-nationalized'. Some of the more obvious signs of Soviet domination were ended and a military career made more attractive to East Europeans. This in turn may have strengthened the reliability of the Pact forces. Beginning in September 1961, Pact forces were involved in multi-national field manoeuvres, which improved their efficiency and national standing. Interestingly, the Hungarian forces, reconstituted after 1956, were not deemed fit to join in major Pact exercises until 1966.

No large-scale multi-national exercises were held in Romania and Bulgaria after 1964, and neither state has a Soviet garrison, unlike the other Pact states. The absence of Soviet troops encouraged Romania's search for autonomy, but Bulgaria remained – and remains – the most determinedly loyal of all the Pact states. Bulgarian leadership was so dependent on Khrushchev's favour that his fall in 1964 led to a – failed – military *coup* in Sofia early in 1965.

The importance of the bloc to the USSR increased as the Sino–Soviet split deepened in the 1960s. Pact forces came to play an actual and not just a nominal role in the common defence and intra-Comecon trade increased. As one writer commented: 'The USSR is unusually dependent upon its political transplants in Eastern Europe. Frequent cross-nation exchanges among government and Party personnel coupled with appropriate doctrinal interpretations, function to preserve something of the weathered and fragmented political faith in international communism.'[10] For this reason, the Prague Spring of 1968 was not allowed to run its course.

By 1968 the USSR had to contend with crisis with China; an unpredictable America, deeply embroiled in Vietnam; the possibility that a Right-wing Republican could win the American Presidential elections of autumn 1968 and usher in a new phase of the Cold War; and the possibility that America's 1967 'bridge-building' to Eastern Europe and the beginnings of Bonn's *Ostpolitik* might unsettle Eastern Europe. In this context, the sudden liberalization of Czechoslovakia in 1968, looked on approvingly by Yugoslavia, Romania and the West European CPs, may have seemed to Moscow like the beginning of a trend which could have unravelled communist control over the Eastern bloc.

On 5 January 1968 the Stalinist Antonin Novotny was replaced by Alexander Dubček as First Secretary of the Czechoslovak CP. Novotny's departure was partly a response to popular and party wishes to move away from the deadening effects of a regime under which the economy had atrophied and morale had sunk, and partly to do with the complicated issues thrown up by the ethnic balance of Czechs and Slovaks in a federal state traditionally dominated by Czechs. Dubček's pedigree was impeccable. Brought up and educated in the USSR, a graduate of the Higher Party School in Moscow, unswervingly loyal to the party and the USSR, he was also a Slovak who was never in control of the battle between reformers and hardliners that continued in the Czechoslovak party throughout 1968. In January 1968 one of his major opponents, Jiri Hendrych, Novotny's right-hand man, described him as 'an honest man but he is indecisive'.[11]

Moscow was happy with Dubček's appointment and although knowing of his ambitions to reform the party, Brezhnev sent him a message of congratulations. The communiqué after their meeting in Moscow at the end of January 1968 spoke of the 'full identity of views on all questions discussed'.[12] However, it is doubtful if Brezhnev knew the character of the reforms that Dubček planned. The apparatus of censorship and repression ceased to function, the media and public openly discussed the faults of the system and called for democracy. Dubček spoke of the need to make the party the servant and not the master of the people. He endorsed freedom of speech and contact with the outside world. This was the beginning of the Prague Spring which enervated politics and public life in Czechoslovakia. Debate widened and 'one issue led to another as the political onion was unpeeled layer by layer; people watched their television screens spellbound and fought to buy newspapers'.[13]

The Russians were deeply concerned, as was East Germany's Ulbricht. At a meeting of bloc leaders in Prague on 25 February, Dubček publicly pledged Czechoslovakia's loyalty to the 'community of Socialist countries' and singled Ulbricht out to promise 'constant opposition to revanchism in West Germany' and attempted but failed to explain his domestic reforms. On 29 March after Novotny had lost the Presidency to General Svoboda who supported Dubček, Brezhnev warned from Moscow: 'The Communist Party is a party of people who not only think as one but act as one . . . Experience has taught incontrovertibly that the

Party needs firm conscientious discipline both when it leads the masses to revolution and when . . . it fights for the creation of a socialist society.'[14] The very next day, Soviet Deputy Foreign Minister Vladimir Semyonov warned Dubček and Svoboda that unless they kept order Soviet troops would intervene. This threat was underlined by the arrival at Red Army headquarters in Czechoslovakia on 31 March of Soviet Defence Minister Marshal Grechko who empowered the 35,000 Soviet troops stationed in the country to impose martial law if necessary.[15]

The Soviets approved of 'order' above most things, therefore the ferment in Czechoslovakia was dangerous because it was unpredictable, appeared out of control and threatened, with the connivance of Dubček, Svoboda and the new Prime Minister Oldrich Cernik, to demote the Communist Party. Soviet fears were confirmed when the Czech 'Action Programme', *The Czechoslovak Road to Socialism* was published in April 1968. It promised an increase in the power of parliament, freedom of speech and the press, and denounced the mistakes and excesses of Novotny's regime. The party was criticized for the 'monopolistic concentration of power in the hands of Party bodies'. The Programme declared: 'Each member of the Party and Party bodies has not only the right but the duty to act according to his conscience. It is impermissible to restrict communists to these rights, to create an atmosphere of distrust and suspicion of those who voice different opinions, to persecute the minority, under any pretext – as has happened in the past.'[16] The Soviet media attacked the Programme as a return to the bourgeois republic of Masaryk and Beneš, but the Czechs attempted to assuage Moscow's doubts. Dubček and Foreign Minister Jiri Hajek went to Moscow early in May, and the Chairman of the Czech Parliament, Josef Smrkovsky, referred to this visit on 15 May when he said: 'We must understand the fears of the Soviet Union which has in mind not only Czechoslovakia but also the security of the whole socialist camp. Even so, the Soviet comrades declared [on Dubček's visit to Moscow] that they do not want and will not interfere in Czechoslovakia's internal affairs.'[17] But when, on 15 June, the Czechoslovak government proclaimed merely the 'leading role' of the CP and not its supremacy and declared that 'socialist state power must not be a monopoly of any party or parties',[18] then, despite Czechoslovak protestations to the contrary, it must have looked to Moscow as though Czechoslovakia was going the way of Hungary in 1956.

Military threats had already been levelled at Czechoslovakia. Polish and Soviet units exercised near the Czech frontier in May, and the Czech–Polish border was closed during the exercise. At the end of May, Kosygin visited Prague to discuss the 'strengthening of the Warsaw Pact', or closer Soviet control over the Czech forces.

In mid-July Prague received an unambiguous warning in the form of the 'Warsaw letter' delivered after the Warsaw meeting of the USSR, DDR, Poland, Hungary and Bulgaria:

> The development of events in your country evokes deep anxiety in us . . . we cannot agree to have hostile forces push your country off the road of socialism and thus jeopardise the interests of the entire socialist system . . . . Anti-socialist and revisionist forces have laid hands on the press, radio and television . . . A situation has thus arisen which is entirely unacceptable for a socialist country . . .Czechoslovakia can retain her independence and sovereignty only as a socialist country, as a member of the socialist community . . . It is our conviction that a situation has arisen in which the threat to the foundations of socialism in Czechoslovakia jeopardises the common vital interests of other socialist countries . . . . That is why we believe that a decisive rebuff to the forces of anticommunism . . . in Czechoslovakia is not only your task but ours too.[19]

A meeting was held at Cierna on the Czecho–Soviet border where Dubček and his colleagues were confronted by the Soviet Politburo and Czechoslovakia's East European critics. The meeting resolved nothing, although the Czechs thought they had convinced the others of their loyalty to the Warsaw Pact, but on the night of 20 August Soviet, East German, Polish, Hungarian and Bulgarian forces crossed into Czechoslovakia. Apparently the Soviets expected that either the Czechs would rally around a pro-Soviet administration, which they hoped would be formed by a special meeting of the Czech Praesidium on the eve of the invasion or, failing that, pro-Soviet leaders would invite Soviet intervention in the name of the Czech people, and Dubček and company would be arrested. But the Czech people opposed the intervention and supported Dubček. President Svoboda refused to lend his weight to Soviet plans and the Praesidium did not vote out Dubček, Cernik and the rest. After being beaten and questioned in Moscow, Dubček and his colleagues were returned to Prague, but the reforms were reversed, Soviet troops stayed and Dubček was finally removed and replaced by Gustav Husak in April 1969.

The invasion was condemned by Romania, Yugoslavia, China and the West European CPs. It damaged Moscow's standing in the Third World and interrupted *détente*, but not for long. As far as the East Europeans were concerned, it laid the ground rules for *détente* and their relations with the West in what was to become known in the West as the 'Brezhnev Doctrine' or 'Doctrine of Limited Sovereignty'. This was spelt out in November 1968 by Brezhnev:

> When internal and external forces hostile to socialism attempt to turn the development of any socialist country in the direction of the capitalist system, when a threat arises to the cause of socialism in that country, a threat to the security of the socialist commonwealth as a whole – it already becomes not

only a problem for the people of that country, but also a general problem, the
concern of all socialist countries.[20]

In his memoirs Brezhnev dismissed the affair in a few lines: 'During the
situation that endangered Czechoslovakia's socialist gains in 1968, the
Soviet Union, Bulgaria, Hungary, DDR and Poland acted on principles
of socialist solidarity. Performing their international duty they came to
the aid of a fraternal nation.'[21]

The Warsaw Pact proved its usefulness militarily and politicly in the
Czech affair, but the ability of the Czech forces to obey Prague rather
than the Pact led the USSR to reform the Pact's command structure in
1969. The East Europeans were given the appearance of more say in the
common defence, while at the same time creating an integrated command under which the Soviet C-in-C had under his direct control a force
of units drawn from all the Pact forces.[22] However, as an indicator of
their true military worth, the East European armed forces continued to
be poorly equipped compared with Moscow's other friends and allies.
The Red Army had the T-62 tank throughout the 1970s and it was
supplied in numbers to Cuba, North Korea, North Vietnam, Syria,
Libya, Algeria, Iraq and Egypt. The same countries, except North
Korea, also received the high-performance MiG 23 'Flogger' which was
only introduced into Soviet service in 1972. However, by 1979 none of
the Pact countries had received the T-62 and only Czechoslovakia had
received – in 1979 – twelve MiG 23s.[23]

None of the satellites repeated Czechoslovakia's mistake. Riots and
strikes in Poland brought down Gomulka in 1970, shook his successor
Edouard Gierek in 1976 and toppled him in September 1980. These
disturbances resulted initially from economic grievances and, on each
occasion, food-price increases had to be abandoned. By 1980 the Polish
economy was being strangled by its subsidies on food and consumer
goods (estimated at $5.5 billion or 25 per cent of the Polish budget in
1980[24]) and an enormous $17 billion hard currency debt. The USSR had
become accustomed to handling Poland gently, especially after the
election in 1978 of a Polish pope and his visit to his homeland in 1979.
However, Soviet patience was to be sorely tried by the emergence of the
10 million-member free trade union Solidarity, led by the Catholic Lech
Walesa, which won official recognition, the right to strike, a lifting of
censorship and quickly became a focus of Polish loyalty and identity that
communism never had been. Soviet threats were naked, but at least put a
brake on Solidarity's activities and therefore forestalled a half-expected
Soviet invasion.

Elsewhere, Romania was allowed to continue her independent foreign
policy line which had been established in the early 1960s. In April 1964
Romania declared that all communist parties were equal and seven
months later she reduced the length of military service from 2 years to 16

months. Chinese Premier Chou En-lai visited Bucharest in June 1966, relations were opened with West Germany in 1967 and maintained with Israel when the rest of the bloc severed relations in 1967. Romania also received state visits from Presidents Nixon and Ford. Supported by Yugoslavia and China, Romania caused the USSR much embarrassment and was subject to a number of veiled threats – some of them military. In June 1974 she refused the request made by the Soviet C-in-C Warsaw Pact Marshal Yakubovsky that Romania give the USSR a land corridor through the Dobruja, Romania's Black Sea province,[25] the very prospect of which must have alarmed Bucharest, Belgrade, Athens, Ankara and NATO.

In 1976 Romania refused to follow its allies and raise defence spending, and the split between Romania and the rest of the Pact was so marked at the December 1978 Warsaw Pact summit, and diplomatic activity among the other Pact countries so unusual that there was speculation in the Western press that either Romania might be preparing to leave the Pact or that the USSR might be considering resolving its Romania problem, or both. In the event, neither happened and Nicolai Ceausescu remained firmly in control. Essentially Romania could do what others could not because Ceausescu's domestic policies were impeccable. There was no prospect of liberalism contaminating his neighbours or of the CP losing control. Also, geography dictated that Romania remain in the Soviet shadow, whatever her wishes. Czechoslovakia, Hungary and even Poland had Western connections and traditions that Romania did not have. Additionally, if Czechoslovakia or Hungary left the Warsaw Pact, a wedge would be driven into the USSR's defences whereas in purely military terms, a neutral Romania did not need to be a danger to the USSR.

In effect, the embarrassment caused by Romania was partially offset by the propaganda value of being able to point to Bucharest as an example of political pluralism in Eastern Europe, as Moscow could also point to Budapest as an example of economic pluralism in the Pact countries. Orthodox in foreign policy, Hungary introduced market forces in 1968 in its 'new economic mechanism' where the government defined the tax, credit and price guidelines, but enterprises decided their priorities and attempted to maximize profits which were taken as the yardstick of efficiency.

All the East Europeans benefited from *détente* in terms of increased trade with and access to the technology and capital of the West, and because *détente* lessened their dependence upon the USSR. The treaties with West Germany signed by Poland in December 1970, the DDR in December 1972 and Czechoslovakia in December 1973 and the Final Act of the Helsinki European Security Conference in 1975 all answered the frontier questions which had been raised by the Second World War. All three states had had something to fear if West Germany had sought to recreate the Reich of the 1930s. Similarly all the East Europeans stood to benefit if the talks on Mutual and Balanced Force Reductions (MBFR) which began in 1973 (and were still continuing in 1980) actually resulted in troop reductions because any reduction of Soviet garrisons would have entailed greater freedom.

Eastern Europe also suffered from the popular expectations raised by the Helsinki Agreement's provisions on human rights. The Orlov group in the USSR had parallels in Czechoslovakia's Charter 77, Poland's Workers' Defence Committee and supporters of singer Wolf Bierman and chemistry professor Robert Havemann in the DDR. The satellites dealt with dissidents as did Moscow, but in Poland protest was widely based among workers and intellectuals and had the often explicit blessing of clergymen if not the Church itself.

The East Europeans provided diplomatic support in the UNO against the West and against China, and a platform from which to try to negotiate favourable trading links with the EEC. They also provided ideological reassurance and sometimes acted as proxies of the USSR. The DDR especially gave active support to national liberation movements in Africa and sent aid and personnel to Angola, Ethiopia, Mozambique and South Yemen. By 1980 Comecon's membership had grown to include Mongolia, Cuba and Vietnam, and it had association arrangements with Finland, Guyana and occasional links with Yugoslavia and North Korea.

Although the Comecon energy bond was expected to weaken in the 1980s if the USSR could no longer guarantee to increase oil deliveries, the economic links were extremely important. In the first nine months of 1978, the socialist states accounted for 59 per cent of total Soviet trade whereas the West's share was 29 per cent. Also, the East Europeans contributed about 50 per cent of joint investments in the USSR in 1975, totalling 500 million roubles, but during the Tenth Plan from 1976–80 this total was expected to be up to ten billion roubles. Comecon contributed money and expertise to major development projects in the USSR, including the 1733-mile (2,772 kilometres) gas pipeline from Orenburg in south-east Russia to Uzhgorod on the western border, a 750-kilovolt powerline linking the Ukraine with Eastern Europe and numbers of major industrial complexes.[26] The East Europeans expanded trade with the West in the 1970s, but intra-bloc trade had helped all their economies, and Hungary and the DDR had developed higher standards of living than the USSR, partly because of internal factors but partly because it was Moscow's policy to keep the East Europeans quiescent even if it sometimes meant treating them in economic terms more favourably than Soviet citizens.

*Eleven*

# THE BREAK-UP OF MONOLITHIC COMMUNISM

Before the First World War the Russian Bolsheviks were just one of many nationally based political groups who considered themselves heirs of the ideas of Karl Marx. Debate, argument and polemic between and within the national groups was constant and often bitter, but all the groups were more or less equal in their ideological legitimacy. The Russian Revolution changed that. Thereafter it was natural that communist parties looked for example, inspiration and guidance to the successful Soviet communists who had actually seized and kept power. When the Communist International or Comintern was set up in 1919 to encourage the overthrow of capitalism it was natural that it should be based in Moscow.

In Stalin's time the Comintern and foreign communist parties became subordinate to the state interests of the USSR, not just to its revolutionary leadership. Indeed foreign CPs obeyed instructions from Moscow even when these were harmful to their national interests.[1] By the late 1940s Moscow had become accustomed to the obedience of other CPs, which were all clients rather than equals.

From 1917 onwards an essential feature of Soviet policy was to maintain communist unity, which actually meant the Soviet direction of world communism. But this was easier to effect before the Second World War when only the USSR and Mongolia had communist regimes than after, when communism seized power in Eastern Europe and the Far East. Once in power, communist parties discovered national interests – as had the CPSU earlier – which sometimes conflicted with those of their co-ideologists.[2] The satellite states had to subordinate their national interests to Moscow, but in the case of communist parties outside the USSR's physical control, this did not happen. National interests were exerted at the expense of the Soviet Union, and the communist monolith was shattered. Yugoslavia, Albania and China broke away from Moscow's hold. New international centres of communist authority appeared in Belgrade, Peking, Havana and Hanoi.

The emergence of Eurocommunism weakened Moscow's ideological leadership still further.

It was a difficult experience for the CPSU to accommodate itself to the collapse of its unquestioned paramountcy in world communism.[3] But whereas most of Moscow's disputes were on ideological grounds – or at least couched in ideological language – the Moscow–Belgrade split was on a straightforward power politics basis.

Alone of the countries of occupied Europe, except the USSR, Yugoslavia under the leadership of Josip Broz Tito's communist partisans, liberated itself from German rule. The communist regime in Belgrade enjoyed far more popular support and commitment than any other in Eastern Europe. This secure domestic base, with the absence of Soviet troops, ensured that Belgrade's relations with Moscow were unique in the Soviet bloc. Tito took an independent line from the start. He complained about the behaviour of Soviet troops passing through north-east Yugoslavia in early 1945. More openly anti-Western than Stalin, he nearly came to blows with British forces over rival Italian–Yugoslav claims to the area around Trieste in 1945, and in 1946 his forces shot down two US aircraft. In both these instances, the Soviet Union had to intervene diplomatically to calm the situation down.

There were disagreements underlying Soviet–Yugoslav relations, apart from differing attitudes towards the West. Belgrade disliked the USSR's activities in joint stock companies which exploited Yugoslavia's natural resources and Moscow was suspicious of Yugoslavia's hold over Albania. On the other hand, Tito and his senior colleagues had the emotional and ideological attachment to Moscow of communists the world over. Tito had participated in the Russian Revolution, and there was no suggestion of Yugoslavia's seeking ideological independence from Moscow immediately after the war. Indeed the choice of Belgrade for the headquarters of Cominform was indicative of Yugoslavia's standing in the communist world. Rather, the split came when Stalin's opposition to three related strands of Yugoslav foreign policy became apparent early in 1948.

Tito too had territorial ambitions. He was the main supporter of the communists in the Greek civil war and had designs on Albania where his supporters were dominant. In 1947 discussions in Yugoslavia with the Bulgarian leader Georgi Dimitrov produced the Bled Agreement on a united south Balkan federation to include the Macedonian provinces of Yugoslavia, Bulgaria and – apparently – Greece. The South Slav federation was also, it seems, to include the non-Slav Albanians, but in February 1948 Stalin, who had not been consulted on the federation, summoned the Yugoslavs and Bulgarians to Moscow. In tense meetings Stalin vetoed the federation and objected to Belgrade's plan to send troops to Albania at 'the invitation' of Albania's Enver Hoxha. He also demanded: 'The uprising in Greece must be stopped.' Dimitrov fell into line, but Tito did not, and on 28 June, four days after the commencement of the Berlin Blockade, the Cominform expelled Yugoslavia and called for a *coup* against Tito.

Stalin was concerned that an independent Belgrade might cut across his foreign policy interests and that Tito's Balkan ambitions might involve the USSR in a conflict with the USA in the eastern Mediterranean. Ultimately, Tito was outside Soviet control and refused to come inside. As Tito said: 'Stalin envisaged us being his satellites after the war . . . . He did everything possible to provoke a fight and had his forces massed on our frontiers in case the opportunity should arise.'[4] Stalin did not invade Yugoslavia because he could not be sure how the West would react, but he could be reasonably certain that the Yugoslav forces could and would put up more resistance than could be overcome with the forces at his immediate disposal in Eastern Europe. But an economic blockade did not work and neither did the expected *coup* materialize. By 1950 Tito had mended some of his fences in the West, and the Korean war made any Soviet military adventure against Yugoslavia too risky, but Yugoslavia remained a defeat and a serious problem for Moscow. Yugoslav independence in foreign affairs, freedom from external control and the ability to deviate from the Soviet ideological model were examples that attracted many people in the satellites thereafter.

Recognizing this, Khrushchev went to Yugoslavia in May 1955. A partial reconciliation was achieved on the basis of a Soviet apology, although Tito did not accept Khrushchev's claim that Beria had been to blame for the original split. He refused to re-enter the Soviet fold and forced Khrushchev to acknowledge 'different forms of socialist development'.[5] In his difficulties with Poland and Hungary in 1956 Khrushchev sought Tito's advice, but the Hungarian uprising discredited Khrushchev's conciliatory line towards Yugoslavia in the eyes of many in the Kremlin and when contacts between Moscow and Belgrade resumed in August 1957, they were not as cordial as they had been a year earlier.

Soviet intervention in Hungary alarmed Belgrade, as did the invasion of Czechoslovakia twelve years later, and both served to reaffirm the Soviet–Yugoslav split. After 1956 Yugo–Soviet relations were ambivalent and never close. Yugoslavia threatened Moscow's position in the communist world for the following reasons: her leadership enjoyed mass support; her market-forces socialism, worker participation and landowning peasantry were envied by neighbours; her willingness to allow her citizens free use of their passports demonstrated a confidence lacking elsewhere in Eastern Europe; she had a leading role in the Non-Aligned Movement and a respected voice in the world. Alternatively, Yugoslavia remained communist and supported many of Moscow's aims, if only indirectly.[6] She had a freedom of action on the international stage possessed by none of the satellites. She also provided another channel to the Third World if the USSR wanted to make diplomatic use of her. Additionally, Yugoslavia took 3.3 per cent of the USSR's exports in 1977, equivalent to 1,093.5 million roubles, and was one of Comecon's major trading partners.

However, the context of Yugo–Soviet relations changed in the late 1970s. Belgrade's relations with China, which had been severed by Mao in 1958, were restored, culminating in a visit to Yugoslavia by Chairman Hua Guofeng in August 1978 and paralleled by the collapse of the Sino–Albania alliance and the consequent muted Albanian overtures to the USSR for the first time in twenty years. Chinese approval gave Yugoslavia even more ideological status than hitherto, but created the risk of Moscow seeing Belgrade not just as a maverick but as Peking's partner. Besides, the death of Tito on 4 May 1980 and his succession by an untried collective leadership introduced a new variable into the equation. Important though Yugoslavia was to the USSR she was overshadowed as a geopolitical and ideological problem for the last twenty, if not twenty-five, years of Tito's life by China. Yugoslavia was a constant irritant and a potential danger by example, but China evoked a visceral response in the USSR.

The Sino–Soviet split became public in 1960, although it was not immediately recognized by the West, possibly because the acrimonious Sino–Soviet debate was couched in ideological terms. Neither country criticized the other openly until 1962, before which the Chinese lambasted Yugoslavia and the Soviets inveighed against Albania. The split centred on Chinese rejection of Soviet leadership, especially on the issue of relations with the West and attitudes towards the 'Revolution'. Peking continued to preach and promote the inevitability of war with capitalism, but Khrushchev argued for coexistence. A sharp debate went on between Moscow and Peking after Khrushchev's Secret Speech (see Chapter 3) advocated coexistence with the West. At the November 1957 Moscow Conference of sixty-four communist parties, Khrushchev only obtained the united 'Moscow Declaration' by including in it Mao's thesis that 'revisionism' was a greater sin than 'dogmatism'. In return the Chinese acquiesced in Moscow's leadership of world communism.

'Revisionism' differed from orthodox Marxist–Leninism in that it no longer claimed that the transition from capitalism to socialism need be accomplished by war. The Soviets did not believe that they were guilty of 'revisionism', which remained a heresy in the USSR. Rather, they claimed, as Lenin had done before them, the authority to interpret Marxist–Leninism to suit the times and the circumstances. When these interpretations, or 'revisions', were rejected by China, the Chinese were accused of 'dogmatism', of clinging too tightly to an outdated dogma. Khrushchev explained the ideological differences at the June 1960 conference of the Romanian CP when he declared: 'We do not intend to yield to provocations and to deviate from the general line of our foreign policy . . . This is a policy of coexistence . . . one cannot mechanically repeat now on this question what . . . Lenin said many decades ago on imperialism, and go on asserting that imperialist wars are inevitable until socialism triumphs throughout the world.'[7]

At the Moscow Conference of eighty-one CPs in November 1960, Albania's Enver Hoxha vilified Khrushchev, and China's Deng Xiaoping accused Moscow of betraying the Revolution and threatened that China intended to wrest the leadership of world communism from the USSR.[8] The final conference declaration papered over the cracks, but the split had surfaced earlier during the Afro–Asian Solidarity Conference at Conakry in Guinea in May 1960.[9] It is interesting to note that the public Sino–Soviet rows coincided with the pricking of Khrushchev's foreign policy bubble. After the optimism of Camp David, the U-2 affair and the failed Paris Summit gave Khrushchev's critics ammunition to use against his 'revisionist' policies.

With hindsight it is obvious that China and the USSR came together reluctantly in the late 1940s. The Red Army turned over Japanese weapons to the Chinese communists in 1945–6, but at the same time it looted Manchuria of some $2 billion of industrial equipment. Stalin urged caution on Mao in his civil war with the Nationalists and only withdrew recognition of Nationalist China five months before the proclamation of the People's Republic of China in October 1949.

While the West was concerned that a communist China would augment Soviet power, Stalin had the example to look to of Yugoslavia, another state where independent communists came to power by their own efforts. Certainly, communist China gave Stalin greater authority in the world as the spokesman of world communism and certainly China helped balance America's hold over Japan, but Moscow always treated the Chinese as less than full partners. Even in the spring of 1949 the Russians concluded economic agreements with the Nationalists in Sinkiang and the communists in Manchuria as though these were independent states. A thirty-year Treaty of Friendship, Alliance and Mutual Assistance signed by China and the USSR in 1950 was followed by a grant of $300 million of Soviet credits to China. This amounted to 50 cents per Chinese, a sum miniscule in proportion to the needs of a country which had been at war since 1927. The treaty emphasized the relationship between the two. It was Mao's first trip abroad and he had to stay two months in Moscow before the discussions were completed. He had to agree to the independence under Soviet tutelage of Mongolia and to joint stock companies in Manchuria and Sinkiang. In return, the Manchurian Railway and its industry were to be returned to China by 1952, but Port Arthur, a 'symbol of Russian imperialism on Chinese soil', was not returned to China until 1955. Only after China entered the

Korean war did Moscow provide military aid, for which Peking had to pay $2 billion.

It is interesting that after Stalin's death the Chinese demanded the return of Mongolia to Chinese sovereignty, and the Soviet commercial agreements with Manchuria and Sinkiang (the 'East Turkestan People's Republic) were phased out. Nevertheless, Moscow provided China with considerable aid. She provided the technical blueprints for and helped build 211 major industrial projects. Up to 10,000 Soviet 'experts' worked in China and about 10,000 Chinese were trained in the USSR which took about 50 per cent of China's exports. Nevertheless, China never received as much Soviet aid as she wanted, and Mao was angered at receiving less than non-communist Egypt and India. Perhaps the Chinese delayed breaking with Moscow because they hoped for lavish aid throughout the 1950s. It may be that Mao was taken in by Khrushchev's boasts about the USSR's economic performance. Mao visited Moscow in October 1957 in the euphoric atmosphere engendered by Sputnik, unaware that Sputnik represented the tip of only a small – compared with the USA – iceberg and that performance in the rest of the economy was sagging. In December 1957 the Chinese claimed: 'The absolute superiority of the Soviet Union in inter-continental ballistic missiles has placed the striking capabilities of the United States in . . . an inferior position.'[10]

In fact, it was Mao's presupposition that there was a united world communist movement that led to the split. Mao believed that the communists had at their joint disposal the weapon which would allow 'a fight to the finish . . . against all who dared oppose the irresistible march towards communism.'[11] He apparently envisaged united communist action against capitalism and was prepared to run the risk of a world war, which he thought communism would win if only because more communists could survive a nuclear war since there were more of them. He also envisaged a movement clinging to orthodox Marxist–Leninism, as interpreted by China, and promoting world revolution. But Khrushchev was moving towards a *modus vivendi* with the West which offered the prospect of a settlement in Europe and greater Soviet influence in the world without having to fight for it. He was aware of the limitations of Soviet nuclear and economic strength and had no wish to be pushed by China's unsophisticated and naïve belligerence into a situation where his bluff could be called and he would be humiliated, or worse, by an America whose military supremacy he recognized even if Mao did not.

Of course the hardline Chinese were simply echoing the warlike line promulgated by Khrushchev at the time of his struggle with Malenkov when he too had claimed that nuclear war would destroy capitalism but not socialism. It is ironic that Khrushchev enjoyed Mao's support in that power struggle. On the eve of the Twentieth Congress he was endorsed by Mao who claimed that 'the great successes of the USSR in foreign and domestic policy in recent years are inseparable from the correct leadership of the well-tried Central Committee of the CPSU headed by Comrade Khrushchev'.[12] The irony is compounded by the poor relations between Khrushchev and Mao, the mutual lack of comprehension and sympathy, Mao's claim to equality with Khrushchev once Stalin was gone and Khrushchev's open distrust of the Chinese. In 1954 he returned from China to claim to his colleagues: 'War with China is inevitable. During my visit to Peking . . . everyone was unbelievably courteous and ingratiating, but I saw through their hypocrisy'.[13] The next year, he even admitted to Chancellor Adenauer of West Germany: 'China already has 600 million inhabitants who live on a handful of rice. Each year there are 12 million more. How is it going to end? . . . I beg you to help us resolve our difficulties with China.'[14]

Prior to the 1960 communist conferences, Moscow and Peking differed on numerous issues. China objected strongly to the Secret Speech and claimed she had been inadequately consulted over it. Khrushchev did not consult the Chinese during the Middle East crises of 1957 and 1958, and refused Chinese encouragement to become embroiled in Iraq in 1958. His *détente* with and visit to America angered the Chinese. His refusal to give them adequate support against the USA over the offshore islands of Quemoy and Matsu[15] and his neutrality in 1959 when China and India clashed in the Himalayas struck the Chinese as a betrayal of the Sino–Soviet treaty.

Furthermore, Mao rejected Khrushchev's proposals in 1959 to build a Soviet controlled radio station on the south-west China coast to maintain contact with the USSR's submarines in the Pacific; and he rejected any suggestion that China should be linked in an East–West diplomatic package with West Germany where both should remain non-nuclear. In December 1957, Khrushchev had promised nuclear aid to China, but he revoked this in June 1959 when it became apparent that he was not going to get the joint control over foreign policy and retention of control of nuclear warheads that he wanted. The Chinese retaliated by attacking 'revisionism', and Khrushchev tried to bring them to heel by abruptly withdrawing the 1,390 Soviet industrial specialists and their blueprints from China. Although this action was intended to remind the Chinese how dependent they were on Soviet technological assistance, in fact, it stiffened the Chinese resolve to become self-sufficient. As Sino–Soviet trade dropped in volume the links between the two states grew weaker.

Efforts at reconciliation failed. Moscow broke off relations with Albania in December 1961. The split grew to include criticisms of each other's social system, and old ethnic and cultural antagonisms surfaced. Khrushchev's successors made concerted efforts to heal the schism, but when Vice Premier Chou En-lai's visit to Moscow in November 1964 proved fruitless, the Politburo turned to the idea of an international communist conference to endorse the USSR's stance. But, by this time, even the appearance of unity was difficult to create. Twenty-six CPs were invited to Moscow in March 1965, but only nineteen attended. The World Communist Conference in June 1969, which had been delayed 8 months because of the problems in Czechoslovakia, was only attended by seventy-five·parties out of a total of 111, while the basic conference resolution on communist unity was in fact ratified by sixty-one parties only. Of the fourteen ruling parties, those of Yugoslavia, North Korea, China, North Vietnam and Albania did not attend and Cuba sent only an observer. Some of the European parties, notably the British, Dutch, Italian, Romanian and Swedish, objected to the principle of casting a fellow CP out of the world communist movement. The Kremlin gave way to demands from the Romanian and Italian parties that conference proceedings should be reported, with the result that speeches by foreign communists appeared in the Soviet press even though they were sometimes highly critical of the Soviet invasion of Czechoslovakia.

This pluralism at the conference, together with the absence of the East and South-East Asian CPs, emphasized the ideological and geopolitical natures of the split. Nevertheless, the conference was a qualified success for Brezhnev who presided over it. At least the schism did not spread. The Romanians and Italians did not go the way of the Chinese. Also, in her absence, China was not able to defend herself against a number of criticisms, notably that she had prolonged the split by rejecting Soviet offers of reconciliation; that her Cultural Revolution from 1966–8 was offensive to many communist hierarchies because it involved an apparent diminution of party control; that her instigation of armed clashes with Soviet troops earlier in 1969 showed her to be an aggressive, expansionist and unpredictable threat to world peace, especially in view of the first Chinese H-bomb test on 17 June 1967.

Until 1969 the Sino–Soviet split remained a war of words, and one that was relatively muted during the Cultural Revolution as China turned in on herself. The 'filthy Soviet revisionist swine' were accused of betraying the Revolution at home, in the Third World and in their relations with the West. In their turn the Chinese were arraigned for 'petty-bourgeois revolution-mongering', and 'military great power chauvinism with pretensions to world hegemony'.[16]

The Sino–Soviet split was mirrored throughout the world. Many CPs split into pro-Moscow and pro-Peking factions and Soviets and Chinese competed for influence in the Third World. But the USSR mounted a very effective political campaign against China in the middle and late 1960s. When China sought to exclude the USSR from the second Afro–Asian Conference in Algiers in 1965, Soviet pressure brought about its cancellation. Moscow's mediation at Tashkent in January 1966 over the dispute between Pakistan and India established her as an Asian great power and confirmed her close links with India. Also, by stepping up her help to North Vietnam, the USSR prised open the solid bloc of pro-

Chinese Asian CPs, confounded Chinese criticism that Moscow was no longer interested in world revolution, diverted American attention from Europe and forced the Chinese to stand guard against the USA in the south while the USSR reinforced her troops along the 4,150-mile (6,677 km) Sino–Soviet frontier.

From the beginning there was a military dimension to the Sino–Soviet split, and Soviet actions both reflected Soviet fears and served as implicit threats to China. In 1964 a Soviet military exercise near Vladivostok assumed a conventional Chinese invasion of the maritime provinces,[17] and Khrushchev was reported to have given serious thought to a strike to 'take out' China's infant nuclear capability.[18] If only for propaganda purposes, Moscow took seriously the border grievances and territorial claims put forward by Mao in September 1963 and the strengthening of defences in the east reflected, in part, Soviet perceptions of the vast, sparsely-populated Siberian and Far Eastern provinces with over-crowded China to the south.

In 1966 the Politburo recognized that Chinese hostility must be endured and countered until after the departure of Mao and 'his gang'. The twelve to fourteen divisions on the border were re-equipped, brought up to full strength, reinforced by three to four further divisions and given tactical nuclear weapons. Two more divisions were stationed in Mongolia: The border guard was increased by 20,000 and local inhabitants were urged to undergo paramilitary training. Unprecedently in such a centralized state, in September 1966, Moscow delegated to local military commanders, the responsibility for dealing with the many incidents along the enormous border.

The Sino–Soviet border became 'the leading symbol, central issue and prime hostage of the frozen relationship' which surfaced as a propaganda weapon in the hands of the Chinese and then gained a life of its own, although not until after the clashes on the border in 1969.[19] Imperial China had long had fluid borders to the north and west: with no civilized neighbours, the Middle Kingdom did not need to delineate its extent, but from the seventeenth century Muscovite Russians nibbled away at lands that were often under only nominal Chinese suzerainty. In 'unequal treaties' China surrendered 594,440 square miles (1,540,000 square km) to Russia (Map 11), but China did not reclaim these lands in 1963. She merely demanded that the USSR acknowledge that the treaties were 'unequal', and by implication that the USSR was profiting materially from Russia's imperialist past. China claimed that the Russians, before and after 1917, seized other Chinese lands without even the benefit of 'unequal treaties'.

On 2 March 1969, Chinese forces ambushed Soviet troops on Damansky (or Chenpao) Island in the Ussuri River. This may possibly have been an attempt to create internal unity after the chaos of the Cultural Revolution by stimulating a common fear of the common

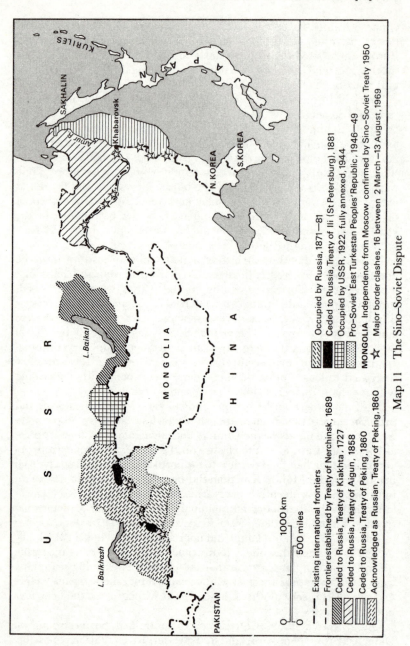

Map 11   The Sino-Soviet Dispute

enemy. Thirty-one Soviets and an undisclosed number of Chinese died in clashes which quickly escalated to involve regiment-sized units. Until September border skirmishing continued as the Red Army probed at Chinese defences from Kazakhstan. The incidents no doubt frightened both principals to the extent that Premier Kosygin went to China in September 1969 and a dialogue opened. But in the interim the USSR had taken soundings in Eastern Europe and the West on a possible strike at China's nuclear forces and there had allegedly been a practice 'dry run' by Soviet aircraft at Chinese cities. In April 1969 small Warsaw Pact units from Poland, Hungary, Bulgaria and the DDR were sent to the Sino–Soviet border, and in November 1969 a new Central Asian Military District was created, which grouped under one command forces in the Kazakh, Kirghiz and Turkmen Republics. In August 1969 a missile specialist, General Tolubko, was given command of the Far Eastern Military District.

Soviet forces on the border were increased to forty-four divisions by 1972 (forty-six by 1980), but although the Kremlin no doubt considered a preventive war against China, her forces were never deployed for it. It is revealing of Soviet perceptions of Eastern and Western threats that throughout the 1970s the thirty-one Soviet divisions in Eastern Europe were kept at or near combat readiness whereas half the units in the Far East were understrength category 2 divisions with only 50–75 per cent of complement. There was no prospect that the relatively unmechanized and unmotorized Chinese army could invade and hold large tracts of the USSR against the advanced Soviet forces. China's military threat was potential, not actual.

Soviet foreign affairs since 1945 were dominated by the USA, but Moscow believed that the strength of America and the West were transient since they would inevitably decline. But how to cope with the Chinese 'who use the identical prism but perceive a different rainbow' and who were as contemptuous of the USSR's future as was the USSR of the USA's – and for similar reasons? The Kremlin saw China as an ascending, not a declining power, and this, combined with China's tremendous material and human potential, meant that the Soviet leadership saw China as an even greater danger for the future when her economic and military strength might grow to match the USSR's.

On the other hand, China felt threatened in turn by the simple fact of the USSR's permanent physical presence in Asia. The US presence in mainland Asia was reduced after 1973 to 33,000 troops in South Korea, and air units in South Korea and Thailand. However, China could never look forward to a time when the USSR would also depart. Rather, with the rapid development of Siberia and the Far East the Soviet presence in the region would only increase. Throughout the period of the split, Moscow pursued towards China the same apparently contradictory policies that she pursued towards others. While making repeated efforts to get the Chinese to improve specific aspects of their relationship and negotiate some of their problems, the USSR simultaneously mounted deliberate pressure against China's foreign interests.

Until Mao died in September 1976 relations remained extremely tense, although diplomatic contacts remained. Border negotiations continued nominally, but they remained stalled during the 1970s by Moscow's refusal to comply with China's prerequisite that all troops be withdrawn from the 'disputed' territories – which were all in Soviet hands. Also, party-to-party contacts were broken off between January 1966 and 1978 when China resurrected her Sino–Soviet Friendship Association and sent greetings to the CPSU on the anniversary of the Revolution.

Further border clashes occurred in 1972 and 1974, and border talks reopened in December 1976 after a break of 18 months. However, nothing else apparently resulted from the USSR's conciliatory efforts after the death of Mao, and Peking even rejected the CPSU's message of condolence. The Russians pinned their hopes on a new generation of Chinese leaders, and their hopes must have been raised when the post-Mao power struggle threw up a Chinese leadership which was just as 'revisionist' as was the CPSU. Nevertheless, although the substance of the ideological dispute had evaporated, other differences remained, even though the Soviet and Chinese press became more restrained about each other and Radio Moscow looked forward to 'the revival of the mighty anti-imperialist alliance of the Soviet Union, China and other socialist states'.[20] But post-Mao China had no wish to re-enter the Soviet fold, and Chairman Hua Guofeng restated the demand in an address to the Chinese parliament in March 1978 that Soviet troops should disengage from the 'disputed' areas. Then in the spring of 1979 China abrogated the Sino–Soviet treaty of 1950. Nevertheless, a modest agreement on river traffic on the Amur and Ussuri Rivers was reached in 1977. Also, at the end of 1979, China and the USSR began talks about talks on the normalization of relations, but these were halted by the Soviet action in Afghanistan which alarmed China.

The USSR sought to isolate China as China sought to isolate the USSR, and Moscow was uneasy at any expansion of Chinese contacts and influence. As early as 1964 Moscow regarded as Western collusion France's extension of diplomatic recognition to and West Germany's discussions about trade and consular agreements with China. China's refusal to sign the Test Ban Treaty in 1963 and the Non-Proliferation Treaty in 1968 was taken as indicative of her hostile intentions. Moreover, China grew in world importance in the 1970s. She entered the UNO in 1971, developed quite good relations with the USA and the West, exchanged ambassadors with America on 1 January 1979 and signed a treaty of peace and friendship with Japan in August 1978. She cultivated Western Europe as a natural ally and gained access to Western trade – including some military equipment which was refused to the USSR. Although China could not compete with the USSR in the value of aid she could offer, she posed an ideological alternative to the Third World and competed with the USSR in socialist politics everywhere. She even offered support to Yugoslavia in the late 1970s and Romania especially in 1971, 1976 and 1978 when relations between Bucharest and Moscow became so strained that there were rumours of a possible Soviet military 'solution' to the Romanian problem.

Ever conscious of the dangers posed by enemies on two flanks, the USSR sought to defuse tension in the West, and although SALT II was not concluded as expected, SALT I enshrined Moscow's nuclear parity with the USA, and even though the Helsinki Agreement created dissident problems, it rounded off the *Westpolitik* which settled Europe's frontiers.

Nevertheless, the Sino–Soviet split damaged Moscow's standing in parts of the Third World, if only because the prospect of fierce competition between Moscow and Peking undercut the moral force of the ideological messages they tried to promulgate. Furthermore, in supporting different sides in the Angolan civil war of 1975, they were seen to be pursuing the kind of power politics that Marxist–Leninism rejects. By using her Cuban ally to swing round the Non-Aligned Movement at its Havana Conference in 1979 to support the USSR, Moscow was widely seen to be willing to subordinate the whole of the Third World to her own interests.

China's search for friends was matched by the USSR's attempts to 'surround' China. In June 1969 Moscow floated an Asian defence pact involving India, Thailand and Indonesia against China. When this did not materialize, she cultivated India, Afghanistan and North Vietnam. Peking saw the Soviet invasion of Afghanistan in December 1979 as a further step in the encirclement of China, the most obvious example of which had been the gradual weaning of North Vietnam away from the Chinese and into the Soviet camp. When China sought to 'punish' Vietnam by her 'limited' invasion of that country on 16 February 1979, she did so in an unsuccessful attempt to force the Vietnamese to withdraw from Cambodia where the Chinese-backed Pol Pot regime had been overthrown by Vietnam.

Vietnam joined Comecon on 29 June 1978 and signed a treaty of friendship and co-operation with Moscow on 3 November 1978. China was, therefore, taking a grave risk, for Moscow's credibility suffered when her new ally was attacked by her old. However, Moscow only intervened diplomatically and gave arms to Vietnam. Moscow realized that to commit troops either against China or in Vietnam would weaken the USSR's propaganda case that China was an unpredictable warmonger of whom the West should be wary; harm the USSR's 'peace loving' image just a few months before the Non-Aligned Conference in Havana; set back *détente* with the USA even further; and invite the kind of military stalemate suffered by the US in Vietnam. Fortunately for the USSR, the Chinese forces did less well than expected against the most experienced army in Asia, and Soviet intervention was never necessary. But the world had seen the dangers inherent in the 'new Cold War' between giants whose ideological and geopolitical interests clashed so seriously.

If the 1970s did not resolve the Sino–Soviet split, then in at least three other ideological areas, Moscow had cause for quiet satisfaction. Burgeoning after the invasion of Czechoslovakia and blossoming in the mid 1970s, the Eurocommunist phenomenon reached a high point at the European Conference of Communist Parties in East Berlin in June 1976. Eurocommunism involved independence from Moscow, stress on the parliamentary rather than the revolutionary road to communism, and rejection of 'the dictatorship of the proletariat'. The Eurocommunists offered the prospect that once elected to office, they could presumably be voted out. The Italian Palmiro Togliatti was the first postwar Euro-communist and his Italian Communist Party (PCI) under Enrico Berlinguer was, with Georges Marchais's French Communist Party (PCF) and Santiago Carrillo's Spanish Communist Party (PCE), the centre of Eurocommunism.

By the end of January 1976, all three had rejected the 'dictatorship of the proletariat'. Their movement was stimulated by the example of Allende in Chile, *détente* in Europe, and the real prospect of coming to – or at least sharing – power not only in France and Italy but also in Portugal after the revolution in 1974 and in Spain after the death of Franco in 1975. Moscow encouraged communists to join governments in Iceland, Finland and Portugal, but was aware that communists in government in France and Italy, where the CPs consistently won at least 20 per cent and 30 per cent of the vote respectively, would upset the European balance of power to a degree the USA might find unacceptable. It could be that Moscow opposed entry into coalition governments by the PCI, PCF and PCE on the grounds that participation without control could compromise them in un-communist decisions, have them rejected at the next election and set back the communist cause. Possibly Moscow did not want them to try to come to power because the Soviets had abandoned the prospects of 'revolution' in the West. Also, if Eurocommunists in government practised what they preached and introduced their policies while allowing an opposition and a free press, then the East European demands for the same could have been overwhelming. Possibly Moscow distanced itself from the Eurocommunists because the Americans would have found it easier to accept the PCI in power in Italy if they thought there had been a split between the PCI and the CPSU; then, after a few years the split could have been healed?[21]

Such speculation was rife in the West in 1976, but by 1980 Carrillo's PCE was reduced to parliamentary impotence. The PCF had broken away from the French Socialists and at the Twenty-third Congress of the PCF in May 1979 had re-entered the Soviet fold. In February 1979 the PCI, whose parliamentary support of the Catholic Christian Democrats had lost it some electoral support, announced its abandonment of the search for cabinet posts. By 1980 Eurocommunism was still significant but it no longer threatened to destabilize Europe and outrun Moscow's ambitions.

When Albania severed links with China in July 1978 because of China's 'revisionism' China lost an important ideological outpost and even though the USSR did not gain one, Albanian propaganda against the USSR lost some of its edge. Furthermore, there was always the prospect that Albania would need a protector again, especially as her dispute with Belgrade over the 1.5 million Albanian Yugoslavs remained alive.

The third occasion for ideological satisfaction was Cuba which, virtually estranged between the Missile Crisis and 1969, had become by 1980 Moscow's chief partner in foreign affairs. Expensively subsidized, but with ambitions that complemented Brezhnev's, Fidel Castro provided the foot-soldiers and Third World legitimacy for much of Soviet policy in Africa and South-West Asia, as well as providing a forum for Soviet views in the Non-Aligned Movement.

Soviet communism had been on the ideological defensive after Czechoslovakia and pluralism continued to characterize world communism in 1980. But, the USSR had 'lost' only Chile in 1973 to counter-revolution and only Laos after 1975 to the Chinese heresy. She had chalked up successes – if only partial sometimes – in Angola, Mozambique, Ethiopia, South Yemen, Afghanistan, Vietnam and Cambodia whose ruling communist parties acknowledged at some time during the 1970s varying degrees of allegiance to Moscow.

# Twelve

# THE SOVIET SUPERPOWER

A superpower can be defined as a state with the ability and will to exert significant, and sometimes decisive, influence throughout the world. Numbers of states have a global importance without being superpowers. China's ideological weight in the world is not matched by military and economic strength: she remains a regional power with superpower potential. West Germany and Japan are economically important in all corners of the world but militarily they are only regional powers, who acknowledge their ideological and military dependence upon the USA. Britain and France have declined from world power status, and although they retain cultural, economic and political interests – including some defence commitments – throughout the world, they no longer possess the military 'reach' or political 'clout' to be effective outside their own regions and the residues of their empires.[1]

The USSR, however, as shown in Egypt, Syria, Ethiopia, Mozambique, Angola, South Yemen, Afghanistan and Vietnam, has developed the means and the will to intervene far from her shores. In sheer size alone, the USSR is a superpower. She has the largest land area, third largest population and third largest economy in the world.[2] But international status depends not just on a country's strength but upon perceptions of that strength by others. It is interesting that the USSR rejected the term superpower as applying only to the 'capitalist imperialist' USA, although most of the world applied this term to the USSR.

The Soviet Union was regarded as a superpower at the end of the Second World War, long before she acquired a global reach, when her status depended upon her war record, her conventional military strength, her possession after 1949 of nuclear weapons, the decline in power and status of the West Europeans, which left the USSR as the only country with even the potential to challenge the USA, and the fact that the USSR had a powerful physical presence in central Europe and east Asia – the two main areas in which the 'world' war had been fought.

Since the Revolution the USSR had had an ideological importance world wide, but in Khrushchev's time Soviet interests became global even if the Cuban Missile Crisis showed that Moscow did not yet possess the power to make her interests stick. It was Khrushchev who set global horizons for Soviet foreign policy and who laid down the arms and naval development programmes which, by the end of the 1960s, enabled the USSR to assume her place alongside the USA as a global superpower in fact and not just in name. But it was the armaments element virtually alone which gave the USSR superpower status. Her GNP was less than half that of the USA.[3] More revealingly, Soviet *per capita* GNP was much lower than that of the major Western democracies.[4] One author argued: 'The Soviet political system is a source of acute embarrassment to foreign communist parties, and its state ideology is a profound irrelevance both to revolutionary movements and to developing countries in search of guidance.'[5]

Soviet Marxism may not be directly applicable to the tribes, grasslands and tropical swamps of Mozambique, but communism was imposed upon Mongolia and the central Asian republics, and Moscow's claims that her ideology was a model for the Third World have been widely listened to. Indeed widespread receptivity to Moscow's ideology was one element of her global influence.

When Khrushchev began the policy of opening doors to the Third World, it marked Russia's first important venture beyond her Eurasian heartland, but she enjoyed few of America's advantages. When US diplomacy became global after the Second World War at least American business and tourism had led the way, and the USA was able to capitalize upon the deep Western cultural penetration of the Third World. America had the enormous advantage that when she burst on to the world stage she found that the language of international trade, finance and transport was English, her own tongue. It has been fashionable to decry US 'Coca-cola culture', but American films, music and popular culture permeated the world in ways that the USSR could not begin to match.

Suspect in many areas of the world because of her ideology and atheism, the USSR was also received warily by some newly independent countries for whom she was an imperialist power with colonies in central Asia, and was in addition, white and relatively rich. Soviet protestations of solidarity with the Third World, while ideologically correct, were often rejected in some quarters as veiled neo-colonialism. Inexperience with the Third World led the USSR to give offence and make mistakes which set back her cause. When Sadat expelled Soviet 'advisers' from Egypt in 1972 he did so with the full support of his countrymen to whom the Soviets had become at least as objectionable in their four years' presence as had the British in their seventy-four years up to 1956. When President Podgorny arrived in Mozambique in March 1977, dressed in lounge suit, overcoat and trilby, and delivered a three-hour public address – in Russian – to the poverty-stricken masses of Maputo, who had so recently despatched their white, Portuguese masters, it must have given the Mozambicans food for thought, if only at the utter inappropriateness of it àll. Perhaps it was partly a recognition of her own gauche behaviour that led the Kremlin to employ Cuba as a diplomatic and military stalking-horse in the Third World.

Economically, Soviet importance in the world was potential, rather than actual, and was, anyway, limited by the erratic performance of her agricultural sector. Nevertheless, in 1977 she was the largest producer of oil at 572.5 million tonnes (and even then was expected to become a net oil importer by the mid-1980s), platinum (25 per cent of world trade) and asbestos (2.46 million tonnes). In 1977 she was the second largest producer of aluminium (1.79 million tonnes), chrome (2.18 million tonnes), gold (245 tonnes), lead (510,000 tonnes); zinc (735,000 tonnes) and nickel smelter products (168,000 tonnes).[6] But the rouble was not a convertible currency and was only used for trade within the Soviet bloc. The USSR was not included in the major conferences on the international economic crises of the mid-1970s. She was not invited to the December 1975 Energy Conference which assembled the Western powers, OPEC and the Third World in discussions on the oil and commodity problems.

In a television address in May 1964 Khrushchev said: 'When the Soviet Union helps the young developing countries, giving them a portion of the wealth amassed by its own labour . . . it is limiting its own possibilities for a certain period of time.' But, he added: 'We would be poor communists, poor internationalists if we thought only of ourselves.'[7] This public attitude did not change under Brezhnev, but Soviet bloc non-military aid to the less developed countries declined from 8 per cent of their total aid receipts in the early 1970s to 2 per cent in 1976. By 1979 India, one of the major recipients of Soviet aid, was paying back more each year in interest and capital than she was receiving from Moscow.[8] Whereas OECD nations gave $13 billion in aid in 1977, the Soviet bloc gave only $800 million,[9] or only 0.05 per cent of GNP, against OECD donations of 0.4 per cent of GNP and a UNO target of 0.7 per cent of GNP.

Most Eastern bloc aid was in the form of credits to encourage export markets. Between 1954–76 the USSR extended $19,277 million in aid credits, of which $9,790 million were taken up. Other East European states offered $6,475 million, of which $2,200 million were taken up. (China offered $3,953 million of which $1,950 million were taken up.) As part of the Soviet bloc aid programme there were about 70,000 technical advisers in the less developed countries in 1976, but it seems that these were not a net cost to the bloc for the less developed countries paid their salaries in hard currency at rates between $15,000–$20,000 per annum. The CIA estimated that the 21,000 advisers in the Middle East and North Africa netted a flow of $200 million in hard currency and equivalent goods to Eastern Europe in 1976.[10]

Another element of aid was the advanced education and technical training provided in the Soviet bloc countries. This programme began after the death of Stalin, but increased from 134 Third World students in the USSR in 1957 to a total of 36,450 enrolled throughout the bloc by December 1976, of whom the majority were in the USSR.[11] By the end of 1976 48,500 students had returned to their native countries taking with them their education and their acquaintance with Eastern bloc culture and politics.

The USSR had a $1.2 billion trade surplus with the Third World in 1976, but this would have been a deficit had it not been for armaments sales which were worth $2.5 billion. Moscow sold arms usually for hard currency, and between 1972–6 she delivered arms worth $10,340 million to the less developed countries (mostly to the Middle East and Africa),[12] apart from deliveries to bloc countries.[13] It was armaments, both her own and those of her satellites, that gave the USSR the means for global military action and upon which she depended for her influence abroad.

The USSR is a militarized state. Preliminary military and political training are part of the formal school curriculum. Military service lasts two years in the army and air force and up to three years in the navy and border guards. The armed forces total 3,658,000, compared with 2,022,000 in the USA, 4,360,000 in China, 495,000 in West Germany, 509,000 in France and 323,000 in Britain. Conscripts have a reserve obligation up to the age of 50. This means that, with Soviet reservists of over 25 million and the 80 million members of the part-time military training organization (DOSAAF), two-fifths of the Soviet population is not only eligible for call-up, but has received at least rudimentary military instruction. Effective military numbers in the event of war would be very much smaller than that of course, and the importance of such numbers lies not so much in there being so many potential soldiers in the USSR, but that they have all been exposed to the reinforcement of socialization and attitudes of acceptance of authority and conformism that are implicit in military training. The USSR has absorbed the lesson of Frederick the Great and Napoleon that mass or conscript armies are not just formidable tools of foreign policy, but engines of social control.

As a one-party police state the USSR mounts its foreign policy on a platform of wide popular support which is rare in the West. Government decisions are not publicly questioned. There is not the informed opinion found in Western countries, since the USSR is politically homogeneous. Alec Nove wrote that: 'There are few countries in the world today where political passivity is so great as in the Soviet Union.'[14] An American President could be circumscribed by Congress, legislation, public opinion or by the refusal of allies to accept and act upon the President's

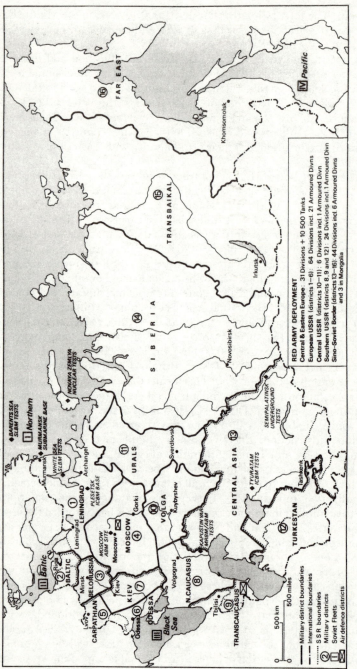

RED ARMY DEPLOYMENT
Central & Eastern Europe: 31 Divisions + 10 500 Tanks
European USSR (districts 1–6): 64 Divisions incl. 21 Armoured Divns
Central USSR (districts 10–11): 6 Divisions incl. 1 Armoured Divn
Southern USSR (districts 8, 9 and 12): 24 Divisions incl. 1 Armoured Divn
Sino–Soviet Border (districts 13–16): 44 Divisions incl. 6 Armoured Divns
                                          and 3 in Mongolia

Military district boundaries
International boundaries
S S R boundaries
Military districts
Soviet Fleets
Air defence districts

Map 12   Soviet Military Strength

wishes. President Brezhnev faced no such constraints.

Brezhnev inherited from Khrushchev the military structure and defence doctrine which allowed him to pursue global policies. After a brief flirtation in 1960 with Western ideas of defence based upon nuclear deterrence, the USSR turned in 1961 to its present defence policy which is that the prevention and avoidance of world war is the prime objective; that a strong military capability is the best way of making war unlikely and of preventing the USA from using her military strength to dictate the outcome of events, as over Cuba in 1962. However, whereas the West's doctrine of 'nuclear deterrence' implies that if the deterrent has to be used then deterrence has failed, the USSR believes that her defence will only have failed if her armed forces are unable to *win* a war. It was this Soviet determination to ensure her security by building armed forces (Map 12) which could *win* a world war, that endowed the USSR with such an array of armed force by the end of the 1970s as to have achieved her original objective but at the cost of alarming the West which had only armed its conventional forces to the level of hoping to *prevent* a war.

Soviet defence policy requires the capacity to win a war on two fronts. Forces on the Chinese border absorbed about 10 per cent of the total defence effort in the 1970s, rising to about 15 per cent per year at the end of the decade.[15] The Far Eastern defence effort is likely to increase in response to signs of more military spending in Japan. At the end of the 1970s Tokyo was urged by China and the USA to play a greater part in her own defence, and Japanese naval units participated in a Pacific exercise 'Rimpac 1980' with US, Canadian, Australian and New Zealand units. This was Japan's first such major naval venture since 1945.

Military strength conferred status on the USSR and Moscow has been prepared to pay very heavily for it. The CIA estimated that despite the expected slowdown of the Soviet economy in the 1980s defence spending would rise from 11 or 12 per cent of GNP in 1980 to 15 per cent by 1985, whereas US defence spending was unlikely to exceed 5 per cent of GNP by 1985. Such an effort obviously imposed strains on the Soviet economy and limited the production of consumer goods but it gave the USSR nuclear parity with the USA, an edge in conventional arms, an effective satellite reconnaissance system, and the long-range air and naval capability to show the flag or intervene far from her shores. Moreover, in the enormous Soviet exercise '*Okean 75*' in 1975, the USSR used its ocean surveillance and communication satellites to effect central control over naval activity around the world, thus demonstrating Moscow's capacity to wield all its military might at once.

Talleyrand defined 'non-intervention' as a political and metaphysical term meaning much the same as intervention.[16] Once the USSR had developed a navy with a world role then the mere presence of Soviet vessels was enough to emphasize the strength and potential of the USSR, which therefore found itself playing roles in local affairs by default as well as by design.

Furthermore, the Soviet Air Force increased its inventory of Antonov-22 long-range transport aircraft from five in 1970 to fifty in 1979, and it was these aircraft that enabled the rapid build-up of tanks and heavy equipment in Ethiopia in November 1977. This long-range airlift capacity, capable of moving four airborne divisions in one lift, was supplemented by the 1,300 Aeroflot airliners, a large proportion of which was first mobilized in the Warsaw Pact exercise 'Shield-72' in 1972. This included a massive airlift of troops to prepositioned equipment in Eastern Europe. But the more obvious sign of the growth of Soviet strength was the development of a 'blue water' navy. The commander and creator of the modern Soviet navy, Admiral Sergei Gorshkov wrote: 'The creation of the Soviet oceanic fleet may be put on a par with the most important events of the recent past.'[17] This is indeed the case for the emergence of the USSR as a naval power was one of the most significant developments since 1945 (Map 13).[18]

Unlike Britain and America the USSR is not dependent upon maritime lines of communication. Her seaborne trade is not great and she can reach all her major allies by land. Therefore she did not develop the kind of 'balanced' navy that Britain and the US developed. The main thrust of Soviet naval development was in submarines. In 1957 Khrushchev appointed Admiral Gorshkov to build and command the Soviet navy. Gorshkov abandoned Stalin's plan of trying to match the West by building large surface ships, and by 1958 the decision had been taken to double production of nuclear submarines to ten per year.

Until Gorshkov's time the prime duty of the Soviet navy was coastal defence, but like the US navy, its main task became strategic. The first ballistic missile submarines were deployed in the late 1960s, and in 1979 the Soviet navy boasted ninety submarines, of which seventy-one were nuclear-powered, mounting 1,028 ballistic missiles. In search of invulnerable positions from which to threaten the US and the West, these submarines were deployed in the high seas and it became the task of the rest of the navy 'to ensure the credibility and operational viability of the ballistic missile submarines'. In practice this meant guaranteeing them access to the high seas by being prepared to disrupt Western anti-submarine warfare efforts in key areas, especially the choke points (the Straits of Gibraltar, the English Channel, etc.).

The second major task was 'sea denial', which involved the capacity to find and destroy the West's ballistic missile submarines and 'deny' particular stretches of water (Black, Barents and Norwegian Seas and Sea of Okhotsk?) to Western navies. The third task, which also incorporated the first two, was the Soviet deployment of a blue water navy: the ability to assert its presence in all the strategically important oceans of the world. In this connection Soviet ship deployments in

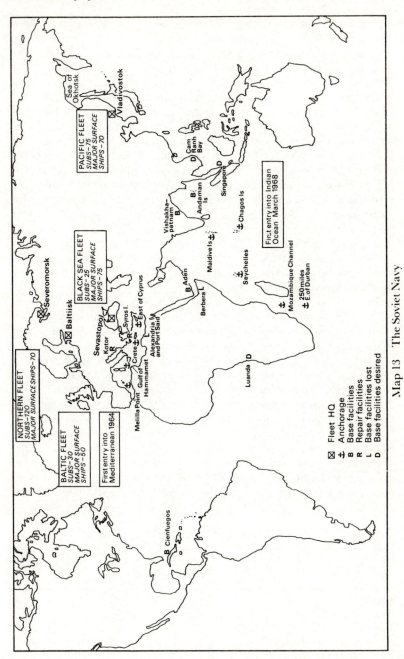

**Map 13   The Soviet Navy**

Legend:

⊠  Fleet HQ
✛  Anchorage
B   Base facilities
R   Repair facilities
L   Base facilities lost
D   Base facilities desired

NORTHERN FLEET
*SUBS-120*
*MAJOR SURFACE SHIPS-70*

Severomorsk

BALTIC FLEET
*SUBS-30*
*MAJOR SURFACE SHIPS-50*

Baltiisk

First entry into Mediterranean 1964

BLACK SEA FLEET
*SUBS-25*
*MAJOR SURFACE SHIPS-75*

Sevastopol

Kotor R

Crete

Syros I.

East of Cyprus

Alexandria and Port Said

Melilla Point

Gulf of Hammamet

Aden B

Berbera L

Maldive Is ✛

Seychelles ✛

250 miles E of Durban ✛

Mozambique Channel

Luanda D

First entry into Indian Ocean March 1968

Chagos Is ✛

Vishakha-patnam B

Andaman Is

Singapore D

Cam Ranh Bay D

PACIFIC FLEET
*SUBS-75*
*MAJOR SURFACE SHIPS-70*

Vladivostok

Sea of Okhotsk

Cienfuegos B

distant waters increased from 2,000 to 22,000 ship-days per year between 1965 and 1976.[19]

It was following the US stationing of Polaris submarines in the Mediterranean in the spring of 1963 and the American request for the Rota base in Spain that the Soviet Mediterranean squadron made its first appearance. By 1968 a regular Soviet naval presence was established in the Indian Ocean, and at the Twenty-third Congress of the CPSU in 1969 Defence Minister Malinovsky announced: 'The creation of the Blue Belt of Defence has been completed.'[20] This was not yet fully apparent in the West, and in September 1969 *The Military Balance 1969–70* declared: 'There has been a degree of naval expansion which suggests that the Soviet Union is in the process of transforming her naval forces from their traditional role as a mere adjunct to land power into an instrument for global support of Soviet interests.'[21] By 1979 the process was well under way, and the deployment of 12,000 marines and eighty-five amphibious ships, including fourteen Alligators capable of landing a battalion plus twenty-five tanks, and two 43,000-ton(ne) Kiev-class carriers (with two more under construction) gave the Soviet navy the capacity to exercise gunboat diplomacy in the classic manner.

In addition to military vessels, the USSR possessed about 20 million tonnes of cargo and fishing ships by 1979, an increase from 1.5 million tonnes in 1958. The merchant fleet earned hard currency by competing in the world sea-freight markets at rates which undercut those of Western shipping lines. All merchant ships were subject to military use if necessary, and many major merchant ships entering service after 1973 had a Ro/Ro (Roll-on/Roll-off) capacity and reinforced decks and ramps for carrying heavy equipment, including tanks. Such ships sealifted tanks to Angola in 1975 and Ethiopia in 1977.

However, one authority wrote in 1978: 'The US navy has outbuilt the Soviet navy by 3.3 million tons to 2.6 million tons since 1958. In the *détente* period [since 1969] the Americans outbuilt the Russians by 12 per cent in ship numbers as well as by 7 per cent in tonnage.'[22] Table 12.1 shows the extent to which the Soviet navy remained inferior to the NATO navies.

Table 12.1    The Strength of the Soviet and NATO Navies at July 1979.[23]

|  | Major surface ships | Attack and patrol submarines | Ballistic missile submarines |
|---|---|---|---|
| USSR | 275 | 248 | 90 |
| Total Warsaw Pact | 280 | 256 | 90 |
| USA | 180 | 80 | 41 |
| Total NATO (excluding France) | 389 | 192 | 45 |
| Total NATO (including France) | 437 | 215 | 49 |

Besides, the Soviet navy operates as four distinct fleets which could not immediately support each other. These fleets all experience difficulties in gaining access to the high seas, and the USSR has major problems in supplying ships at sea, providing air cover for its fleets and hiding its submarines from the extremely sophisticated NATO detection gear. Soviet diplomacy made major efforts to secure bunkering and repair facilities for its merchant shipping throughout the world and bases for its naval vessels but even the overseas base facilities that were gained did not compensate for the fact that Soviet ships on the high seas have to operate a long way from home and, unlike the US navy with its 13 carriers, have to operate as a rule without air cover. Also, at the beginning of the 1980s, the Soviet navy had reached the phase of 'block obsolescence', the period when – assuming a ship life of twenty years – Gorshkov's first generation of vessels needed replacing at about the same time, whereas Western vessels needed replacement at more regular and less disruptive intervals.

In the 1970s Soviet strength matured and in September 1979 ex US Secretary of State Kissinger warned: 'Never in history has it happened that a nation achieved superiority in all significant weapons categories without seeking to translate it at some point into some foreign policy benefit.'[24] But of course the USSR had already derived benefits from her military strength in Angola and Ethiopia and was to venture into Afghanistan. Western attempts to understand Soviet foreign policy since the Second World War have asked whether it was a product of Marxist–Leninist ideology or Russian power politics. This, however, remained unanswered by 1980.

# NOTES AND BIBLIOGRAPHY

## Chapter 1

1. Quoted in Arthur M. Schlesinger Jr., *The Crisis of Confidence* (André Deutsch, 1967) p. 159.
2. Quoted in André Fontaine, *History of the Cold War*, vol. II (Secker & Warburg, 1970) p. 490.
3. Nadezhda Mandelstam, *Hope Abandoned* (Collins and Harvill, 1974).
4. Many good books deal with the origins and development of Soviet communism. See especially, David Lane, *Politics and Society in the Soviet Union* (Martin Robertson, rev. reprint, 1977) and Leonard Schapiro, *The Communist Party of the Soviet Union* (Eyre & Spottiswoode, 1970). Brief, but very good, is G. F. Hudson, *Fifty Years of Communism* (Penguin, 1968).
5. Lane, op. cit., p. 128.
6. G. N. Curzon, *Russia in Central Asia* (Longmans Green, 1889) p. 315.
7. V. I. Lenin, *Collected Works*, vol. 31, *Left-Wing Communism – An Infantile Disorder*, Moscow 1920, p. 70 (also Lawrence & Wishart, 1966).
8. Louis J. Halle, *The Cold War as History* (Chatto and Windus, 1967) p. 46.
9. Daniel Yergin, *Shattered Peace: The Origins of the Cold War and the National Security State* (André Deutsch, 1978) p. 10.
10. Sir William Hayter, quoted in William Manchester, *The Glory and the Dream* (Michael Joseph, 1973) p. 410.
11. Quoted in John W. Spanier, *American Foreign Policy Since World War Two* (Nelson, 4th ed., 1972) p. 102.
12. George Ball, *Diplomacy For a Crowded World* (Bodley Head, 1976) p. 87.

## Chapter 2

1. Alan Clarke, *Barbarossa: The Russian German Conflict 1941–45* (Penguin, 1966) p. 70.
2. Montgomery Hyde, *Stalin* (Michael Joseph, 1972) p. 547.
3. See *Soviet Union* No. 3 (300) 1975, *Mezhdunarodnaya Kniga*, Moscow and Ian Grey, *The First Fifty Years: Soviet Russia 1917–67* (Hodder and Stoughton, 1967) p. 404.
4. The American billion, i.e. 1000 million, is used throughout.
5. According to Khrushchev the drought of 1946 led to localized famines in 1947 when thousands died of hunger. See Eric de Mauny, *Russia Prospect* (Macmillan, 1969).
6. Alec Nove, *Stalinism and After* (Allen & Unwin, 1975) p. 107.
7. Edward Crankshaw, *Khrushchev: A Biography* (Sphere, 1968) p. 152.
8. John Dornberg, *Brezhnev: The Masks of Power* (André Deutsch, 1974).
9. N. S. Khrushchev, *Khrushchev Remembers* (André Deutsch, 1971) p. 229.

10. See Solzhenitsyn's harrowing account of his own and others' experiences on being condemned to the labour camps, Alexander Solzhenitsyn, *The Gulag Archipelago* (Collins/Fontana, vol. 1 1974, vol. 2 1975).

11. See Nikolai Tolstoy, *Victims of Yalta* (Hodder and Stoughton, 1978) for a condemnation of Britain's duplicity in this rather squalid affair, and see the counter argument by Reuben Ainsztein in *The Sunday Times*, 12 March 1978.

12. Hyde, op. cit., p. 531.

13. Crankshaw, op. cit., p. 163.

14. Brian Crozier, *The Future of Communist Power* (Eyre & Spottiswoode, 1970) p. 36.

15. Interestingly, while the Cold War was brewing up the xenophobia of the *Zhdanovschina* was directed ultimately against the ideas exemplified by the USA, while McCarthyism in the USA – which ruined careers and compromised principles, but did not butcher people – was directed against the ideas exemplified by the USSR.

16. Schapiro, *The Communist Party of the Soviet Union.*

17. Robert Conquest (ed.), *The Soviet Police System* (Bodley Head, 1968), p. 47.

18. Robert Conquest, *The Great Terror: Stalin's Purge of the Thirties* (Macmillan, 1968) p. 335.

19. Adam B. Ulam, *Stalin: The Man and His Era* (Allen Lane, 1974) pp. 408–9.

20. Lane, *Politics and Society in the Soviet Union*, p. 79.

21. Isaac Deutscher, *The Prophet Outcast: Leon Trotsky, 1929–40* (OUP, 1970) p. 306.

22. *Vozhd* translates inadequately into 'leader' or 'boss', but means much the same as *führer*, *caudillo* or *duce*.

23. Lazar Pistrak, *The Grand Tactician: Khrushchev's Rise to Power* (Thames and Hudson, 1961) p. 165.

24. The 1936 or Stalin Constitution required a party congress – the font of party authority – to meet every three years.

25. Khrushchev only needed to absent himself on vacation for a matter of weeks in 1964 and he was overthrown.

26. Professor Meissner, quoted in Roy MacGregor-Hastie, *The Mechanics of Power* (Frederick Muller, 1966) p. 39.

27. The Secretaries of the Moscow, Leningrad and Ukraine parties were important enough in their own right, especially if they also had full seats on the Politburo, to bid for the ultimate position of power, the General Secretaryship of the CPSU. They had the advantage over Government Ministers in that they had had the opportunity to fill important posts in their party organizations with their own men.

28. This at any rate was Khrushchev's opinion. See Khrushchev, op. cit., p. 250.

29. See Alexander Solzhenitsyn, *The First Circle* (Fontana, 1970) for a novel which deals with three days at one such establishment.

30. Dornberg, op. cit., p. 116.

31. Khrushchev, op. cit., p. 311.

32. Milovan Djilas, *Conversations With Stalin* (Penguin, 1969) p. 140. This very revealing little book gives a considerable insight into Stalin's governmental style in the late 1940s.

33. Alec Nove, op. cit., p. 106.

34. See Louis Fischer, *The Life of Lenin* (Harper and Row, 1964) pp. 430–34.

35. Marr argued that with the spread of communism, language difference would wither away and there would become one universal language. Stalin, however, disagreed with this rather Marxian analysis and wrote that language was a fundamental basis of society and fundamentals do not change.

36. Ulam, op. cit., p. 435.

37. Stalin's favourite and Leningrad Party boss Sergei Kirov died in mysterious circumstances in 1934, and within three years all his main Leningrad party appointees had been executed.

38. For details of the Leningrad Affair and the suggestion that Beria and Malenkov had instigated the affair to rid themselves of dangerous rivals see ibid., pp. 706–10.

39. In his novel, *The Living and the Dead*, published in the Khrushchev 'thaw', Konstantin Simonov, no devotee of Stalin, described the enormous emotive response of the Soviet people to Stalin's broadcast of 3 July 1941, two weeks after the German attack, when he addressed his countrymen for the first time not as 'Comrades' but as 'My Friends, Brothers and Sisters'.

40. Khrushchev first floated these proposals on behalf of Stalin at the Nineteenth Congress, and in so doing attracted the attention of and some support from those who had never previously imagined him as a party thinker.

41. Khrushchev, op. cit., p. 314.

42. Averell Harriman, *Peace with Russia?* (Gollancz, 1960) p. 103.

43. There are excellent biographies of Stalin by Ulam, Hyde and Deutscher. The reader who wishes to pursue the character of Stalin ought also to read Trotsky's study and two recent views of the pro- and anti-schools: Ian Grey, *Stalin* (Weidenfeld & Nicolson, 1979) which portrays Stalin as Lenin's heir and Ronald Segal, *The Tragedy of Leon Trotsky* (Hutchinson, 1979). However, an interesting insight into the character of Stalin is offered in Mervyn Jones, *Josef* (Jonathan Cape, 1970), a novel.

44. R. W. Davies in *The Times Higher Education Supplement*, 21 December 1979.

## Chapter 3

1. Known as Praesidium between 1952–66.

2. From the encyclopaedia *Rossiya SSR*, quoted in Alexander Solzhenitsyn, *The Gulag Archipelago*, vol. 2 (Fontana, 1976) p. 191 footnote.

3. de Mauny, *Russia Prospect*, p. 283.

4. Tibor Szamvely in *The Sunday Telegraph*, 3 March 1968.

5. Hyde, *Stalin*, p. 602.

6. Another version of the fall of Beria has been attributed to Khrushchev, in which Beria is strangled by Malenkov and Mikoyan at a Praesidium meeting on 27 June 1953. See G. F. Hudson, *Fifty Years of Communism: Theory and Practice 1917–1967*, p. 163.

7. MacGregor-Hastie, *The Mechanics of Power*, p. 37.

8. See Khrushchev, *Khrushchev Remembers*, for the text of this seminal speech.

9. Palmiro Togliatti in an interview with *L'Unita*, 17 June 1956, quoted in Crankshaw, *Khrushchev: A Biography*, p. 232.

10. Nove, *Stalinism and After*, p. 142.

11. Isaac Deutscher, *The Unfinished Revolution: Russia 1917–1967* (OUP, 1967).

12. K. S. Karol, *La Chine de Mao* (Paris, 1966), quoted in de Mauny, op. cit., p. 274.

13. Subscribers to the Great Soviet Encyclopaedia of 1957 were asked to remove the 'incorrect' three-page entry on Beria and replace it with the 'correct' three-page article on the Bering Straits.

14. It is still a great honour to have one's remains interred at the Kremlin wall, and in 1970 a bust of Stalin was set up above his grave.

15. Sir William Hayter, *A Double Life* (Hamish Hamilton, 1974) p. 129.

16. Hedrick Smith, *The Russians* (Times Books, 1976) p. 245.

17. Fontaine, *History of the Cold War*, vol. II, p. 265. See also the account of the Kremlin reception on 31 December 1956 in Wolfgang Leonhard, *The Kremlin Since Stalin* (OUP, 1962) p. 232.

18. Carl Linden, *Khrushchev and the Soviet Leadership 1954–64* (Johns Hopkins UP, 1966) p. 52.

19. The General who almost brought down the Third French Republic in 1888–9. See James Harding, *The Astonishing Adventure of General Boulanger* (W. H. Allen, 1971).

20. Better known in the West is the work by Tito's ex-confidant, Milovan Djilas, *The New Class* (Allen & Unwin, 1966) on the same theme of ideals betrayed.

21. Not only did Khrushchev believe that abstract artists were betraying Soviet realism and undermining the party, he sincerely found abstract art to be deeply objectionable. While in Britain in April 1956 Khrushchev claimed that Epstein's statue of Lazarus,

which he saw in Oxford, had given him nightmares. See Hayter, *A Double Life*, p. 138.

22. Crankshaw, op. cit., footnote 16, p. 303.
23. Khrushchev, op. cit., p. 457.
24. *Pravda*, 7 November 1957, quoted in Linden op. cit., p. 60.
25. *Pravda*, 28 January 1959, quoted in Linden op. cit., pp. 82–3.
26. A worker who regularly exceeded his allocated quota of work, after a miner, Alexei Stakhanov, who was publicized as an example for all to follow.
27. Marxist–Leninism argued that the society moving from socialism to communism would give rise to the 'new socialist man' who would be free from the taints of greed and superstition.
28. See Peter J. Mooney and Colin Bown, *Truman to Carter: A Post-War History of the United States of America* (Edward Arnold, 1979) pp. 78–9.
29. Quoted in I. Deutscher, *Russia, China and the West 1953–1966* (Penguin, 1970) p. 289.
30. Smith op. cit., p. 245.
31. de Mauny, op. cit., pp. 73–4.
32. Conor Cruise O'Brien, in *The Observer*, 18 March 1979.
33. See Robin Edmonds, *Soviet Foreign Policy 1962–73*. (OUP, 1975) p. 33.
34. See Lane, *Politics and Society in the Soviet Union*. p. 241.
35. See Michel Tatu, *Power in the Kremlin* (Collins, 1969).
36. Crankshaw, op. cit., p. 270.
37. Quoted in L. Churchward, *Contemporary Soviet Government* (Routledge & Kegan Paul, 1968) p. 287.

## Chapter 4

1. Edmonds, *Soviet Foreign Policy 1962–73* p. 89.
2. See the very interesting chart of political opinion in the USSR in Zbigniew Brzezinski, *Ideology and Power in Soviet Politics* (Praeger, 1967) p. 117.
3. See Dornberg, op. cit. for Brezhnev's early career. See also Leonid I. Brezhnev, *Brezhnev – A Short Biography* (Pergamon Press, 1978).
4. See de Mauny, op. cit.
5. Set up by Khrushchev in 1962, it had the power to remove party or government officials from their posts.
6. A. Brown and M. Kaser (eds.), *The Soviet Union Since the Fall of Khrushchev* (Macmillan, 1978).
7. So named by the French commentator Michel Tatu.
8. Quoted in Dornberg, op. cit., p. 237.
9. ibid., p. 265.
10. A photograph on the front page of *Pravda*, 19 December 1974, showed the apparent change in rank of the two men. See the article by Victor Zorza in the *Guardian*, 15 January 1975.
11. *Pravda*, 17 April 1975.
12. As President, Brezhnev for the first time had the protocol rank to outrank heads of government and to deal on equal terms with other heads of state. While General Secretary of the CPSU he had technically only ranked with, for example, Ron Hayward, General Secretary of the British Labour Party while the Labour Party was in government from 1974–9.
13. *Pravda*, 15 October 1976.
14. See Brown, op. cit., pp. 312–13.
15. See Lane, *Politics and Society in the Soviet Union*, for text of the constitution, pp. 553–6.
16. Moscow could now claim that Westerners who accused the USSR of not honouring the human rights elements of the 1975 Helsinki Agreements (see page 132) had only to look at the 1977 Constitution to see that the USSR did guarantee human rights.
17. *The Observer*, 2 December 1979.
18. See Jerry F. Hough, 'The Generation Gap and the Brezhnev Succession' in *Problems of*

*Communism*, vol. XXVIIII July–August 1979.

19. Stephen White, 'The USSR: Patterns of Autocracy and Industrialism', in A. Brown and J. Grey (eds.), *Political Culture and Political Change in Communist States* (Macmillan, 1977) p. 42.
20. *The Daily Telegraph*, 20 December 1977.
21. Smith, *The Russians*, p. 341.
22. The *Guardian*, 15 September 1979.
23. In 1979 Britain had a population of 56 million, with approximately 44,000 people in prison.
24. *The Economist*, 13 December 1975.
25. See Smith, op. cit., pp. 8 and 86.
26. The *Christian Science Monitor*, 17 October 1977.
27. *New Society*, 24 May 1979.
28. See Michael Binyon in *The Times Higher Education Supplement*, 28 December 1979.
29. See the article, 'The Giant Grows Sluggish', *The Economist*, 29 December 1979.
30. Lane, op. cit., p. 513.
31. ibid., p. 261.

## Chapter 5

1. Robert Kaiser, *Russia: The People and the Power* (Secker & Warburg, 1976) p. 322.
2. ibid., p. 316.
3. May McAuley, *Labour Disputes in Soviet Russia, 1957–1965* (OUP, Clarendon Press, 1969).
4. *The Sunday Times*, 30 March 1975.
5. Alexander Shelepin was head of the trade unions from 1967–75. His knowledge of negotiating and personnel matters had doubtless been acquired in his previous appointment – head of the KGB.
6. de Mauny, *Russia Prospect*, p. 94.
7. They were applied experimentally in a Ukranian coal mine early in 1965 and resulted in increased coal production of 33 per cent, reduced costs and large bonuses for the miners.
8. Brian Crozier, *The Future of Communist Power*, p. 53.
9. Dornberg, *Brezhnev: The Masks of Power*, p. 194.
10. Lane, *Politics and Society in the Soviet Union*, p. 280.
11. Dornberg, op. cit., p. 243.
12. Keith Bush, 'Soviet Economic Growth: Past, Present and Projected', in *Nato Review*, no. 1 (NATO, Brussels, 1974).
13. Dornberg, op. cit., pp. 253–4.
14. Harriet Ward, *World Powers in the Twentieth Century* (BBC and Heinemann Educational Books, 1978) p. 295.
15. Central Intelligence Agency, *The Soviet Economy in 1976–77 and Outlook for 1978* (CIA, August 1978) p. 2.
16. Ward, op. cit., p. 295.
17. Lloyds Bank, *Economic Report, USSR*, March 1979.
18. CIA, op. cit., p. 14.
19. CIA, op. cit., p. 4. This included machinery and amenity costs. Productive investment in agriculture was 20 per cent of total Soviet investment, but less than 5 per cent of total US investment.
20. *Time*, 1 September 1975.
21. CIA, op. cit., p. 2.
22. For the Great Grain Raid see James Trager, *Amber Waves of Grain* (Arthur Fields Books, 1974).
23. *The Financial Times*, 26 July 1979.
24. *New Scientist*, 11 December 1975, p. 620.

25. Lane, op. cit., p. 286.
26. The *Guardian*, 2 June 1976.
27. See R. Conquest (ed.), *Agricultural Workers in the USSR* (Bodley Head, 1968) for details of Khrushchev's policies towards the peasantry.
28. Dornberg, op. cit., p. 191.
29. Khrushchev, *Khrushchev Remembers*, p.387.
30. L. I. Brezhnev, 'The Virgin Lands', *Novy Mir*, November 1978. See the review in *Problems of Communism*, vol. XXVIII January–February 1979, p. 48.
31. See Conquest (ed.) op. cit., p. 55.
32. A. Brown and M. Kaser (eds.), *The Soviet Union Since the Fall of Khrushchev*, p. 7.
33. de Mauny, op. cit., p. 117.
34. *The Economist*, 8 March 1980, p. 54.
35. Peter Wiles, quoted in *Problems of Communism*, vol. XXVI, May–June 1977, p. 1.

## Chapter 6

1. Contribution to 'Critique of Hegel's Philosophy of Law', K. Marx and F. Engels, *On Religion*, Moscow 1955, p. 42 (also Lawrence & Wishart, 1972).
2. In R. Conquest (ed.), *Religion in the USSR*, (Bodley Head, 1968) p. 7.
3. In de Mauny, *Russia Prospect*, p. 288.
4. Bohdan R. Bociurkiw, 'Religion in the USSR After Khrushchev', in John W. Strong (ed.), *The Soviet Union Under Brezhnev and Kosygin* (Van Nostrand Reinhold, 1971) p. 150.
5. *Pravda*, 2 March 1964, quoted in Michael Bourdeaux, *Religious Minorities in the Soviet Union* (Minority Rights Group, 1970).
6. Bociurkiw, op. cit., p. 143.
7. On 25 October 1962 an *Izvestia* article signed by Patriarch Aleksei called on 'the entire Christian world to immediate, decisive protests against the aggressive acts of the USA over Cuba'.
8. Smith, *The Russians*, p. 434.
9. Lane, *Politics and Society in the Soviet Union*, p. 256.
10. *The Observer*, 1 April 1979.
11. Tamara Dragadze, 'A Muslim Way of Life in the Soviet Union', *New Society*, 10 January 1980, p. 56.
12. See William C. Fletcher, *Religion and Soviet Foreign Policy* (OUP, 1973) especially pp. 121–33.
13. Teresa Rakowka-Harmstone, 'The Dilemma of Nationalism in the Soviet Union', in Strong (ed.), op. cit., p. 115.
14. Editorial in *Kommunist*, quoted in ibid., p. 127.
15. These included a Dutch, a French and even a tiny British unit.
16. Ann Sheehy, *The Crimean Tartars and the Volga Germans*, report no. 6 (Minority Rights Group, 1971).
17. R. Conquest, *The Nation Killers* (Macmillan, 1970) p. 103.
18. Decree of 5 September 1967 rehabilitating Crimean Tartars, quoted in the *Guardian* 29 December 1977.
19. See *The Economist*, 9 October 1971.
20. *Christian Science Monitor*, 19 February 1979.
21. T. H. Rigby, *Soviet Studies*, vol. 28 (University of Glasgow Press, 1976) p. 615.
22. The *Guardian*, 30 July 1977.
23. See Michael Rywkin, 'Central Asia and Soviet Manpower', in *Problems of Communism*, vol. XXVIII January–February 1979, p. 3 and *passim*.
24. John Hazard, 'Soviet Law and Justice', in Strong (ed.), op. cit., pp. 93–4.
25. Andrei Amalrik, *Will the Soviet Union Survive Until 1984?* (Allen Lane, 1970) pp. 8–14.
26. Santiago Carrillo, *Eurocommunism and the State* (Lawrence and Wishart, 1977) p. 161.
27. Smith, op. cit., p. 417. For text of the letter see *The Sunday Times*, 3 March 1974.
28. See the interview with Nikolai Bokov in the *Guardian*, 12 May 1976.

29. See Dornberg, *Brezhnev: The Masks of Power*, pp. 234–6.
30. Two of the men, Mark Dymshitz and Edward Kuznetsov, together with Alexander Ginzburg and two others, were flown to the USA in April 1979 in exchange for two Soviet spies, Valdik Enger and Rudolf Chernyayev.
31. *Tass* quoted by Peter Reddaway in *The Sunday Times*, 1 August 1976.
32. The *Guardian*, 4 October 1977.

## Chapter 7

1. Numbers of high-ranking Red Army officers who fell victim to the Great Purge of 1937–8 were exiled to the Far East where, consequently, the quality of military leadership was higher than it was in European Russia, e.g. General (later Marshal) Zhukov, in disgrace, won the battle of Kalkin Gol against the Japanese.
2. George Kennan, *Memoirs 1925–50* (Hutchinson, 1968) pp. 560–61.
3. Hyde, *Stalin*, p. 36.
4. See Richard Pipes, 'Détente: Moscow's View', in R. Pipes (ed.), *Soviet Strategies in Europe* (Crane Russak, 1976) p. 9.
5. George E. Mowry, *The Urban Nation* (Macmillan, 1967) pp.160–61.
6. For the factual details of the Potsdam provisions see Keesing's Research Report No. 8, *Germany and Eastern Europe Since 1945* (Scribner's, 1973) and for an anecdotal account of the conference itself see Charles L. Mee Jr., *Meeting at Potsdam* (André Deutsch, 1975).
7. Arthur Bryant, *Triumph in the West* (Collins, 1959) p. 90.
8. Lord Moran, *Winston Churchill: The Struggle for Survival 1940–65* (Constable, 1966) p. 279.
9. Grey, *The First Fifty Years: Soviet Russia 1917–1967*, p. 409.
10. For discussions of the nuclear diplomacy issue see Gar Alperovitz, *Atomic Diplomacy: Hiroshima and Potsdam* (Simon and Schuster, 1965) p. 241, Barton Bernstein, 'Roosevelt, Truman and the Atomic Bomb', *Political Science Quarterly* No. 90, Spring 1975, pp. 23–69 and Chalmers M. Roberts, *The Nuclear Years: The Arms Race and Arms Control 1945–70* (Praeger, 1970) p. 10.
11. Negotiations between Japan and the USSR in the 1970s, aimed at joint exploitation of Siberian minerals, were made difficult by Japanese demands for the return of the Kuriles, which were symbolically important to Tokyo, but of immediate strategic significance to Moscow.
12. Ulam, *Stalin: The Man and His Era*, p. 625. See also Manchester, *The Glory and the Dream*, pp. 499–500.
13. Yergin, *Shattered Peace: The Origins of the Cold War and the National Security State*, pp. 64–5.
14. See the discussion in Mooney and Bown, *Truman to Carter: A Post-War History of the United States of America*, p. 34.
15. James E. King Jr. 'NATO: Genesis, Progress, Problems', in Gordon B. Turner and Richard D. Challener (eds.), *National Security in the Nuclear Age* (Praeger, 1960) pp. 150–51.
16. Robert E. Sherwood, *Roosevelt and Hopkins* (Harper, 1948) p. 793.
17. According to US Ambassador Harriman, quoted in ibid., p. 892. When Truman was made aware of the reactions of his allies he reinstated Lend–Lease deliveries to Russia and Britain until the end of the Japanese war.
18. Yergin, op. cit., pp. 64–5.
19. Lucius D. Clay, *Decision in Germany* (Heinemann, 1950) p. 320.
20. W. S. Churchill, *The Second World War*, vol VI (Cassell, 1960) pp. 227–8. Churchill offered Stalin a 'Balkan Deal' of 90 per cent influence in Romania, 75 per cent in Bulgaria (which was not at war with the USSR) and 50 per cent in Yugoslavia and Hungary. Britain was to have the other 50 per cent in Hungary and Yugoslavia and 90 per cent in Greece.
21. Eden, quoted in Schlesinger, *The Crisis of Confidence*, p. 112.
22. Djilas, *Conversations With Stalin*.

23. James F. Byrnes, *Speaking Frankly* (Harper & Brothers, 1947) p. 30.
24. The murder was revealed by the Germans in April 1943. Moscow blamed it on the Germans, but although the full details are not known, it is known that the 10,000 Poles were in Russian hands in 1939.
25. It is widely held that Rokossovsky's forces were exhausted and needed to re-supply and regroup before attempting to take Warsaw, even if Stalin had wanted to help the anti-communist and anti-Russian Home Army, which is very unlikely. See Alan Clarke *Barbarossa* (Penguin, 1966) pp. 421–2, and Alexander Werth *Russia at War* (Pan, 1964) pp. 778–90.
26. The then Chief of the German General Staff reported, however, that before abandoning the Poles to their fate, Rokossovsky made two attempts to force the Vistula and take Warsaw, on 25 July and 2 August 1944, and that both these attacks were repulsed by the Germans with heavy Soviet casualties (see Colonel–General Heinz Guderian, *Panzer Leader* (Futura, 1974) pp. 358–9). If surprise had failed it made military sense for Soviet forces to regroup before attempting a frontal assault on the city.
27. When Molotov was asked what would happen to them, he gave the memorable response: 'The guilty ones will be tried.'
28. Alfred Grosser, *Germany in Our Time* (Pall Mall Press, 1971) p. 31.
29. Harry S. Truman, *Memoirs: 1945 Year of Decisions*, vol. 1 (Signet Books, 1955) p. 455.
30. The Soviet economy was not gearing up for war: 1946 was dubbed 'the Year of Cement' and major speeches in the campaign for elections to the Supreme Soviet in February 1946 concentrated on reconstruction, not foreign affairs.
31. Quoted in Joyce and Gabriel Kolko, *The Limits of Power: The World and United States Foreign Policy 1945–1954* (Harper and Row, 1972) p. 33.
32. Walter Bedell Smith, *My Three Years in Moscow* (Lippincott, 1950) p. 37.
33. Truman letter to Byrnes, 5 January 1946, quoted in Roger Morgan, *The Unsettled Peace* (BBC Publications, 1974) p. 67.
34. Djilas op. cit., p. 141. Following the withdrawal of support and the Yugo–Soviet split of 1948, the Greek insurrection collapsed.
35. Harry S. Truman *Memoirs* vol. 2 (Doubleday, 1955) p. 106.
36. Halle, *The Cold War as History*, p. 159.
37. See Grosser, op. cit., p. 65.
38. See D. F. Fleming, *The Cold War and Its Origins 1917–1960* (Allen & Unwin, 1961), and also Fontaine, *History of the Cold War*, vol. I.
39. Cabell Philips, *The Truman Presidency* (Macmillan, 1966) p. 186.
40. The US issued a similar declaration almost simultaneously with the pronouncement of her 'containment' policy which appeared under the title 'The Sources of Soviet Conduct' by X in the July 1947 edition of *Foreign Affairs*. The 'X article' by the foremost US Russian specialist, George Kennan, said that US policy 'towards the Soviet Union must be that of a long-term patient but firm and vigilant containment of Russian expansive tendencies'.
41. Kolko, op. cit., p. 214.
42. See the fascinating account in Fontaine, op. cit., pp. 352–6. Possibly Finland was allowed to go its own way as part of the Soviet propaganda offensive in 1948 to convince the Scandinavians that Moscow was peaceable and that they did not need to join NATO.
43. Djilas, op. cit., p. 68.
44. USSR, Poland, Bulgaria, Czechoslovakia, Romania, Hungary, Yugoslavia, France, Italy and later Holland.
45. Andrei Zhdanov, 22 September 1947, in *The Strategy and Tactics of World Communism*, supp. I, (US Govt. Printing Office, 1948) pp. 212–30.
46. A. J. P. Taylor, *The Course of German History* (Methuen, 1961) p. 2.
47. Byrnes, op. cit.
48. Keesing's Research Report No. 8, p. 12.
49. The French made no bones about wanting to partition Germany, and the Anglo–

American moves to merge their zones into Bizonia were easily portrayed as breaches of the Potsdam Agreements to maintain German unity.

50. Hannes Adomeit, 'Soviet Risk-Taking and Crisis Behaviour', Adelphi Papers No. 101 (International Institute for Strategic Studies (IISS), 1973) p. 8.

51. See the account of the American Military Governor in Clay op. cit., p. 367.

52. Yergin, op. cit., pp. 396–7.

53. This Soviet–Israeli link was broken at the end of 1952 when Stalin used the anti-Semitic element of the Doctors' Plot (see page 18) to sever relations with Israel.

54. Ulam, *Stalin: The Man and His Era*.

55. It may be fanciful to suppose that Stalin timed the Soviet absence from the UN deliberately to enable the USA to obtain UN backing so that she would not feel dangerously isolated in her aid for South Korea. UN involvement broadened the issue and meant that the war would not be portrayed simply as a military confrontation between the superpowers. Besides, if Stalin really had miscalculated, then the UN could act as a brake upon the US because the UN would never have condoned an American nuclear strike against China or the USSR.

56. Khrushchev, *Khrushchev Remembers*, p. 368.

## Chapter 8

1. The first US H-bomb was tested on 1 November 1952. The USSR followed on 12 August 1953. The original American nuclear lead had been cut from four years to less than one, but to the surprise of the West, the USSR's crude nuclear parity with the USA – parity in that Moscow had the H-bomb as well – made the USSR less, not more, intractable.

2. See George Quester, *Nuclear Diplomacy: The First 25 Years* (Dunellen, 1972), Fig. 3 on p. 295, showing a graph of respective American and Soviet round-trip capable aircraft.

3. America's first ICBM was launched in February 1958, and although the USSR may have deployed 50 ICBMs to the USA's 27 for a few months at the end of 1960, the total American delivery capacity far outweighed the Soviet capacity to strike at North America. See Quester, op. cit., Figure 4 on p. 296 and also Mooney and Bown, *Truman to Carter: A Post-War History of the United States of America*, chapter 11.

4. Jean Lacouture, *Ho Chi Minh* (Allen Lane, 1968).

5. Khrushchev quoted in D. W. Bowett, *The Search for Peace* (Routledge & Kegan Paul, 1972).

6. Quoted in Crozier, *The Future of Communist Power*, p. 32.

7. Khrushchev, *Khrushchev Remembers*.

8. See Philip Noel-Baker, *The Arms Race* (Atlantic Press, 1958) pp. 12–20.

9. H. S. Parmet, *Eisenhower and the American Crusades* (Collier-Macmillan, 1972).

10. Solution of the nuclear arms control issue foundered on the rock of 'verifiability' – the ability of $x$ to assure himself that $y$ has only as many weapons as the agreement allows – until the deployment by both the USA and USSR in the 1960s of photographic reconnaissance satellites made verifiability possible.

11. A fascinating and little understood episode, the Soviets gained in withdrawing from Austria. They furthered their peaceful co-operative image, especially among neutrals and Third World states. They made some West Germans consider reunification on Moscow's terms. They removed the British military presence from the frontiers of Yugoslavia and Hungary, and they complicated NATO's cohesion and logistics by severing the alliance in central Europe: thereafter, troops and supplies could not travel direct from Munich to Northern Italy over the Brenner Pass, they had to go via France. In return Moscow gave up the opportunity she had never really seized, to make Austria, or even just the Soviet zone, communist. Her withdrawal might also have encouraged other occupied peoples to think of an Austrian-type solution. However, like the withdrawals from Finland in 1945, Azerbaijan in 1946, North Korea in 1948, Port Arthur (in China) in 1955 and Porkkala in Finland in 1955, the withdrawal from

Austria did not convince the West of Moscow's peaceful intentions.
12. Halle, *The Cold War as History*, p. 354.
13. This argument might seem unreal to the Western reader, but it worried the Russians. See Adam B. Ulam, *Crisis and Coexistence, 1917–1967* (Secker & Warburg, 1968) p. 630.
14. Adomeit, op cit., p. 10. See also Roger Morgan, *The United States and West Germany 1945–1973* (OUP, 1976) p. 78.
15. Halle, op. cit., p. 361.
16. Fontaine, *History of the Cold War*, vol. II, p. 326.
17. Traditionally leaders do not risk diplomatic failure so they usually only attend summits when agreement is near: a promised summit implied an agreement on Berlin.
18. Spanier, *American Foreign Policy Since World War Two*, p. 167.
19. Possibly this was the 60 megaton device tested on 30 October 1961.
20. This was a development of the Rapacki Plan proposed in the UN by Polish Foreign Minister Adam Rapacki in October 1957. The plan proposed a nuclear free zone in central Europe, including Czechoslovakia, Poland and the Germanies. The West opposed the plan because it favoured the USSR with her preponderance of conventional power.
21. Ulam, *Crisis and Coexistence*, p. 631.
22. The official American and Soviet versions claim that Gary Powers's U-2 was shot down by a new kind of surface-to-air missile, but the intriguing story that the U-2 was sabotaged on the ground before take-off is told in Kaiser, op. cit., p. 455.
23. Until after a new President had been inaugurated in the USA. Nevertheless, the terms in which Khrushchev talked publicly about the affair were so bellicose and his departure from Paris on 18 May 1960 so abrupt that the Americans feared he was going to precipitate a major crisis by signing a separate peace with East Germany. American forces were put on a world-wide alert.
24. Halle, op. cit., p. 380.
25. The CIA sponsored invasion of Cuba at the Bay of Pigs on 17 April 1961 turned into a military and diplomatic fiasco for which Kennedy publicly accepted the blame.
26. He had disapproved of the independence of action over the Congo displayed by the UN Secretary-General Dag Hammarskjöld.
27. Philip Windsor, *City on Leave: History of Berlin 1945–1962* (Chatto and Windus, 1963) p. 223.
28. Fontaine, op. cit., vol. 2, p. 420.
29. Paul-Henri Spaak, *The Continuing Battle: Memoirs of a European* (Weidenfeld & Nicolson, 1971).
30. As well as Windsor, op. cit., see also David Shears, *The Ugly Frontier* (Chatto and Windus, 1971) and Curtis Cate, *The Berlin Wall* (Weidenfeld & Nicolson, 1978).
31. See Spanier, op. cit., p. 171 and Ulam, *Crisis and Coexistence*, p. 654.
32. Fontaine, op. cit., vol. 2, p. 171.
33. Hayter, *The Kremlin and the Embassy*, p. 146.
34. Recently supplied Soviet aircraft and their Soviet crews were scattered to airfields outside Egypt at the beginning of November 1956, and Soviet technicians were ordered to the Sudan. When Soviet aircraft overflew Turkish airspace and the USSR asked Turkey's leave to send Black Sea warships through the Straits, these were further threats, but there was never any intention of becoming militarily embroiled.
35. Indeed, Nasser outlawed the Egyptian CP.
36. Fontaine, op. cit., vol. 2, p. 262.
37. Ulam, *Crisis and Coexistence*, p. 615.
38. Khrushchev, op cit., p. 507.
39. *The Observer*, 11 November 1962.
40. Moscow furthered her image in the Third World by endorsing the non-interventionist principles adopted by the first Non-Aligned Conference at Bandung, Indonesia, in April 1955.
41. The American failure to push through the Bay of Pigs affair may have been as

worrying to the Russians as if the US had invaded and conquered the island. Outright aggression in defence of an obvious national interest was understandable, but vacillation and hesitation were unpredictable and therefore supremely dangerous in the nuclear age because they made it correspondingly difficult to arrive at the correct countermove.

42. Castro only declared his communism in December 1961.
43. MRBMs had a range of approximately 2,000 miles (3,218 kilometres) and IRBMs 1,300 miles (2,092 kilometres). Between them they would have brought most of America within range of missile attack.
44. See Linden, *Khrushchev and the Soviet Leadership 1954–64*, p. 153.
45. For the text of the correspondence see Robert F. Kennedy, *The Thirteen Days: Cuban Missile Crisis* (Macmillan, 1969).
46. Khrushchev letter to Kennedy, 28 October 1962, quoted ibid., p. 179.
47. Theodore Sorensen, *Kennedy* (Hodder and Stoughton, 1965) p. 713.
48. Graham T. Allison, *Essence of Decision: Explaining the Cuban Missile Crisis* (Little Brown, 1971) p. 138.
49. ibid., p. 141.
50. Khrushchev, op. cit., p. 494.
51. Khrushchev to the Supreme Soviet, *Pravda*, 13 December 1962.
52. Although the self-confident Kennedy may well have created more fuss about them than did President Carter over the Soviet combat brigade in Cuba in 1979 (see page 135).
53. See Spanier, op. cit., pp. 176–7 for this argument.
54. Such an eventuality must have looked distinctly possible to the Russians in 1962. Britain and France were already nuclear, and the Multilateral Nuclear Force was being seriously discussed in NATO. This would have given Bonn some say in nuclear affairs.
55. Ulam, *Expansion and Coexistence*, pp. 661–9.
56. Arthur M. Schlesinger Jr., *A Thousand Days: John F. Kennedy in the White House* (Fawcett Cress, 1967) p. 759.
57. Castro got his own back. He warned other Third World leaders that the Soviets could not be trusted and that the first time he had heard that Moscow was to withdraw the missiles was on a radio news broadcast. Mohamed Heikal, *Sphinx and Commissar: The Rise and Fall of Soviet Influence in the Arab World* (Collins, 1978) p. 122.
58. The first of the new Echo class nuclear-powered attack submarines, equipped with Cruise missiles and designed to counter the American carrier, appeared as early as 1962.

## Chapter 9

1. These principles were enshrined in the Brezhnev Constitution of 1977. See Lane, *Politics and Society in the Soviet Union*, p. 559.
2. *The Military Balance 1969–70* (IISS, 1969) p. 57.
3. The issue of Soviet defence costs is a study in its own right. However, the dollar costs of American and Soviet defence in the decade 1966–77 were roughly equal, even though the USSR steadily increased the rate by which it outspent the USA in the 1970s. It has been asserted that Western estimates of Soviet defence spending were based on incorrect assumptions before 1976 when the CIA revised its analytical techniques and said that defence cost 11–13 per cent of Soviet GNP as against previous estimates of 6–9 per cent. See the original argument that is often misread or unread: *A Dollar Cost Comparison of Soviet and US Defense Activities, 1967–77* (CIA National Foreign Assessment Center, January 1978).
4. ibid., p. 55.
5. The deployment of strategic weapons, enough of which would survive a major nuclear attack, in turn to be able to inflict an 'unacceptable' response.

6. A. Brown and M. Kaser (eds.), *The Soviet Union Since the Fall of Khrushchev*, p. 55.
7. MAD is the capacity – after absorbing a surprise 'first strike' – reliably and massively to retaliate in kind and degree. It was enunciated by US Secretary of Defense Robert McNamara in 1962. See Robert McNamara, *The Essence of Security* (Harper and Row, 1968) p. 52.
8. Lynn Etheridge Davis,'Limited Nuclear Options', Adelphi Papers No. 121 (IISS, 1975–6) p. 1.
9. Malcolm MacKintosh, 'Soviet Strategic Policy', *World Today*, vol. 26, No. 7, July 1970, p. 272.
10. By 1973 over half the officers in the navy were graduate engineers.
11. For discussion of Soviet military and defence policies see John Erickson, *Soviet Military Power* (Royal United Service Institution, 1971) and for the Soviet view (Marshal) V. D. Sokolovsky, *Soviet Military Strategy*, trans. Harriet F. Scott (Crane Russak, 3rd edition, 1975).
12. Alistair Buchan, *The End of the Post-War Era* (Weidenfeld & Nicolson, 1974) p. 39.
13. Richard Lowenthal, 'Changing Soviet Policies and Interests', Adelphi Papers No.66 (IISS, March 1970).
14. See V. A. Aspaturian, 'Moscow's Options in a Changing World', in G. K. Bertsch and T. W. Ganschow, *Comparative Communism* (W. H. Freeman, 1976) p. 370.
15. J. W. Fulbright, *The Arrogance of Power* (C pe, 1967) p. 122.
16. Heikal, *Sphinx and Commissar: The Rise and Fall of Soviet Influence in the Arab World*, p. 167.
17. Edmonds, *Soviet Foreign Policy 1962–73*, p. 78.
18. See Mooney and Bown, *Truman to Carter: A Post-War History of the United States of America*, p. 200.
19. Nove, *Stalinism and After*, pp. 172–3.
20. See Lane, op. cit., p. 114.
21. Corrall Bell, *The Diplomacy of Détente: The Kissinger Era* (Martin Robertson, 1977) p. 120.
22. The word used is *razryadka*.
23. Sir William Hayter, *Russia and the World* (Secker & Warburg, 1970) p. 4.
24. *Pravda*, 5 June 1973.
25. *Soviet News*, 2 March 1976.
26. Kissinger, 'Statement to Senate Finance Committee', Department of State *Bulletin*, April 1974, p. 323.
27. *Pravda*, 16 August 1973.
28. *Time*, 3 January 1972, p. 11.
29. Interestingly, the Russians were still using this term, rather than *détente*, in their public utterances.
30. See *The Military Balance 1972–3* (IISS, 1972) pp. 83–6 and *Strategic Survey 1972* (IISS, 1973) pp. 14–19.
31. *The Military Balance 1979–80* (IISS, 1979) p. 89.
32. Smith, *The Russians*, p. 243.
33. Dornberg, *Brezhnev: The Masks of Power*, p. 238.
34. Headline in *The Sunday Times*, 9 August 1970, referring to the ceremony at which the foreign ministers initialled the treaty prior to its formal signing.
35. Aidan Crawley, *The Rise of West Germany* (Collins, 1973) Chapter XIII.
36. The *Guardian*, 4 March 1978.
37. Ian Greig, *The Communist Challenge to Africa* (Foreign Affairs Publishing Co., 1977) p. 15.
38. Avigdor Haselkorn, *The Evolution of Soviet Security Strategy* (Crane Russack, 1978).
39. The *Guardian*, 17 February 1975.
40. See the *Christian Science Monitor*, 9 July 1979.
41. Heikal, op. cit., pp. 13–14.
42. ibid., p. 283.
43. Although reports appeared at the end of 1979 that some Soviet warships were being

refuelled and repaired there and that there were Soviet advisers there (*The Sunday Times*, 26 November 1979).

44. Edward Gonzalz, 'Complexities of Cuban Foreign Policy', in *Problems of Communism*, vol. XXVI, November–December 1977.
45. *Pravda*, 27 October 1965, quoted in Greig op. cit., p. 53.
46. See Colin Legum, *After Angola, The War Over Southern Africa* (Africana Publishing, 1978).
47. Greig, op. cit., p. 211.
48. Department of State *Bulletin*, April 1976.
49. Brezhnev to All-World Conference of Peace-Loving Forces, *Pravda*, 27 October 1973, in Edmonds, op. cit., p. 161.
50. Anwar al-Sadat, *In Search of Identity* (Collins, 1978) p. 187.
51. The USSR had the use of Egyptian airfields from which Soviet aircraft could reconnoitre NATO naval deployments in the Mediterranean, and the Soviet navy had access to naval facilities at Alexandria and Mersa Matruh.
52. The Soviets tried and failed to get Sadat to accept a ceasefire. See ibid., pp. 250–66.
53. With Cuban, East German and Soviet advisers in the country and a twenty-year treaty of friendship signed in October 1979.
54. *The Observer*, 17 November 1974.
55. The mutual culture shock involved – and therefore effectiveness of the operation – can be imagined.
56. Haselkorn, op. cit., p. 93.
57. *Strategic Survey 1979* (IISS, 1980) p. 54.
58. In the BBC's 'Analysis' broadcast on 23 January 1980 on Afghanistan, two distinguished authorities on the USSR, John Erickson, Professor of Politics at Edinburgh University and Hal Sonnenfeldt, US Under-Secretary of State in the Kissinger era, both argued that the role of the military in Soviet decision-making has increased and that the military have the casting vote over questions of security.
59. A device used by Soviet diplomacy. Stalin – of all people – used to claim difficulties with his Politburo as a reason why he could not agree to certain proposals. President Roosevelt used to believe him.
60. 'When the Himalayan peasant meets the he-bear in his pride He shouts to scare the monster who will often turn aside' – Kipling, quoted in *The Economist*, 15 March 1980, p. 11.

## Chapter 10

1. And parts of Yugoslavia too. See Djilas, *Conversations With Stalin*, pp. 70–74.
2. For details of the communist take-over of Eastern Europe see Martin McCauley, *Communist Power in Europe 1944–49* (Macmillan, 1977) or Richard Mayne, *The Recovery of Europe* (Weidenfeld & Nicolson, 1970) pp. 134–46.
3. Bulgaria – 10 July 1947; Czechoslovakia – 11 July; Hungary – 14 July; Yugoslavia – 25 July; Poland – 4 August; and Romania – 26 August.
4. The CPs of the USSR, Poland, Bulgaria, Czechoslovakia, Romania, Hungary, Yugoslavia, France, Italy and (later) the Netherlands. It was wound up in April 1956.
5. Yergin, *Shattered Peace: The Origins of the Cold War and the National Security State*, pp. 348–9.
6. Compare this with what the de Gaulle and Atlee governments were doing in France and Britain at this time.
7. For one man's experiences in this period see William Shawcross, *Crime and Compromise: Janos Kadar and the Politics of Hungary Since Revolution* (Weidenfeld & Nicolson, 1974) Chapter 3.
8. Fontaine, *History of the Cold War*, vol. II, p. 227.
9. For an excellent discussion of the Pact's early years see Malcolm Mackintosh 'The Evolution of the Warsaw Pact', Adelphi Paper No. 58 (IISS, June 1969).

10. Nish Jamgotch Jr., 'Soviet Foreign Policy Perspectives', in James A. Kuhlman (ed.), *The Foreign Policies of Eastern Europe: Domestic and International Determinants* (A. W. Sitjhoff International Publishing Co., 1978).
11. Pavel Tigrid, *Why Dubček Fell* (Macdonald, 1971) p. 13.
12. Hayter, *Russia and the World*, p. 35.
13. Tigrid, op. cit., p. 44.
14. Dornberg, *Brezhnev: The Masks of Power*, pp. 222–3.
15. Tigrid, op. cit.
16. Harry Schwartz, *Eastern Europe in the Soviet Shadow* (Abélard Schuman, 1973) p. 75.
17. Hayter, op. cit., pp. 38–9.
18. Crozier, *The Future of Communist Power*, p. 93.
19. Hayter, op. cit., pp. 40–41.
20. ibid., p. 66.
21. L. I. Brezhnev, *Brezhnev – A Short Biography* (Pergamon Press, 1978).
22. For details of the reorganization see Malcolm Mackintosh, 'The Warsaw Pact Today', *Survival*, May/June 1974 (IISS, 1974) pp. 123–4.
23. See the annual issues of *The Military Balance* (IISS).
24. *The Economist*, 12 January 1980, p. 69.
25. ibid., 6 July 1974, pp. 12–13.
26. Lloyds Bank *Economic Report, USSR*, March 1979.

## Chapter 11

1. The French CP did not oppose the German occupation of France until after the German attack on Russia abrogated the Hitler–Stalin Pact of 1939.
2. See Hudson, *Fifty Years of Communism: Theory and Practice 1917–1967*, chapters 7 and 17.
3. A process that was paralleled by the loss of empire and political influence by Britain and France (and America in the 1970s) which limited their strength and self-confidence – although the analogy should not be pursued too far.
4. Phyllis Auty, *Tito: A Biography* (Penguin, 1970) p. 254.
5. Fontaine, *History of the Cold War*, vol. II, p. 198.
6. Some of the ships that delivered military aid to and supported the MPLA (Popular Movement for the Liberation of Angola) forces and the Soviet and Cuban intervention in the Angolan civil war in 1975 were Yugoslav. See *Strategic Survey 1975* (IISS) p. 31.
7. John Gittings, *Survey of the Sino–Soviet Dispute* (OUP, 1968) p. 346.
8. Edward Crankshaw, *The New Cold War: Moscow versus Peking* (Penguin, 1963) Chapter 12.
9. See Sadat, *In Search of Identity*, p. 155.
10. *World Culture*, 20 December 1957, quoted in Crankshaw, *Khrushchev: A Biography*, p. 267.
11. Mao in October 1957. See Fontaine, op. cit., vol. II, p. 278.
12. See George Paloczi-Horvath, *Khrushchev: The Making of a Dictator* (Little Brown, 1960) p. 193.
13. Khrushchev, *Khrushchev Remembers*, p. 466.
14. Fontaine, op. cit., vol. II, p. 133.
15. See Colin Bown, *China 1949–75* (Heinemann Educational Books, 1977).
16. See Strong (ed.), *The Soviet Union Under Brezhnev and Kosygin*, p. 201.
17. M. J. Mackintosh, 'The Soviet General's View of China in the 1960s', in R.L. Garthoff (ed.), *Sino–Soviet Military Relations* (Praeger, 1966) p. 187.
18. P. Van Ness, 'China and the Third World', in *Current History* (Philadelphia, September 1974) p. 108.
19. Harry Gelman, 'Outlook For Sino–Soviet Relations', in *Problems of Communism*, vol. XXVII September–December 1979, p. 57.
20. The *Guardian*, 5 November 1976.
21. See Neil McInnes, *The Washington Papers*, vol. IV, No. 37, *Euro-Communism* (Sage

Publications, 1976) pp. 74–8.

## Chapter 12

1. When French troops intervened to prop up the Mobutu government in Zaïre in 1978 they had to use US Air Force aircraft to get there.
2. Soviet GNP had been overtaken by Japan's by 1980.
3. Soviet GNP in 1977 was estimated at $930 billion. American GNP in 1978 was $2,106 billion.
4. Soviet *per capita* GNP in 1977 was about $3,500. But *per capita* GNP for the West in 1978 was: West Germany – $10,000; USA – $9,500; France – $8,500; Japan – $8,000; Britain – $5,400; Italy – $4,500. *The Military Balance 1979–80* (IISS, 1979).
5. Colin S. Gray, *The Geopolitics of the Nuclear Era: Heartland, Rimland and the Technological Revolution* (National Strategy Information Center Inc./Crane Russak, 1977) p. 50.
6. Lloyds Bank, *Economic Report, USSR*, 1979, pp. 19–21.
7. Milton Kovner, 'Soviet Aid to Developing Countries: A Look at the Record', in Strong (ed.), *The Soviet Union Under Brezhnev and Kosygin*, p. 71.
8. *The Economist*, 28 April 1979, p. 46.
9. The *Guardian*, 21 October 1977.
10. *Communist Aid to the Less Developed Countries of the Free World* (CIA, 1977).
11. There were 86,000 foreign students in Britain in 1979.
12. ibid.
13. It is worth noting that besides the substantial quantities of arms sold by Britain, France and other Western countries, the USA exported arms worth $11.4 billion in the financial year 1976–7 alone. *Strategic Survey, 1977* (IISS, 1978).
14. Nove, *Stalinism and After*, p. 174.
15. William Hyland, 'Soviet Security Concerns in the 1980s' in *Prospects of Soviet Power in the 1980s*, Part II, Adelphi Papers No. 152 (IISS, 1979).
16. See Bell, *The Diplomacy of Détente: The Kissinger Era*, p. 158.
17. See Admiral Sergei Gorshkov, *The Sea Power of the State* (Pergamon Press, 1979).
18. See Eric Morris, *The Russian Navy: Myth and Reality* (Hamish Hamilton, 1977).
19. See Worth H. Bagley, 'Sea Power and Western Security: The Next Decade', Adelphi Papers No. 139 (IISS, 1977) p. 14.
20. Haselkorn, *The Evolution of Soviet Security Strategy*, p. 33.
21. *The Military Balance, 1969–70* (IISS, 1969) p. 6.
22. Bell, op. cit., p. 76.
23. *The Military Balance, 1979–80* (IISS, 1979).
24. Quoted in *The Economist*, 8 September 1979.

# INDEX